Praise for *Defendant*

"The most readable book about a psychiatric trial that one is going to get to read for many a year. And the questions it raises go deep into the nature of professionalism and responsibility."

—Norman Mailer

"A detailed, dramatic narrative . . . written with skill and remarkable restraint."

—Saul Bellow

"A book that should be read by every physician, would-be physician, and person who cares about the practice of quality medicine. (It won't hurt lawyers to read it too.) . . . It's a real cliffhanger and an education about both law and medicine."

—Ann Landers

"*Defendant* is courtroom drama. Tense. Emotional. Factual. But it is more. It also tells the story of what is happening in health care and what the epidemic of malpractice suits . . . is doing to the practice of medicine."

—*Chicago Tribune*

"The implications of various psychiatric diagnoses and technicalities of medical malpractice litigation are lucidly presented. . . . The authors effectively portray the personalities involved [in the trial]: the lawyers— one calm, incisive, and confident, the other increasingly aggressive and out-of-control; the judge—sharp, ironic, and evenhanded; the impassive jury; and the witnesses, few of whom seem to tell the truth, the whole truth, and nothing but the truth, but rather their self-serving versions of the truth."

—*Los Angeles Times*

"Because *Defendant* is thoughtful, objective, current, and well researched, it will interest lawyers, insurers, health-care providers, and, above all, the patients who pay a price for this dilemma, even when they seek medical attention from caring, competent, and careful physicians."

—*Kansas City Star*

"Since malpractice suits have become so common, a book such as this, filled with insight and strengthened by the personal equation, is invaluable. One may read it as a case study, or more sensibly, as the fascinating story of a psychiatrist who will never be the same because of her frustrating experience."

—*Chicago Sun-Times*

DEFENDANT

A Psychiatrist on Trial for Medical Malpractice

AN EPISODE IN AMERICA'S
HIDDEN HEALTH CARE CRISIS

Sara C. Charles, M.D.
and
Eugene Kennedy

Vintage Books
A Division of Random House
New York

FIRST VINTAGE BOOKS EDITION, November 1986

Copyright © 1985, 1986 by Eugene Kennedy and
Sara C. Charles, M.D.

Library of Congress Cataloging in Publication Data

Charles, Sara C.
    Defendant, a psychiatrist on trial for medical malpractice.

Reprint. Originally published: New York: Free Press, 1985.

    1. Charles, Sara C.—Trials, litigation, etc.
2. Trials (Malpractice)—Illinois—Chicago. 3. Psychi-
atrists—Malpractice—Illinois—Chicago. 4. Physicians
—Malpractice—United States.   I. Kennedy, Eugene C.
II. Title.
[KF228.C454C45   1986]   346.7303′32   86-40147
ISBN 0-394-74663-5 (pbk.)   347.306332

Manufactured in the United States of America
10 9 8 7 6 5 4 3 2 1

FOR

Elizabeth Lucia Tower Troy, M.D.

CONTENTS

Acknowledgments   *xi*

Preface to the Vintage Edition   *xiii*

Introduction   *xvii*

What Is Medical Malpractice Litigation   *1*

The Beginning . . .   *3*
   First Session   *3*
   The Accident   *5*
   The Complaint   *6*

PART I   The Plaintiff

The Trial—Day One   *11*
   Opening Statements   *11*
   Concerning Confidentiality   *22*

Day Two   *23*
   A Psychiatrist's Notes   *23*
   The Plaintiff's Case   *24*
     The Mother   *24*

The Mother—Cross-Examination   32
The Son-in-Law   37
The Sister   43
The Father   44

Day Three   49
The Plaintiff's Strategy   49
The Plaintiff   59

Day Four   66
The Plaintiff Continued   66
The Plaintiff—Cross Examination   69
The Best Friend   74

PART II   The Experts

Some Relevant Definitions   79

Devising the Case   81

Day Five   88
Plaintiff's Expert I   88
Plaintiff's Expert I—Cross-Examination   91

Day Six   97
Plaintiff's Expert II   97
Plaintiff's Expert II—Cross-Examination   100

Day Seven   110
Defendant's Expert   110

Day Eight   117
Defendant's Expert Continued   117

PART III   The Defendant

Day Eight Continued   123
The Defendant   123

Day Nine   137
The Defendant Continued   137

Day Ten   153
The Defendant Continued   153
Closing Arguments   160
Going Home   171

PART IV   The Patients

Understanding the Malpractice Litigation Crisis   *175*

The Scope of Malpractice Litigation   *178*

Medical Negligence: A Protean Concept   *184*

A Generation of Malpractice Crisis   *194*

Malpractice Litigation: A Crisis Getting Worse   *208*

Side Effects on Doctors and Patients   *216*

Final Arguments   *227*

ACKNOWLEDGMENTS

We would like to thank the Honorable J. Frank McGarr, chief judge of the Northern District of Illinois, for his permission to review and transcribe the audio recording of the federal trial that is the subject of this book. We would also like to thank Mr. Victor Villaflor for his great help in accomplishing this task. Our secretary, Ms. Mary Louise Schniedwind, worked diligently on this project and aided us immeasurably during the period of preparation and the trial itself. We are also grateful to Mr. Max Sonderby of the Cook County Jury Verdict Reporter, and to Dr. Richard Warnecke, Ms. Micaela Sullivan, Dr. Jeffrey Wilbert, Mr. Kevin Franke, M.A., and Mr. Richard Lichtenberg, for their research contributions. The research facilities of numerous institutions were made generously available to us, including those of the University of Illinois at the Medical Center in Chicago; Loyola University of Chicago; the University of Miami, Miami, Florida; and the American Medical Association.

We express our gratitude to Dr. Lester Rudy, Chairman of the Department of Psychiatry at the University of Illinois; to Dr. Alfred J. Clementi, chairman, board of trustees, of the Illinois State Medical Society along with its leadership and staff; Mr.

Thomas Sullivan and the staff of the Illinois State Medical Inter-Insurance Exchange; the leadership and staff of the Chicago Medical Society; Mr. Richard Layton, former Vice-President for Marketing of the American Medical Assurance Company; and Ms. Cynthia Baines of the University of Illinois.

To the many physicians throughout the country—and especially those in Illinois—who have generously participated in and supported our research projects, we are most grateful. And we cannot permit thanks to Mrs. Lois Wallace to go without saying.

Without the dutifulness of the following, this book would not have been written at all: Theresa A. Buschek, Charles R. Eby, Rita M. Janos, Kathleen M. Kirby, Thomas L. Scarborough, LeVerne M. Sullivan, Richard L. Thomsen, and Cheryl J. West.

We are particularly grateful to Erwin A. Glikes.

PREFACE TO THE VINTAGE EDITION

When, as a result of the trial experience, I first began to look into the effects of malpractice litigation on the delivery of health care, I wondered if the problem, then largely perceived as one of liability premium costs for doctors, would not resolve itself before I finished my research. Instead, it has worsened beyond anyone's power to anticipate or imagine it. While physicians have been caught between the jaws of escalating insurance payments and exploding legal accusations of malpractice, the real victims of this truly national problem are the ordinary citizens, the recipients of medical care. Few, however, seem aware of the changes litigation has imposed on their medical care. Perhaps the ambivalence Americans feel toward their doctors contributes to their inability to see clearly the enormous impact that the malpractice litigation crisis has had on the culture of medicine in the United States.

Rachel Carson, sensing the insidious long-range effects of the pesticides that seemed to offer such wonderful short-term benefits, foresaw a "silent spring." Nature's life would finally be stilled by the profligate use of chemicals, and people would understand the cause too late to save that fragile and irreplaceable wonder.

America is headed for a silent spring in health care—for a doctor shortage rather than a doctor glut, for a time when the availability of superior health care will be so compromised because, among other things, of the destruction of the fragile environment of professional medical practice, that doctors will not be available, treatment options will be limited, and the horizons of medical research will be severely shrunken. The short-term gains of massive litigation—America has lived up to its reputation as a litigious society—have blinded us to its long-range destructive impact on America in general and on health care in particular. The intended message of the first edition of this book has become all the more urgent in the three years since it was first written. The final sections have been extensively revised and updated so that they reflect the deepening urgency of this extraordinary national problem.

This book is not meant as a special pleading for doctors. Its real concern is for the patients who ultimately pay the bills and suffer the losses in care that result from the battering of professional medicine—in turn the result of the largely unwarranted number of negligence actions that have been brought against the profession over the past generation. It is true that ordinary citizens are beginning to taste the crisis of liability coverage in the rise in their own insurance rates and in those of their school districts, parks, and municipalities. They have begun to suspect that suing for any and every contingency of life ultimately works against the nature of life itself. You cannot cover every possibility of accident or injury without ultimately closing the streets and skies. Ordinary persons understand that life is inherently risky, that they have some responsibility for their existence and conduct, that a society run by legal action will, like that of Athens, lose its vitality and slowly recede. Ordinary persons do not yet fully appreciate that in the long run *they* are the victims of the massive short-range legal onslaught against their physicians. This onslaught is well advanced, as can be seen by examining the evidence provided in this book about early retirement and career changes by doctors because of professional and personal demoralization resulting from the excessive use of lawsuits against them. The impact can also be seen in the diminished numbers of applicants to medical school and in changes in medical practice itself. In addition to defensive medicine, these include the refusal of physicians, because of fear of lawsuits, to perform procedures for which they are well qualified, and their reluctance to treat certain patients perceived as potentially litigious. These losses are translated into diminishing quality and availability of health care for Americans.

The most serious casualty of this phenomenon is the doctor-patient relationship itself. There can be no real care without trust; this essential ingredient of treatment has been notably clouded by the large-scale legal assault on medical competence. Despite contrary assertions, the enormous increase in malpractice suits has not purified or improved medical care. It has not weeded out bad doctors and, in reality, has no real concern with disciplining them or ousting them from the profession. The avalanche of legal action has, however, affected deeply the spirit of the nation's finest physicians, driving them to modify their practices if not to leave practice altogether.

This book is written to make clear the real wounds a society inflicts on itself when it embraces solutions such as excessive litigation without realizing that the presumed cure may kill. It is written in the firm belief that Americans are not going to understand the issues until all participants lower their voices. Nothing will change about the crisis of malpractice and associated litigation in our lives until patients and citizens, as well as professionals, understand how it, like the pesticides that once seemed so wonderful, can bring death to the very people it claims to save.

Sara Charles, M.D.

INTRODUCTION

My first feelings after being charged with medical malpractice were of being utterly alone. Suddenly I felt isolated from my colleagues and patients. Since then I have learned, in the course of my own suit and trial and in the research I have conducted, that this feeling of aloneness is not at all unusual, that almost every physician accused of being negligent has a similar reaction. I also understand that what I experienced during the five-year span of my own case—that it swallowed up my life completely, demanded constant attention and study, multiplied tension and strain, generated a pattern of broken sleep and anxiety because I felt my integrity as a person and as a physician had been damaged and might be permanently lost—are the common reactions of most doctors accused of negligence.

Like everyone else, I was fully aware of the horror stories about patients who had suffered from negligent doctors. Until I was sued, however, I had no idea that similar stories existed about doctors who had been involved in what they considered unjustified malpractice suits. I learned not only that large numbers of physicians felt isolated and ashamed of the compromises with their professional judgment that they made through practicing "defensive medicine," but that many had been permanently damaged as persons and practitioners by the impact of legal action in their lives. Many felt angry at what they perceived as the injustice of the accusations against them. Others reported that they had lost the edge of their confidence as well as the enjoyment they had formerly experienced in their professional activity. The more I studied the more I realized how widespread and unpublicized were the effects of malpractice litigation on the nation's doctors. The number of doctors involved is almost overwhelming. It is estimated, for instance, that one of every two physicians in Illinois has already been sued for malpractice. The doctor-owned Illinois State Medical Inter-Insurance Exchange, which insures 9,348 doctors, reports that during the year 1984–85, 2,647 negligence suits were filed against their physician clients. In the following year, during intense efforts to introduce tort reform measures in Illinois, 2,213 physicians insured by this company were sued between July 30 and November 30, 1985. Doctors might feel isolated, but they are hardly alone in facing the unique challenge of malpractice litigation.

I understood this better when one evening, quite by chance, I was seated next to one of my former medical school professors at a dinner party, a distinguished physician, regarded as one of the world's leading experts in his field of specialization. As we sat and talked he told me many things about himself and his family, including the tragic death of his son in an automobile accident just the year before. It was only after that sad revelation, however, that he mentioned his experience of being named in a malpractice action along with a group of other doctors. They chose to settle the case and he did not have the opportunity, as he put it, "to clear my name and reputation." His own isolation was still obvious as he described his shame at practicing "defensive medicine," by ordering tests that, in his clinical judgment, he deemed unnecessary simply to protect himself against potential litigation for not doing so.

Doctors not only feel ashamed of practicing medicine defensively, they also feel chagrin and regret that the specter of litigation hovers in the background of their relationships with their patients. What most doctors identify as essential to good medicine, healthy and open relationships with those they treat, is now shadowed with hesitation and uncertainty. As they see it, something has been lost in the heart of their life work that is markedly affecting the quality and the delivery of American health care. Doctors, caught up in conflicting advice from insurers and lawyers about the malpractice phenomenon, experience a sense of helplessness about dealing successfully with a problem that has devastated so many of their colleagues and is a constant threat to them.

I have written this book to explore dimensions of the malpractice problem that have major implications for America's doctors and their patients. The first three sections of the book are the story of my own trial for medical malpractice. The concluding section is based on the research that has been carried out by me and others on the nature and effects of malpractice litigation.

The documentary account of the trial is based not only on personal notes and firsthand observations, but also on the audio recording of the proceedings that was made available by the Federal Court in Chicago. A complete transcript of the trial was developed from this recording and it is the source of all trial quotations used here. The recording, of course, also made possible an accurate description of the dramatic qualities—the emotions, tones of voice, pauses, and incidental sounds—of the proceedings.

Although the plaintiff, Terry Walker (not her real name), waived all privilege concerning the confidentiality of all aspects of her treatment sessions, only those materials have been used that, through depositions and trial testimony, have become part of the public record. The re-creation of the psychotherapy is based on my firsthand knowledge of the events and from the testimony given under oath by the principals. It is not meant to be a case history in classic psychiatric form; it focuses primarily on matters that are relevant to the legal construction of the negligence case. So, too, the tight concentration of the trial, as the legal tradition demands, necessarily omits many of the motions and other maneuvers that occurred before and during that event. For the most part, the reader will experience the trial, with its slow revelation of people and events, just as the members of the jury did.

The reconstruction of the dated therapy sessions was based not only on my process notes, but also on the sworn testimony of other principals in depositions taken before the trial began. The words and thoughts attributed, for example, to Terry Walker as she climbed to the roof of her apartment house are not fictionalized suppositions but are taken from her own sworn account of the event. This same principle applies to all other conversations, such as those between her and her former therapist, and members of her family. Sworn depositions by several other persons who did not testify at the trial (such as the New York psychologist and Dr. Edward Wolpert, plaintiff's expert) were drawn upon to check the accuracy of the narrative. Details, for example, of the chapter on how the case was devised are based on depositions, as well as letters, notes, and memoranda that were part of the record. Every effort was made to present exactly what the principals said about themselves and their own thoughts in their own words.

Terry Walker, as I have said, is not the plaintiff's real name. The names of other Walker family members, friends, and former therapists have also been changed.

Although my husband and I worked on every page of this book together, his is the voice that describes the therapeutic sessions and narrates the malpractice trial.

Sara C. Charles, M.D.

DEFENDANT

WHAT IS MEDICAL MALPRACTICE LITIGATION?

Charges of medical negligence constitute a tort or civil rather than a criminal legal action. The vast majority of medical malpractice suits are based on claims of negligence, the doctrine of which entitles the injured plaintiff to damages if it can be proved that the defendant's failure to meet the standard of care due to the plaintiff was the cause of the injury.

Unlike other negligence suits, the standard of care in medical cases is established not by the jury, but through the expert testimony of other members of the medical profession. What is testified to as the "usual and customary" practice within a certain location, a general uncodified rule, becomes, by definition, the applicable standard of care. Recently, there have been efforts on the part of trial lawyers to hold by statute not only board certified but all physicians to a national standard of care irrespective of the nature or location of their practice (P. M. Danzon, *The Frequency and Severity of Medical Malpractice Claims,* Rand Report R-2870, Institute of Civil Justice, Santa Monica, Calif.: Rand Corporation, 1982). The members of the jury in a malpractice trial are, then, the "tryers of fact." They evaluate, on the basis of the evidence in a specific case, whether the defendant physician conformed to the standard set by the experts.

As in any tort action, a negligence suit begins with the filing of a complaint that lists the allegations against the defendant. No proof for these charges need be adduced in order to file such a legal action and the fee for this step in the proceedings is small. The defendant makes a formal legal response and this is followed by a period known as "discovery," during which the opposing sides, through depositions, taken under oath, of relevant witnesses, including medical experts, develop the evidence that will be presented at the later trial. Each side is supplied with copies of all the materials that are generated during this time, which may last many months or even years. An indication of how this period of time is increasing in malpractice litigation is demonstrated in the 1980 report of the National Association of Insurance Commissioners. Paid claims that took an average of thirty-seven months in 1975 from incident to disposition, in 1978 took an average forty-six months. For claims that resulted in no payment, an average twenty-six months elapsed in 1975 from claim to disposition; in 1978, it required an average thirty-eight months to settle or dispose of the claim (*Closed Claim Study,* Brookfield, Wis.: National Association of Insurance Commissioners, 1980, p. 21).

The parties to the suit may agree, during this period, to a settlement through which, without any admission of fault by the defendant, a sum of money is paid to the plaintiff and the charges are dropped. Failing such a formal agreement, the case proceeds toward a trial date. Where there is a diversity of jurisdiction, when the plaintiff comes from a state, for example, different from that in which the alleged tort occurred, (and if the plaintiff asks for damages exceeding $10,000) the trial is filed in a federal rather than a state or circuit court. If a physician proceeds to trial, the carrier for his liability insurance provides a lawyer and pays for the costs of the defense. Should the defendant retain a personal lawyer as well, he or she must pay such legal fees. These are the rules of the law and of the court; the contest, however, is always one between human beings.

THE BEGINNING . . .

First Session—December 9, 1974

It was near the end of a mild fall in Chicago, on that last short bridge of the year between Thanksgiving and Christmas, that Terry Walker called Dr. Sara Charles, a psychiatrist, for a session to evaluate the possibility of entering psychotherapy. One of Terry's supervisors at her graduate program in clinical psychology had suggested it. Persons who planned to be therapists could never learn too much about themselves. Terry stepped into the elevator at the McClurg Court complex and pushed the button for the fourth floor. It was not just her supervisor's idea to get into therapy. There were things she wanted to talk about herself.

She rang the bell of Suite 401-A where Dr. Charles greeted her and ushered her into a large full-windowed office that had been a living room before a number of similar apartments had been leased to doctors, mostly psychiatrists. Dr. Charles was also a professor at the University of Illinois Medical School. They walked together across the shag rug to easy chairs that were placed at an angle to each other at the far end of the sun-filled room.

The young woman—sharp featured, thin, shrugging off the knap-sack in which she carried textbooks—seemed alert, curious, as cautious as a rabbit nosing into unfamiliar ground. She wore the casual clothes common to college and graduate students, a lumpy coat over a green T-shirt, brown slacks, and scarred suede boots.

"What is your interest in getting into psychotherapy?" Dr. Charles asked. Terry settled herself and explained the recommendation of her supervisor. Dr. Charles had been one name on the list. Terry was going to check out two other doctors before choosing a therapist.

Terry did not speak easily and the doctor took the initiative, prompting her with mild questions. The young student viewed her life as if it were a television documentary; she could see and talk about herself from the audience, criticizing, theorizing, but not feeling much. She spoke in a flat voice about her training to be a clinical psychologist, edging cautiously toward her main concern. Arnie, whom she had met during her junior year of college, was moving to Chicago later in the year.

"And I know he expects to move in and live with me. I lived with him in Boston when I was there doing research last year. But I don't know, I just don't know. Arnie's been going with somebody else since then and doesn't think it should make any difference to me. But I told him it did. And he's coming and I have to make up my mind about that. . . ."

"You have real concerns about this boyfriend," Dr. Charles said. "But to help you I need to learn a little about your background." Terry seemed defensive, so the psychiatrist proceeded gently to elicit her case history.

"I'm from the Bronx in New York City," Terry responded. "My family still lives there." Arnie, a law student at Harvard, was all right, but it was his family, warm and concerned, that Terry really liked. Terry had been strongly attracted to the mothers of other boyfriends, too. There had been Sherman, her best friend in the high school they attended in New York. "I hated it, it was a long way to travel every day. After school I'd often go home with Sherman to his house. I was comfortable with his mother, I liked being there with her. Then I'd go to my own home as late as possible. . . ."

"Why don't you tell me a little more about your own family?" the psychiatrist asked. . . .

Terry Walker's Had an Accident—November 16, 1975

It was 1:30 on Sunday afternoon when the phone rang in Dr. Charles's apartment. It was the psychologist supervisor who had originally referred Terry Walker for therapy. "Have you heard what happened?"

"No, what do you mean?"

"Terry Walker's had an accident. Yesterday. She's in Northwestern Hospital, in intensive care, very serious. I wondered if anyone had called you. . . ."

Terry in an accident? Dr. Charles had spoken to her just yesterday. The young woman had talked about going home to see her parents for a few days. She had made an extra appointment to discuss things on Monday morning. An accident?

"She fell off the roof of her apartment building yesterday. . . ."

What could have happened? Terry had weathered some crises in the past few months. She had been making real progress. . . .

Dr. Charles called the hospital and reached Terry's father. He had meant to call her, he said in a choked voice. Terry had asked him to call her specifically, but in all the confusion he had not done it. But Terry did want to see her. Could the doctor come? Yes, Dr. Charles said, she would be there in a few minutes.

Dr. Charles stepped out of the elevator into the alcove near the intensive care unit. A tall, gaunt man stood about ten paces across the reception area. Dr. Charles introduced herself to Terry's father who explained that he had flown in from New York the previous afternoon. He rubbed his eyes as he sat down with the psychiatrist on the bench that was just large enough to hold the two of them.

Terry had been upset the day before, Mr. Walker explained, Terry had called her family, the family had called her brother-in-law, a medical intern in Boston. There had also been phone conversations with a former therapist of Terry's in New York. And Mr. Walker had flown out, bringing medicine for Terry; he had flown out but it had been too late. . . .

Mr. Walker sobbed. Yes, surely, Dr. Charles could see Terry as soon as Terry's sister and brother-in-law came out of the unit.

Terry Walker, her eyes wide with fear, lay on a Stryker Frame in the intensive care unit. She had undergone a tracheostomy, the insertion of a tube in her throat to make it possible for her to breathe. Tethered to the breathing machine and the intravenous equipment, she resembled a small bird trapped cruelly in a net of steel. She struggled to speak.

Yes, Dr. Charles replied, her father had explained a little about what had happened. Terry flashed an anxious signal to the psychiatrist with her eyes as she formed words with her lips. Dr. Charles repeated them to make sure she understood.

"How many people know about this? I don't want them to know at school; I don't want anybody at school to know. I'm afraid of what they'll think of me. . . ." She paused. "I'm afraid if they find out about this they'll also find out about what happened to me in my first year of college. . . ."

The Call from the U.S. Marshal—October 13, 1976

What could the call mean?

Dr. Charles had received a variety of anxious messages from her answering service during the years of her psychiatric practice, but never one from a federal marshal. There was no indication of urgency, or even of great importance, no request to call back right away. She was tied up as an examiner of candidates for national board certification in psychiatry and neurology. When she returned the call during a break in the schedule, the marshal told Sara calmly, almost offhandedly, that he had left something at her office. So it was at the end of a long day of judging the skills of psychiatrists as they interviewed patients that she returned to her office and picked up the marshal's bulky envelope.

Alone in the room in which for years she had listened to the painful life stories of scores of men and women, with the late afternoon sounds of the city rising as though from a great distance around her, she opened the envelope.

The unfolded paper in her hand was a summons with an attached complaint that accused her of being a negligent doctor, of being a careless and indifferent physician who had done grievous harm to Terry Walker. She was being sued for $10 million.

The "factual allegations" of the complaint ran paragraph after paragraph. It was a version of her relationship with Terry Walker that was unrecognizable to her. Section 16 read:

The Defendant, a trained Psychiatrist and Medical Doctor, was negligent in her actual therapy sessions with the Plaintiff by not taking the Plaintiff's depression and suicidal tendencies seriously, joking about them, insulting and degrading and in other ways which only caused the Plaintiff to go into a deeper depression, to distrust her self-worth and ultimately to attempt to commit suicide.

It further alleged that Dr. Charles had "admitted to plaintiff's parents that [she] may have made a clinical error."

What in God's name could have happened? Dr. Charles had continued to see Terry as a patient at the Rehabilitation Institute until Terry had discharged her in March. But there had been no accusations. No hint of anything like this. What was this all about anyway? The psychiatrist stared down at the summons, at the title that had so suddenly been given to her. For unrelieved months and years to come she would be known as *the defendant*.

PART I

The Plaintiff

THE TRIAL—DAY ONE

Opening Statements

Dr. Charles never recognized the seriousness of it.

—Patrick Murphy

Dr. Charles . . . had no part in it.

—William Maddux

Ninety degrees at midmorning. We make our way through the crowded Loop streets to the Dirksen Federal Building on Dearborn Street. After four years and as many changes in the trial date, we are heading for the courtroom resolution of the malpractice case against Sara. I hurry along in step with our personal lawyer, Thomas Boodell, as Sara moves swiftly ahead of us caught up in conversation with William Maddux, the lawyer who will defend her at the trial. Everything is on the line now. Our life has already been profoundly affected by the charges. A finding against Sara will alter it permanently. I know what she feels inside, even when she smiles at Maddux and says that she wished she were in Italy. The square-jawed Maddux smiles as though we were all about to begin a great adventure together, and asks genially, "What would you want to be there for?"

"Because then I wouldn't be here," Sara replies.

The courtroom, softly lit, half again the size of a tennis court, is dreamlike. Maddux tells me and Boodell to sit in the back benches with the spectators. "We don't want to look like we're ganging up on them," he says tersely. Then he turns to Sara, "And don't take any notes." Boodell—tall, distinguished-looking, Princeton and Harvard—has worked on the case for years, has taken the most significant depositions. Now, along with me, he must sit on the sidelines.

The plaintiff's lawyer, Patrick Murphy, a forty-year-old bachelor in a rumpled summer suit, stands at a table on the jury box side of the courtroom. With wispy blond hair askew above the brow of his narrow-eyed Irish baby face, Murphy flips through the pages of a legal pad. He is acting Public Guardian for the state of Illinois and often appears on local news shows as a crusader for the underdog.

"Terry Walker versus Sara Charles," the court clerk snaps as though calling out the name of a commuter station, "On trial!" The plaintiff, Terry Walker, arrives during the judge's preliminary remarks to the jury. The doors of the courtroom are thrust open and she rides her electric wheelchair down the aisle into the well of the court, bumping it against the table at which her lawyers sit. Sharp featured beneath Tiny Tim hair, Terry looks harsh and broken. Murphy leans over to speak to his client before standing to introduce his case.

"If it please the court," he says softly, looking up at Federal Judge J. Frank McGarr, the courtly, nobly wattled, sweet-voiced jurist who will preside.

Murphy speaks solemnly. "I want to make a contract with you now," he says to the six jurors and two alternates. "And that is, I'm going to tell you what I believe the evidence shows. I want you to hold me to it. I want you to recall each and every thing I tell you." He turns his head toward the defense table and raises his voice. "And I want *Mr. Maddux to write it down* so in final arguments he can get up here and tell you if I told you something that wasn't said on the witness stand, something that wasn't true. . . ."

He glances at Judge McGarr who has begun to make notations on a legal pad. At a desk below and to the side of the judge, the clerk of the court, a man always in the midst of other people's troubles, stamps a document, *ker-chunk*. That sound, like a judgment sealed, will counterpoint the tense proceedings for the next ten days. It is a symbol of the world going about its business while this private event flows into and becomes indistinguishable from the great river of human woe.

"This case," plaintiff lawyer Murphy says, "involves negligence and malpractice. Judge McGarr will read you the law at the proper time and tell you what standards you're to apply to the physician who may or may not have been guilty of malpractice. We will present witnesses who will tell you about Terry Walker—parents, sister, brother-in-law, and others—and tell you about a young woman who was full of life from her formative years. . . .

"A young woman who grew up in New York City," Murphy continues in slightly husky tones. "The Bronx. Had everything going for her. Two, three times in her life, witnesses will tell you, something happened. It was crazy. We're told we're not supposed to use words like 'crazy,' 'nuts.' Because those are the words we used when we were kids for people who were not all there. There are new words: psychotic, schizophrenic, manic-depressive, borderline personality, character disorder, neurotic, so on and so forth. These are the fancy terms. They describe behavior we're aware of. Different degrees of craziness you'll hear the experts talk about. For situations which might be hard to explain. . . ."

Murphy looks again toward his client. "But when you're going down, when one is going down that slippery slope into the abyss, reaching out for help, trying to say, 'I don't know what's going on. I don't know why I'm acting irrationally. I might even know what is supposed to be rational but I don't know why I'm in this situation.' The experts will talk, and one thing we're asking is that you as the jury try to understand the concept of people who are not operating rationally. . . .

"Twice in her life, Terry Walker did not act rationally. First year of college, Terry was eighteen years old. Nothing to fear in school. Suddenly, she starts phoning her sister every day, two, three times a day. Then she started phoning her parents. She didn't make sense. She said, 'I'm worried about school, I'm worried about my boyfriend.' And they, in their naiveté, they thought there was something wrong with Terry at school—even though she's getting straight *A's*—and that there was something wrong with Terry and her boyfriend. . . . But she kept getting worse.

Family and sister, like any family that's close and strong and works together, went up to Cornell and 'Let's try to deal with this.' Ultimately, Terry had to come home. She continued to act crazy." Murphy sweeps a gesture toward his client. "She would talk nonsensically to her parents, to her mother. She would stand by open windows and would stare out." The lawyer, continuing to gesture with his free hand, speaks dramatically as he offers a glimpse of life in the Walker household. "The mother got so she was afraid to take a shower. She had to keep the door open to make sure Terry was in her sight at all times. One time she caught Terry with her leg out the window. Pulled her back. And for the first time in his life, her father slapped Terry. 'Don't go near the window. We live ten floors up.' " Murphy is almost out of breath. "She had a fixation with open windows."

The lawyer speeds up his narrative; the words come tumbling out. "Terry started seeing the psychiatrist. Again, Terry continued to fall down that slippery slope of irrationality. And at one point the mother, Mrs. Walker, and Terry went to her sister's dormitory—the sister was in college in New York—and Mrs. Walker left Terry alone for a minute and the next thing they know Terry was in front of an open window and it took two people to pull her from that window. Again she was screaming and acting irrationally.

"Finally, [they] got her downstairs, took her to the psychiatrist's office. She broke loose again and ran down Park Avenue screaming. In the middle of New York City, in the middle of the afternoon. They chased after her, grabbed her, and pulled her back. The psychiatrist had to come down and said, 'For God's sake, get her into a hospital.' They took her to a hospital. Terry was admitted. In a psychiatric hospital for three months." Murphy's voice is calmer. "She didn't do very well. Then she improved under the therapist, Dr. Waxman." Marvin Waxman, a psychologist in White Plains, New York, has already given a deposition in the case. He will not appear in court, although he will be a presence.

Murphy describes Terry's recovery, her successful completion of college, and her entering a graduate program in psychology. "She wanted to see a therapist. So she paid *good money* to Dr. Charles, the defendant in this case, to try to understand, to try to get help for whatever it was that bothered her. When she went to see Dr. Charles she was an average graduate student." Murphy speaks dramatically again. "And then, in the summer of 1975, Terry began to gradually show some of the same signs she had exhibited four years before. Maybe no one could tell. And as she moved into the fall, they kept getting worse. She would tell Dr. Charles such things as 'I'm out of control,' 'I feel like I did the first year of college;' 'I can't sleep, I wake up in the middle of the night.' She would relate these things to problems she was having with school. Same thing she did in [her] first year of college. Dr. Charles, the witnesses will say, mistreated her as if the problem were the boyfriend and the problem was school instead of the problem being this much deeper, emotional craziness that was going on. Terry talked about her break, her breakdown, first year of college. She called Dr. Charles many, many nights, one time four days in a row, obsessing. She, as Dr. Charles points out, just saying, 'I don't know what to do, I don't know whether I can stay in school or not, I don't know. . . .' "

Murphy has hinted, in citing Sara against herself, at a body of materials central to the case for both sides. These are Sara's personal notes that through a series of preliminary motions she resisted turning over to Murphy. They not only contained potentially damaging information about Terry Walker, but also about members of her family and friends. Although she had been ordered by the judge to let Murphy and the plaintiff's psychiatric experts examine them in preparing the case, Sara is still fighting to keep them out of the trial itself. A final argument will be made on the issue the next morning.

"In the meantime," Murphy resumes, "she was doing very well in school. 'I don't know whether to date my boyfriend, I don't know whether or not to go out.' She called Dr. Charles at one and two in the morning. She started calling her parents and her sister—all hours of the day and night. There's much other evidence you will hear. I'm just giving you a brief outline." He glances down at the tumbled yellow pages in this hand. "Finally, her sister's husband, . . . Dr. Lester Walston, called Dr. Charles on November 13 and said, 'I want to share something. Terry was acting the way she did in the first year of college. We're very concerned. She's calling two straight weeks between one and five in the morning. And obviously not sleeping.' " He resumes his account of the brother-in-law's phone call. "He said,

'I talked it over with colleagues of mine at the hospital and they said use *Mellaril, she needs something strong, an antidepressant.* . . .' Dr. Charles says, *'I'm the doctor.*'"

The plaintiff's lawyer bends forward. "Two days later Terry continued, the thirteenth, the fourteenth, in this downward slide. Grasping, trying to cry out. You know there's a number of ways that people cry out for help. Terry would go to Dr. Charles and plunk down her money and say 'Help me, you're a professional, you're a psychiatrist.' The other way in which it's communicated, Terry did. It's reflected all the way through." Murphy refers again obliquely to the notes. " 'I'm losing control, please help me, I can't sleep.' The message was coming across. But what was coming back was no help. When Terry said, 'I'm losing control,' *no help!* When Terry said, 'I feel like cardboard,' *no help!* And so on until, finally, on the fifteenth, on Saturday, she's calling her parents, she's talking to her former therapist, who's a good friend at this point, Dr. Waxman in New York. . . . 'Our kid's the same way she was when she was standing in front of those open windows. Something is going to happen! She is crazy. We've got to do something.' " Murphy presses hard toward the fateful moment. "Terry called Dr. Charles, the defendant, on that morning, the fifteenth, and said, 'Maybe I should get some Mellaril, maybe I could get some help. . . .' Dr. Charles says, 'I'll give you Valium or . . . a sedative.' Which our experts will testify that that would not only have done no good, but would have been counterproductive." He shifts his papers. "Through all these Terry is calling for help. Parents heard the call for help and finally the father boarded the plane and flew to Chicago to try to help." He pauses. "It was too late. Terry had leapt off the roof of her building. . . ."

Murphy takes a breath. "Now the defense will be that Dr. Charles didn't push her off the roof. . . . a young woman who was without rationale or without reason, in a *deep depression.* You know there are levels of depression. There is the Grand Canyon when you fall into this clinical depression. This Grand Canyon, the experts will tell, you don't think rationally, you don't think about 'Maybe I can get out.' There's no time. You go *down, down, down.* . . ." His voice trails off.

"The evidence will show," he continues, "that Dr. Charles was negligent in various ways. Number one, when Terry Walker came to her, Dr. Charles never took an accurate history. The physician has to take a history. . . . Terry at the third session told Dr. Charles 'I was hospitalized.' This was a year before the jump. 'I was hospitalized for a psychiatric illness.' Dr. Charles, the defendant, *never once* attempted to contact [Terry's] former therapist, never once called the hospital, never once asked for the hospital notes to find out how serious this was. Even though Terry said she went in for suicidal tendencies, because she was suicidal, and it's reflected. Dr. Charles knew that. She never once followed up to determine how serious was the suicide. Dr. Charles has written" Murphy speaks as a man does lowering a trump card "an article and she said seventy percent of all people who threaten suicide, attempt suicide. So Dr. Charles *knew* that seriousness of it. Terry was one of those seventy percent. And then when Terry, six or eight months into therapy, began acting crazy, began obsessing, told Dr. Charles 'I'm panicking, I don't know what I'm doing.' . . . at least, Dr. Charles, the experts will say 'to *for God's sake, find out what's going on.* . . .'

"What happened? Her [Dr. Charles] testimony will be she only went into the former hospitalization when Terry brought it up and then she didn't inquire about it—of Terry Walker—about the suicide. . . . The danger signs were all there. But not recognizing it, because of lack of taking an adequate history, Dr. Charles let Terry Walker go, thinking she was apparently dealing with a boyfriend situation, a situation involved with class. . . ." Murphy inhales. "But when Dr. Charles, day in and day out, in September, October, November of 1975, Dr. Charles should have known, that that person sitting in front of her and calling at one or two in the morning, 'My God, I'm dealing with a serious case here.' And what comes across is that Dr. Charles *never* recognized the seriousness of it, and even assuming she did, she was even negligent in that situation because she should have taken steps, and they would have been let's increase the visitation. 'You have to see me three or four times a week.' Or 'Let's talk about an antidepressant drug. You're very depressed. Let's do something about that depression.' Or 'Terry, you may not like it but you've got to go back in the hospital. . . .' "

Murphy pauses and speaks in more measured tones. "Besides negligence in this case, we'll talk about damages. . . ." He looks down at the young woman seated in the wheelchair a few feet away from him. "Would Terry Walker be happier with $10 million dollars or with the ability to ski, or the ability to walk, or the ability to stretch, or the ability to go to the toilet without the humiliation and embarrassment of having people to help her? Or even telling her—she has no sense of feel if she soils herself— or without going around with tubes in her because it's the only way she can relieve herself? Whether she'd be happier boating, going for a walk along the lake, or be in a situation to meet young men? Or where any twenty-six- or twenty-seven-year-old woman would like to be instead of being confined in some apartment? She can never get herself to get outside even though, as you'll hear, she had demonstrated a great deal of raw courage coming back from a situation where she could move only her head a couple of years ago, where now she can move around with the help of a wheelchair, and a situation where she's about to get her Ph.D."

Murphy surveys the jury members. "With that kind of culpability," he says, "you pay the damages." He pauses, sighs, and speaks dispassionately. "We want you in this trial to keep an open mind." He recapitulates again the procedure of the trial. Then he turns toward his client. "Terry will not be able to attend all the sessions. She'll be here as much as her stamina permits her. Hope you will not hold it against her. . . ." He speaks a few more sentences urging a verdict for his client, says calmly that he wants recompense, and sits down.

Defense lawyer Maddux rises from his chair. He carries no notes nor has he prepared a formal opening statement. His style is to listen intently to the opposing lawyer and to design his remarks in response. Maddux is a veteran trial lawyer, raised in Boys Town, once mayor of the famous institution, who went to Notre Dame University and Georgetown Law School. Unlike Murphy, whose large staff of assistants shuttles in and out of the courtroom with books and notes, Maddux prefers to function on his own. His brown hair is flecked with gray above features that are weathered but still boyish. If Murphy is the streetfighter, Maddux is the lone eagle.

"At this time, . . ." he begins quietly. "It really should be our proper role at this time to acquaint you with the evidence of the case." Maddux moves closer to the jury box. "I was challenged to write it down." He hunches his shoulder in Murphy's direction without looking at him. "That's what he said. 'Hold him to it.'" He pauses again, letting Murphy's opening pact with them stand fleetingly in the jurors' memory. "I'll have to confess to you, I didn't get many notes. Because I didn't hear much about why Dr. Charles is here to defend this case." His tone is dry and skeptical. "Didn't hear much from what he said about why she's supposed to be responsible for this. So I guess I'll have to wait for the evidence to hear that.

"But I think the evidence is going to show that the plaintiff in this case, yes, she did have a problem. She had a basic character disorder. . . . that is called borderline personality. She has a problem where she needs therapy, psychiatric therapy. The purpose of the therapy from the time that she first engaged Dr. Charles in late 1974—because the incident took place on November 15, 1975—during that period of time the role of Dr. Charles as the therapist was to try to make the plaintiff, Terry Walker, aware of what her character disorder was and help her to come to grips with it so that she could live a normal life.

"And she was doing pretty well." There is an affirming tone in Maddux's voice. "She was doing pretty well. She really was. And from time to time she had a little crisis involving not being able to make a decision. And the doctor would help her know and understand her own decision making. So whether she should go away for a weekend with her boyfriend or not, you know, really serious problems like what courses to take or not to take in school. But this young lady was functioning very well. She was living independently in Chicago, with her parents in New York, her family in New York. She was doing well in school. She went to school every day. She was functioning: she had a job, she had activities, she had a social life. She had all that. She was carrying on all that at the same time. And you wouldn't look at her and say 'There's something wrong.' You wouldn't. There was everything normal about her life and activities."

Maddux faces the jury directly, his arms at his sides. "She had a couple of crises—one in October—that she got over. And, again, the role of the therapist is to try to help someone with this particular problem. These are problems themselves and she can handle them. And she was doing it." He pauses slightly. "And she wasn't getting progressively worse. There were not these fantastic frantic phone calls. In the last couple of—in the period of time prior to the time that she, that this episode happened—probably no more than eleven phone calls. We'll recount them for you. The evidence will show the facts. Dr. Charles has an answering service—and she returns calls promptly. The evidence will show that she talked to Terry Walker every time she called. She has records of them."

Maddux steps back a pace, moving his arms in an explanatory gesture. "So, what really occurred was this young lady, in the circumstances, wasn't 'crazy,' as was said to you. She had this character disorder. She was facing up to it. . . . She wasn't having any insomnia, or any problems sleeping. She was sleeping the proper time. She wasn't psychotic. She wasn't neurotic. She was in the borderline category. And she went through another of those little very human crises that she'd already gone through before but had come out of all right." Maddux stands perfectly still in front of the jury box. "And this time there was some interference from some outside parties that interfered and interrupted the psychiatrist-patient relationship. That was the response of Dr. Waxman, who was not a medical doctor, not a psychiatrist, but a psychologist in New York. And Terry Walker called him just prior to this on November 15—and he did some things that no person should ever do, especially a psychologist, who certainly should know better than to do it. He told her she was sicker than she thought she was. And told her that she needed a lot of things, that she needed help. And the family formed a plan, and then they informed Terry Walker that they would send someone to Chicago to get her and bring her back to New York, hospitalize her, drug her—do all those things to her. And she herself got panicky—and that's because with this little episode she went too far. And she knew it. At a time when she was trying to be independent, and she was trying to make her own decisions, and at a time when she was trying to get along in society as well as she could, she got this problem with Dr. Waxman started, kept it going, and then she was in a corner. And had to make a decision about what she was going to do. She thought rationally and quite consciously, she thought the answer to her problem was to jump off the roof." Maddux speaks quietly. "Dr. Charles didn't do it, had no part in it."

He makes a quarter turn in the space of a pause. "The significance is that, the evidence will show that—this is Saturday, November 15, 1975—that Terry Walker had talked to Dr. Charles that morning, after she had talked to this Dr. Waxman, and told Dr. Charles that she wanted a certain kind of medicine. And in Dr. Charles's opinion it was not the right medicine for her to take.

It was not good for her. It was not part of her therapy. So Dr. Charles suggested an alternative. And that was the last contact. It is also significant to know that Dr. Charles talked to Terry about what she had been doing and what her plans were for the rest of the day. And she made Dr. Charles aware that she was functioning all right, and she had plans and goals. She had things she was going to do. She had them all mapped out in her mind and there was nothing that was really that wrong. All this other business with Dr. Waxman and her parents—all that, that all happened *after* Terry Walker had talked to Dr. Charles. She had no more contact with Dr. Charles. And it was because of that interference, because of that *pressure drawn by the family*, because of Dr. Waxman's telling her she was sicker than she really was, that she had prompted a response she didn't really want. She was going to be taken out of school and be put in a hospital, and all those things. Her independence was going to be destroyed. She would be captured, taken back. That's when she jumped off the roof."

The only sounds that can be heard in the courtroom come from Murphy's flipping over legal sheets as he makes hurried notations.

"The clear and simple point is that Terry Walker has a responsibility for herself—not to injure herself. We think the evidence will clearly show that not only did Dr. Charles not do anything that caused or contributed to the injury of Terry Walker—Terry Walker was an adult, a rational being who made a conscious decision to solve her problems in her particular way. That is not the fault of Dr. Charles. It's unfortunate. But the evidence will show—clearly an unfortunate circumstance that will evoke a good deal of sympathy—but it isn't the fault of Dr. Charles. And at the conclusion of this case—and I think based on the evidence— you will agree with me that a verdict in favor of Dr. Charles is indicated."

Maddux turns and walks quietly past Murphy. Judge McGarr looks benignly at the jury. He has the manner of a man who reassures you that it is all right for you to go home because it means he can go home as well. He makes a slip of the tongue that reveals his feelings about the trial, which, delayed many times, has finally begun. "I suggested to the attorneys that we'd adjourn for the day after *closing* arguments because I thought jury selection would take a little longer than it did. . . ."

Concerning Confidentiality

Excerpt from *Mental Health and Developmental Disabilities Confidentiality Act,* Illinois, 1979

Article 1, Section 2, Number 4
  "Personal notes" means:
  (i)   information disclosed to the therapist in confidence by other persons on condition that such information would never be disclosed to the recipient or other persons;
  (ii) information disclosed to the therapist by the recipient which would be injurious to the recipient's relationships to other persons, and
  (iii) the therapist's speculations, impressions, hunches, and reminders.

* * *

Medical confidentiality, as it has traditionally been understood by patients and doctors, no longer exists. This ancient medical principle, which has been included in every physician's oath and code of ethics since Hippocratic times, has become old, worn out, and useless; it is a decrepit concept.

> "Confidentiality in Medicine—A Decrepit Concept"
> by Mark Sigler, M.D.
> *The New England Journal of Medicine*
> December 9, 1982, p. 1518.

* * *

DAY TWO

A Psychiatrist's Notes

They prove our case.

—Patrick Murphy

Judge McGarr has not only ordered Sara's personal notes surren-
dered to the plaintiff's lawyer, Patrick Murphy and his experts,
but has also allowed Terry Walker to read them. Standing at a
rostrum facing the benign-looking judge—the jury is absent for
the discussion—Tom Boodell now argues for their exclusion from
the trial in a loud clear voice. "Personal notes . . . are not notes
that are intended for use by anybody but the psychiatrist. That
is what the subsequent law [of Illinois] here sought to protect.
That is what psychiatrists have been taught and believed for years.
And that is the way they take their notes, that . . . the meaning
of which is only known to the psychiatrist and can only be interpreted by the psychiatrist." Even if the judge allows them in,
Boodell continues, plaintiff's counsel should explain which sections he intends to use so that "we're not left at the end of the
case with a lot of arguments from words and phrases from those

notes that we haven't heard a lot about in the conduct of the case."

Murphy calmly responds that there is a "compelling need" for admission of the notes. He quotes several snatches from them, "Again and again we see these indications in the notes that should have been telling Dr. Charles that you're dealing with a very sick person, particularly if Dr. Charles related that back to what happened the first time around." He is animated. "It's very important to get them in. They prove our case. They prove what Terry will testify from the stand." Judge McGarr lifts his copy of the notes, Solomon with the baby in his hand. "I find that they are relevant, probative, admissible, and that the plaintiff has demonstrated a compelling need for them and, therefore, once again, I will deny the motion for exclusion of the notes from evidence."

Sara, who has not even let me read the notes during the long years of preparation for the trial, has lost her last chance to shield them from public exposure. The judge signals the bailiff to bring in the jury.

The Plaintiff's Case

THE MOTHER

It was a nice, small family.

—Gerda Walker

Everything is finally locked in place. The six women and two men of the jury—solemn, not even allowing themselves a sideways glance at each other—settle into their chairs. Terry Walker is not in the courtroom. "Proceed, Mr. Murphy," the judge says, picking up his yellow legal pad. Murphy rises and turns as a stockily built woman in her early fifties, henna hair piled above a pale complexion, edges past the plaintiff's table toward the witness stand. Gerda Walker, Terry's mother, clutches a handkerchief in her right hand. She is sworn in, and as she spells her name at Murphy's request, she struggles for breath.

"It's understandable and common," Judge McGarr says gently. "Everybody here is friendly and will be kind to you. And all we want is the information you have to give us."

"That's what I'm here to tell you," she says earnestly, twisting her handkerchief.

She explains emotionally that she came to the United States in 1939 when she was twelve. "I ran away from Hitler's Germany." She settled in New York City and married Mitchell Walker just before her twenty-first birthday. They have two daughters, Terry, twenty-eight, and Carol, who is three years older and married to Lester Walston. Murphy asks her about Terry.

Mrs. Walker sighs. "Miss Popularity would be the first thing that would come to my mind. She had many friends, boys as well as girls. She loved music. . . ." Her voice is warm, proud, gushing. "She took the guitar very seriously. I think when she was in high school and her teacher was so enamored of her and her ability he said to her 'You know, one of these days you might even be better than Judy Collins!' We thought that was going quite a ways." Mrs. Walker explains that Terry was so popular that even though her high school did not have valedictorians, the students requested that she be given that honor.

"And, Mrs. Walker, what was your family like?" Murphy asks, "with Terry, Carol, and your husband?"

"Well, it was a nice small family." Mrs. Walker's tones are those of cozy recollection. "We were very close with one another. The girls were close enough in age, they were very good friends besides being sisters." Murphy steps aside so that his witness can have center stage. "We did many things together. There was a time we wanted, for instance, to get tickets to the Metropolitan . . . and you couldn't get tickets for it. And finally we were lucky, we were able to get tickets. It was on a Friday night. And I said no, Friday night is positively out, that is always family night. I light my candles, we have the traditional dinner. The children never accepted dates—they didn't go out either until very much later. What would happen generally was their friends would come to the house. Friday night we were together." Mrs. Walker pauses briefly, clears her throat.

"We went on vacation trips together. One year we took our daughters to Rome. We showed them the magnificent cathedrals, the beautiful antiquities of Rome, and the Roman environs. . . . And then we took them on a skiing trip to Zermatt, Switzerland. Terry was not as adept as her older sister. It seemed the air was too pure for her. She would blanch sometimes and would have to leave the slope for a lower slope."

Murphy interrupts with a question. "Would you characterize the family, then, as very close?"

"Oh, yes; oh, yes," she responds effusively, "our family was very close. Every member was as important as the next one to one another. The kids were concerned with us. Oh, they made up parties we didn't know about. Anniversary parties. The first party they threw us was when we were married fifteen years. That would make Carol twelve and Terry nine years old. And we really knew nothing about it and the two of them shopped. The grandparents and friends offered to give some money and help. They didn't want any of it, they spent their own money, they put it all together. They made up menus—love tomato juice, love this, love that. You know everything was love and kisses and all that kind of stuff. . . . Obviously these kids must have liked their parents."

Mrs. Walker pours herself a glass of water after explaining that her daughter Terry went to college at Cornell "up in Ithaca."

"Mrs. Walker, did anything unusual happen during Terry's first year in college?"

Mrs. Walker's voice quakes. "She started to get very nervous. . . . She was making calls to our home."

Her voice is filled with anguish as she describes the calls—frantic and incoherent—coming one after the other. "She began to tell me that she couldn't live her life that way any more, she was afraid of what was happening to her . . . she couldn't cope, she couldn't function, she couldn't do the work she was there to do, and 'I think I'm going to jump in the gorge.' What is the gorge? She says it's a place that people jump off. I had not seen that gorge until some time later when everything was better and we visited her at Cornell. . . ." She speaks breathlessly, beside herself in recollection. "When I saw *that gorge* I think my heart stood still. I've never seen anything . . ." she takes a deep breath, "where there was such a deep drop into like a river of water—I don't know, maybe a rocky bed. But when I saw where the drop, my heart, honest to God, it stood still."

The family decided that Terry's father and sister should go up and see her. "He said her room was a *shambles!* It was not to be believed. And while he was there. . . . he walked her to class. She couldn't do her work and they went back to her room and she tried to tell him she'd be all right. . . . Then my husband decided that he would come back home and he went to the airport. But he called her and she says, 'Daddy, you'd better come back,

I don't think I'm gonna make it, I will have to come home with you.' So he went back again, as best I can remember, and she stayed." Later on, Mrs. Walker explains, Terry complained again and Carol went to bring her home.

"Could you describe how she was acting?" Murphy asks.

Mrs. Walker groans. "Well, for those of you here who have seen *The Exorcist* I might," and she wrinkles the surface of her narrative with a laugh. "I might best put it that way. Her voice didn't change, I recognized her voice, but the things that were coming out of her mouth were not to be believed. They were so frightening, they were so foolish, they were insane. I heard my daughter's voice but these were not words that would normally flow from her. . . . She kept saying to me, 'You don't understand, you don't understand.' She said, 'You think I can't read, wait, I'll show you I can read.' She grabbed the nearest newspaper, went into her room, was there for a few minutes, came out again. 'I can't read, I can't really put it together. I think I have a problem.' "

The Walkers sought help for Terry when she came home from college. There were a few visits to one doctor, then another, and finally to a Park Avenue psychiatrist, who, after a short period of time, agreed with Terry's request to return to school. She was there for about a week when the phone calls began again. Terry couldn't cope with things and her sister went up and brought her home.

"And how was she at home on the second occasion?" Murphy asks quietly.

Mrs. Walker answers gravely in a low voice. "Very bad. Very bad. The same thing . . . the same carrying on. She couldn't read, she couldn't function, she said there's no point to her living. . . ." Mrs. Walker's voice has a hint of distance in it as she concludes, "She was pretty crazy."

"Did you take any precautions?"

"Oh, yes, yes," Mrs. Walker answers eagerly, tensely. "I really couldn't leave her sight, I absolutely couldn't leave because, first of all, she threatened suicide constantly. She pauses for a breath and returns with a low-pitched aside, "And I wasn't having it. I only have two children. I don't have any to spare. . . ." Mrs. Walker sobs. "So I made her sleep in my husband's bed. I took showers with my bathroom door open. Excuse me, but I went to the john with the door open. I watched her all the time. . . ." Mrs. Walker presses her handkerchief against her sigh. "I was living on the edge of a sword practically. . . ."

Defense attorney Maddux cuts through the heightened emotion in matter-of-fact tones, "I have an objection to the running commentary by the witness and ask the court to restrain the testimony to the normal, customary questions."

The judge turns toward the startled witness and asks Mrs. Walker to limit her answers specifically to the questions.

Chastened, her tears dried, Mrs. Walker says, "I will try. But I'd like everyone here to understand that this is my first visit to a courtroom of any sort," and she pauses ever so slightly, "other than to become a citizen."

Murphy draws her back. "Besides Terry speaking suicidal things, did she ever do anything?"

Mrs. Walker sighs. "One fine Sunday—we were having a very hard day with her—she walked into her room—and I was close behind her—put one foot over the windowsill and said, 'Mom, this is it, I'm going.' " Mrs. Walker heaves with dramatic intensity. "I dragged her in physically. By her hair. By her arms. I pulled her the length of the corridor between her room and mine, dragged her into the bedroom by her hair, by her arms—it was a brutal thing I was doing—and screaming. And this was the first time my husband ever hit her. He had never laid a hand on her before."

"Did anything like that happen afterward?"

Mrs. Walker takes a deep breath. "One day we had to bring her to the doctor. . . . We went to Carol's dorm to wash up and brush our teeth to take Terry to the doctor . . . and Carol and Terry went up to Carol's dorm and I parked the car and I got there some ten or fifteen minutes later. And I said, 'Where's Terry?' Well, we saw her come in, we don't know where she is. I began looking for her. She was standing in front of a huge open window. It was a window that was almost from ceiling to floor, larger than an ordinary window. And I walked over and I said, 'Terry, what are you doing!' She just gave me one of those stares. She said, 'I'm thinking,' or words to that effect. And I tried to get her out but I couldn't." Mrs. Walker describes wrestling Terry to the floor and out of the room with the help of another student. She gulps a breath. "Then we had to get ready to go down to the car to see the psychiatrist . . . and when we were approaching the car she started to make a run for it and I grabbed her and Carol grabbed her and we started to restrain her. . . . And we finally got her in the car. . . . It was a two-door car—and I had her on my lap. And when we arrived at our destination . . . she bolted for it. I took off after her. I tackled her and nailed her to the ground. And she began to get away from me and I began to scream. On fancy Park Avenue. . . . Finally, the doctor had to come out and he subdued her and took her into his office." Mrs. Walker explains the doctor's decision to hospitalize her.

Carol and Mrs. Walker, joined by a friend of her husband's, took the struggling, resisting Terry to the hospital, which was connected with the Cornell Medical School in White Plains, New York. Terry escaped from the car as they neared the hospital and had to be tackled and subdued again. "She fought going," Mrs. Walker says, "she didn't want to go. She wanted to wait to see her father." Ultimately, however, Terry signed herself in.

Mrs. Walker moves on to describe Terry's hospital progress. "When she first went in there wasn't any, there wasn't much happening. . . . Then the gentleman by the name of Dr. Waxman took over. And the change was remarkable. It just seemed to go so quickly. One after the other she made a very, *very* rapid, very noticeable improvement."

After leaving the hospital, Terry returned to college at Cornell. "She was terrific." After graduation she went on to graduate work in clinical psychology in Chicago.

"At any point," Murphy asks, focusing on her graduate study, "did you notice anything unusual about Terry's behavior?"

Mrs. Walker leans forward, speaking slowly, "Ahh, between a month to three weeks prior to her trying to take her life, she was making the phone calls again." She pauses. "But they weren't, may I say, they weren't, uh, as urgent as the time . . . they weren't as nervous at the time, uh, but they were beginning to come. . . . I tell you very frankly I wasn't as concerned myself this time because she had chosen a psychiatrist, she was under her care, and I felt she was safe."

"Did you know the name of the psychiatrist?"

"No, I didn't. I knew it was a woman."

Mr. Walker was on a business trip to Hong Kong at the beginning of November 1975. He called his wife on his way home.

Mrs. Walker speaks carefully. "And I said, 'You know Terry

was sick again, was sick last night, and I've been getting phone calls from her and Carol's been getting some calls, and I had the feeling something was brewing.' So he said, 'Well, she's got a doctor there.' I said, 'Yeah, well, that's helpful and I'm glad about that but maybe you ought to stop off to see her, you know.' It was on the way anyway."

Maddux cuts across the story. "You know, I have an objection to these hearsay conversations between her and her husband. . . ."

"All right," Mrs. Walker says contritely. "I'm sorry."

"The thrust of your testimony," Judge McGarr says softly, "should be what happened."

Mrs. Walker regains her bearings. Her husband did go to Chicago to see Terry. He returned on Thursday and Terry began to call again. Mrs. Walker thought she was a little nervous, perhaps overworked. She urged her daughter to come to New York for the weekend. They would go to the theater, have dinner, Terry could sleep in her own bed. " 'And if you feel like calling Dr. Waxman'—who was like a colleague by this time because she was enrolled in a psychology program herself—so I thought she would, you know, speak to him as a colleague, and tell him, you know, what's happening. And she thought at first it was a good idea and as the calls kept progressing she was losing touch with herself again. . . ."

"And this was Friday as well?" Murphy asks.

"Friday wasn't so bad. . . . she said to me 'I think I'm gonna be all right, I spoke to daddy earlier, I was very upset but I think I'm gonna be all right.' And a few hours later she called again. . . . She was very nervous, she was concerned, she says, 'I'm floundering, I'm getting nervous, I can't do my work, I'm afraid that the same thing that happened to me before, it's happening to me again.' "

Mrs. Walker was not overly concerned. "And I said, 'Call your doctor, see what she'll say to you, uh, but I would like you to come home anyway, we haven't seen you for a while. . . . Come with us and have a little fun.' "

The next day, Saturday, was "bedlam" with renewed calls from Terry. "It wasn't so much what she said. The calls kept coming . . ." Mrs. Walker catches her breath, "and we would hang up, and we would tell her, please come, just come. 'Get on a plane, tell us what flight you're on and we'll meet you at the airport. Don't even take luggage, just come as you are.' "

What, Murphy asks, did Terry talk about during the Saturday phone calls? Terry complained, her mother says, of not sleeping, of not being able to function. "I said, 'I'm not your doctor.' I said, 'Speak to her, see what she'll do for you. I'm not qualified to give you any advice. I would like for you to come home.' Most of all, that's what I really wanted her to do."

Terry told her mother that she had called the doctor: ". . . and the doctor thought she was fooling around, it wasn't all that necessary and she wouldn't give her medication. . . ." Mrs. Walker shifts to a tone of disdain. "She made her feel as though she was game-playing. . . ."

As Murphy begins another question, Mrs. Walker breaks down in tears. Judge McGarr calls for a brief recess, and as the jury steps out, Mrs. Walker shakes with sobs. After the interruption she explains that she and her husband decided that Mr. Walker would fly to Chicago that afternoon.

". . . We were not able to get medication in all of Chicago! Terry needed medication, it seemed, and she wasn't able to get it in Chicago. . . . It was a question of getting her Mellaril because she was severely depressed." Mr. Walker got the medicine and flew to Chicago. After he left home, Mrs. Walker reports, "we got very frightened because the calls stopped and I couldn't reach anyone in Chicago. . . . About five-thirty . . . I'm not sure of the time . . . I got a phone call from someone at Henrotin Hospital that Terry fell off a roof."

Tension binds the courtroom as Mrs. Walker weeps. "I called my very oldest girlfriend. . . . She had just walked in with her husband and they turned right around and came to my home." She refers to Jack and Marie Konig. Mrs. Walker, breathing heavily, explains that Jack Konig flew with her to Chicago, where they arrived at two or three in the morning. They went directly to Northwestern Hospital, to which Terry had been transferred. They met Mitchell Walker there.

"Now, Mrs. Walker," Murphy asks softly, "would you, to the best of your ability, describe Terry's condition when you saw her?"

Mrs. Walker begins to cry. "Her face was swollen, her arms were swollen, her hair was pulled back into pigtails. She looked like a little bitty girl. She was more dead than alive. . . ." Mrs. Walker sobs heavily and the judge intervenes.

"Just take your time. We can stop now and wait until after lunch . . ."

"No," Mrs. Walker says, taking a deep breath, "I, I don't know what I'm gonna be like after lunch. Maybe a lot worse. . . ."

Mrs. Walker visited her daughter during the months she was at Northwestern and later when she was at the Rehabilitation Institute. "They cut her throat and they put a tube in there and she was breathing through that. . . . every half hour—whatever—they had to turn her over. She was like a flapjack being turned from one side to the other and, uh, she doesn't move, she's crippled. . . ." Mrs. Walker dabs at her eyes as Murphy asks about the Stryker Frame on which her daughter lay. "It was kind of a stretcher she was tied into . . . and she had a weight hanging from the back of her head to keep her still. Uh, they would have to turn her so that she wouldn't get bedsores. . . . It's like a thing that, like a barbecue spit, for heaven's sake. It rotates. . . ."

Murphy has one last question about Terry's condition and Mrs. Walker, distraught, distracted, snaps out a final sentence, "If, if I had known *what kind of doctor we were dealing with!*"

Maddux objects and the judge, glancing at the clock, says, "We're close to lunchtime. In any event, Mrs. Walker will resume again at two o'clock."

THE MOTHER—CROSS-EXAMINATION

Okay, if I said that, then that should stand.

—Gerda Walker

Shortly after two o'clock, Mrs. Walker settles into the witness chair again. Maddux folds his left arm across his chest, touches his right hand to his jaw and addresses her, "Mrs. Walker . . ." He pauses as if lost in thought. Mrs. Walker eyes him carefully. Maddux asks about Terry's making up the college time she lost during the 1971 hospitalization. His tone is pleasant, almost chatty, an old friend catching up on family news.

"And . . . after her hospitalization, she functioned very well in school?"

"Magnificently." Mrs. Walker speaks softly, proudly. Terry

then entered graduate school and lived in Chicago through 1974 and into 1975. Maddux continues his quick, amiable questions.

"Getting along?"

"Yes."

"Independently?"

Mrs. Walker hesitates, "Well, wait. No. When she first came to Chicago, she, uh, shared an apartment with a couple of friends of a friend of hers. . . ."

"When did she get her own apartment?"

Sometime in the summer of 1975, Mrs. Walker answers, and Terry lived there alone, following a normal school and work routine.

"And all through that spring and summer of 1975, she did things normally, functioned very well?"

Mrs. Walker's voice is barely audible. "Yes."

"Getting along fine."

"Uh, huh."

"You were aware that she had a psychiatrist in Chicago?"

"Absolutely." No, Terry never divulged the psychiatrist's name to her.

"You got the idea she did not want to tell you?"

Mrs. Walker answers dispassionately. "She wanted this to be a very private kind of thing. As a matter of fact, I had asked her at one point, because she was doing so well, why do you want a psychiatrist? She says, 'I want to learn something about myself and, hopefully, prevent this from happening again.' When I heard that, I was all for it. She didn't say who. She was an adult and I didn't think I should pry. I took her answer for whatever she wanted to tell me."

Maddux abruptly shifts the subject. "Well, didn't you ever obtain any records as to the payments made to Dr. Charles for the . . ."

Mrs. Walker cuts him off, spacing her words out slowly. "No . . . I believe that she paid for that herself."

"Were you aware that Mr. Walker wanted to deduct those expenses from his income tax?"

She will have no part of that. "I really don't know. You might ask Mr. Walker. I really don't know."

Maddux reminds her that she had seen her daughter in September 1975.

"And she was fine then?"

"She was very good." Mrs. Walker pauses. "But let me say, she was very good. I didn't see any real telltale signs yet. She was tired, she said. Nothing that I would really think and worry about." Terry was, Mrs. Walker agrees quickly, a hardworking student.

Maddux moves to the Wednesday before the incident, the day her husband visited Terry and returned home. "And it was reported to you that she was slightly nervous. And that was about it."

"Well, that, I already knew that from her myself, having had a telephone conversation."

"So you had direct knowledge from having talked with her. . . . She's fine up to that point except she's a little nervous. Right?"

Mrs. Walker nods in agreement, "Yes."

Maddux folds his arms and changes the focus again. "Now you know, and you were aware from the first hospitalization, that she didn't want to go in a hospital, weren't you?"

Mrs. Walker looks carefully at the attorney. "She didn't want to go the first time. Yeah, that's right."

"You were aware, then, that she wasn't treated with any drugs?"

"No, I don't believe she had any drugs at the time."

Maddux touches his chin, deep in concentration. He turns again to the witness. "This gentleman, Mr. Waxman . . ."

Mrs. Walker corrects him. "*Doctor* Waxman . . ."

"A psychologist?"

"Yes."

"He's not a medical doctor?"

"No. He was not the first doctor that she saw," she says flatly. She reviews the various doctors Terry had seen. None of them had worked out.

Maddux pauses, shifts a quarter turn away, then looks back at Mrs. Walker. "Did you ever have any family counseling sessions with Dr. Waxman? . . . to talk about the family relationship and its effect on Terry Walker?"

Mrs. Walker shifts uneasily in her chair. "I don't know whether the family relationship or whether he wanted to find out the dynamics of the thing, or what had happened—I don't really know. I don't know the purpose. . . ."

Maddux's tone is direct. "Do you recall that there was a statement made by him that this family togetherness you had was a myth?"

"Yeah," she says, as though she were speaking to herself. "You know I couldn't remember that. At one time, I don't know why, but I mentioned that to my husband. He said, 'Yes, that statement was made.' So the statement was made."

"In fact, it provoked such a violent reaction from the family there was a big fight and it broke up after about twenty minutes."

The weight of the witness's life can be felt in her explanation, "Well, my daughter thought that he was not speaking to us enough. And she felt we were being attacked as opposed to being spoken to."

Maddux reminds Mrs. Walker that Terry hadn't wanted to go to the hospital under any circumstances. "Wasn't that right? . . . She didn't really want to go the first time?"

Mrs. Walker's eyes flash. "No, she didn't want to go."

"After this unfortunate episode occurred, you talked with your daughter?"

"Uh, huh."

Maddux's voice softens. "And asked her why she jumped?"

"Uh, huh."

"What did she tell you?"

"She was very confused. She was very depressed. She hadn't slept. . . ."

"Didn't she tell you that she did it because she thought you were coming to Chicago . . ."

"No!"

". . . to take her to a hospital?"

Mrs. Walker's voice is strained and thin. "Uhhh . . . that's not what she said to me."

Every eye follows Maddux as he crosses the utterly quiet well of the court, retrieves a binder of deposition testimony from the defense table, and flips through the pages. "Another moment, your honor," he says and the judge nods. Maddux puts his finger on a page and looks back at Mrs. Walker. "You had discussed with Terry since her accident why she jumped and didn't she say she was afraid you were going to hospitalize her again? And that was the furthest thing from your mind. . . ."

Mrs. Walker's voice is drained of emotion. "She said that to my husband and then I guess we talked about it. I don't know. . . ."

Maddux stands directly in front of her holding the book of previously sworn testimony. "Well, I'm going to refresh your memory."

Mrs. Walker shakes her head, "I wish I had put her in the hospital, that's all I can tell you. . . ."

"Excuse me, ma'am," Maddux says evenly, "do you remember when your deposition was taken in this case?"

"Yes, I do remember that. . . ."

"That was in New York?"

"Uh, huh."

"On October the seventh [1977]?"

"Yeah," then, almost eagerly, "I want to go with the deposition because my mind was a little fresher at that time. It was earlier on and I was not in as nervous a state as I am at present."

"That's my next point. Your memory was better in 1977 than it is in 1980?"

"Yeah, because it was closer in time."

"Some questions were asked of you in a deposition . . ."

"Yes."

"And you were sworn under oath . . ."

"Yes."

". . . to tell the truth. There was a court reporter present, like there is now?"

"That's right."

"Taking down questions and answers?"

"Yes," she says almost inaudibly.

"Weren't these questions asked and weren't these answers given at that deposition?

Mrs. Walker, at any time since Terry's injury have you ever discussed with her why she jumped?

Answer: Yes.

Question: Has Terry told you why she jumped?

Answer: She was afraid we were going to hospitalize her again and that was the furthest thing from our mind.

Mrs. Walker breaks in quickly. "Okay, if I said that, then that should stand."

Maddux looks directly at her. "Thank you." He turns away, "No further questions."

Murphy asks Mrs. Walker if Terry was not very distraught

when she visited her in the hospital. Mrs. Walker, reorienting herself, agrees. She has been technically "impeached" through this public revelation of the disparity between the account she has just given for her daughter's reasons for jumping and the account she had given under oath three years previously. "You're excused, Mrs. Walker," the judge says. "You may step down." Mrs. Walker looks exhausted as she rises and moves past the defense table, past the empty space that had been filled by Terry's wheelchair the day before. She will listen to the testimony of her son-in-law, daughter, and husband and then leave the courtroom, never to return during the remaining eight days of the trial.

THE SON-IN-LAW

> *. . . people spent a lot of energy on each other.*
> —Lester Walston, M.D.

Gerda Walker walks slowly, almost abstractedly, to the back of the courtroom and moves stiffly into the last row of benches to sit at its far end. She sighs and rests her head against the wall, watching through half-closed eyes as Lester Walston enters the courtroom to take the stand. In his early thirties, he is short, bearded, self-conscious in his stride down the aisle.

"By the way," Murphy asks after Walston is sworn in, "where did you go to medical school?"

Walston answers quickly, "At Harvard Medical School . . ."

"And where did you do your internship?"

"At the Beth-Israel Hospital and the Cambridge Hospital . . ." he pauses, takes a breath, "which are both part of the Harvard system." He specializes in internal medicine and geriatrics. "And," he adds brightly, "and I teach at Harvard Medical School." Yes, he knew the Walker family and Terry at the time of her hospitalization in 1971. What, Murphy asks, is the young doctor's opinion of the cause of Terry's problem at that time.

Walston exhales. "Cause," he says professorially, "is a hard word in that we don't really understand a lot of causes of mental illness. But the label it would have been given was an agitated depression."

Murphy inquires about the Walkers. What kind of family were they?

"It was a warm family, it was a very close family. People spent a lot of energy on each other and, like any other family, it had its ups and downs but . . . it was very much like my own family in that it was small and closely knit."

Murphy asks if anything unusual happened in the fall of 1975 while Terry was at graduate school. Walston briefly describes the phone calls he and his wife received from Terry and their concern that the same thing that happened in 1971 was happening again.

Walston decided to call Terry's therapist in Chicago. "I was concerned," he says, "that perhaps the therapist didn't know that Terry had been very depressed, hospitalized, and suicidal back when she was at Cornell. . . . By, like the second week of November, I felt that as a family member as well as somebody with a medical background it was important for me to call her therapist and just talk with her and let her know what our perceptions of what was going on were."

"Did you discuss this with anyone before you made any calls?"

"Yeah," Walston replies. "I spoke with a number of colleagues at Harvard in psychiatry to make sure I wasn't overreacting. . . ." Walston comes finally to describe his conversation with Sara. "And I specifically wanted to make sure that she knew that Terry had in the past been hospitalized for mental illness and had talked at that point back when she was in college about killing herself and that we in the family were very worried that that was looking like it was starting up again. . . ."

"What, if anything," Murphy wants to know, "did Dr. Charles say to you at this point?"

"She said that she was aware of Terry's past medical history and that was not news to her. . . ." The young doctor frowns. "Again it was a hard thing to say, being out of town and not really on the scene and also being someone in medicine, it's difficult to call up another doctor and say, you know, why don't you try such and such. But we were worried enough that I was willing to risk, you know, seeming improper and say, have you thought about trying her on some antidepressants or some major tranquilizers . . . and she said, uh, 'No, I'm not going to be doing that' and, uh, 'You know, Terry will work this thing out for herself.' Something to that effect."

Dr. Walston concludes his direct testimony by describing further calls from Terry to him and his wife. "She was just totally disorganized," he says. "She couldn't make up her mind about anything."

Mrs. Walker watches carefully from the rear corner as Maddux rises and walks toward the witness stand.

Maddux's tone is sprightly. "Your involvement in this now is from the perspective, not of a physician taking care of Terry Walker, but as a brother-in-law . . ."

"With significant medical background," Walston hurriedly adds.

Maddux studies him a moment, then asks offhandedly, "Been to medical school. That right?"

"I'm on the faculty of Harvard Medical School."

"What year did you graduate?"

"Medical school? 1974."

Maddux speaks slowly, "Now 1974 was the year that Terry Walker graduated from college. Right?"

"Yuh . . . I guess."

"So that when she had her first hospitalization in 1971, what were you, a first-year medical student?"

"Seventy-one?" He pauses, "I was a second-year . . ."

"Second year," Maddux repeats slowly. "You called to be sure that Dr. Charles was aware, if I understand you, the Thursday before the incident occurred on that Saturday in November of 1975, you called Dr. Charles. . . . And your purpose was to be sure that she knew—she being Dr. Charles—knew about the prior hospitalization."

Walston responds carefully. "Right. And to let her know that Terry was behaving in a very bizarre way toward the family and to make sure that she was also behaving in that bizarre way to Dr. Charles, that she would know what state Terry was in. . . ."

"As a physician," Maddux says conversationally, "you're aware that if it's important to know about the previous hospitalization, it's important to know some *facts* about that hospitalization. Isn't that true?"

Walston nods, "Um, hmm."

"What the diagnosis was?"

"Mm."

"What treatment was given?"

Walston's "Mmm" is barely audible.

"Did you check all that out?"

"What do you mean," Walston draws the words up through a dry throat, "did I check it out?"

"Are you aware," Maddux asks evenly, "that Terry Walker was hospitalized from March first of 1971 until May 18 of 1971? . . ."

"Oh, of course. I went to visit Terry when she was hospitalized. . . ."

"Now then," Maddux says, drawing a line under the episode that has been described so often. "You became aware that she wasn't treated with any drugs during that hospitalization?"

"Mm, hmm," Walston responds.

The courtroom is silent as Maddux steps closer to Walston. "Were you aware that she had informed the attending psychiatrist, Dr. Kent—you knew him, Dr. Kent?" No, the witness did not know him. He never called him.

"Well, did you check in there to find out whether or not she [Terry] had denied whether she had any anxiety or any suicidal thoughts to the psychiatrist taking care of her in the hospital?"

"No," Walston answers quickly. "I was not her physician. I was a family member. . . ."

"Wouldn't that be significant," Maddux says, staring intently at Walston, "if you were a physician looking after Terry Walker?"

The physician looks away. "I've never looked after Terry Walker. . . ."

Murphy is on his feet. He does not want Maddux to explore the facts of Terry's hospitalization in 1971. "I'd like to propose an objection! I presume Mr. Maddux intends to show at some point . . . to tie this up with the fact that that's what Terry said. This is a hypothetical which is based on no fact at the present time."

"Are you in a position to support that?" Judge McGarr asks Maddux.

Maddux responds calmly, "He and I had a stipulation to admit these [hospital] records into evidence, I thought." He turns toward Murphy, "You don't want to put these records into evidence?"

Murphy speaks sarcastically. "Well, if Mr. Maddux wants to showboat in front of the jury, I'm not going to stop him. He's a much more experienced lawyer than I am. But I thought what Mr. Maddux was trying to do was far below the dignity of most lawyers. I have an objection standing, your honor. Tell Mr. Maddux to tie it up and not make showboat plays in front of the jury."

Maddux indicates that Murphy had agreed to allow the Cornell Hospital records into the trial. He cocks his head toward Murphy as he speaks to the judge. "Well, I have to ask him first then, is Dr. Wolpert going to testify? I can if Dr. Wolpert is going to testify." Wolpert has been Murphy's chief expert, the psychiatrist who for the past three years has coordinated the materials for the case against Sara. Murphy withdraws the agreement, technically known as a stipulation. His objection is sustained and Maddux must start again.

Walston studies Maddux nervously as he reviews the doctor's reasons for calling Sara on November 13, 1975, concluding dryly, "And she told you that in her opinion she [Terry] was not a candidate for medication?"

"Mm, hmm."

Maddux uses hard, direct tones. "Were you aware in 1975 that she [Terry] had no medication when she was in the hospital in 1971?"

"I don't remember what my recollection of that was."

"Well, did you become aware of that since this case has gone to trial?"

"Since Terry tried to kill herself," Walston says directly, "the family has discussed this for hundreds and hundreds of hours. And that fact came up since 1975."

"So you didn't know that in 1975 when you talked to Dr. Charles?"

"Right," Walston says, hurrying on to say that his purpose in calling Dr. Charles was to make sure that she considered the possibility of giving medication to Terry. "And whether she considered it because Terry suggested it or I suggested it was not of interest to me."

Maddux appraises the satisfied-looking witness. "You're not a psychiatrist?"

"No, I'm an internist."

"Psychiatry is a different branch of medicine than that which you practice?"

"Right."

"Yours is internal medicine."

"Right."

"And geriatrics?"

"Right," in a softer tone.

"That's taking care of old folks, isn't it?"

"Right."

"Okay," Maddux says calmly, "and if you have a psychiatric disorder you see a psychiatrist . . . ."

Walston breaks in, "Not necessarily. I'm trained in primary care internal medicine, which is a branch of internal medicine which specializes in taking care of the whole patient. And, therefore, I have a small amount of training, although not as much as a psychiatrist, in psychiatry and gynecology and minor surgery and a number of other fields."

"Well now," Maddux asks evenly, "aren't there different boards?"

"Yeah. I'm not boarded in psychiatry. . . ."

"But there are recognized specialties. . . ."

Walston speaks rapidly. "But there are new training programs that have come into existence in the last ten years in which internists are trained in various fields outside internal medicine so that they can take care of the whole patient. And I've had that sort of training. So I've had systematic, although not extensive, training in psychiatry."

Maddux touches his right forefinger to his lips thoughtfully. "And you wouldn't consider yourself as expert as a board certified psychiatrist?"

"Oh, by no means . . . no means."

"And what was best or not best for that patient," Maddux continues, "you'd leave it up to the board certified psychiatrist?"

Walston hesitates, then says, "If the psychiatrist was making appropriate decisions, sure."

Maddux pauses, letting the jury carefully inspect the witness. Walston answers a few more questions and Maddux walks back toward the defendant's table as though he were all finished. Then he turns and asks again about the time Dr. Walston received phone calls from Terry in the fall of 1975.

"October, late October. November."

Maddux begins to sit down. He glances back at Walston and fires a question, "Did you turn off your phone at some point?"

"For a while," Walston admits and goes on to explain his need for sleep.

"No further questions," Maddux says and finally does sit down.

Murphy rises and attempts, with a few questions, to reestablish the basic facts of his theory that Terry was suicidal in 1975.

Maddux stands up as Murphy sits down, "That prompts one more question. In this close family togetherness . . . didn't Mrs. Walker ever tell you, when you had these hundreds of hours of discussion about this episode, that she [Terry] didn't appear to be as bad in 1975 as she did in 1971?"

Walston seems irritated. "Yes, I was aware that to some extent her parents did not pick up on it as early as we did."

"Well, were you aware that her father was there—here in Chicago—on the Wednesday before the Saturday when she jumped?"

"Of course."

"Well, wasn't he in a position to know?

"To know what?"

"Whether she was better or worse in 1975 than she was in 1971?"

Walston looks away from the lawyer, snapping the tension. "Oh, by that point, I think all of us agreed that she was in very rough shape and tantamount to as bad as she was before. Absolutely."

Maddux looks down at the witness for a moment. "No further questions."

Walston lowers his head as he moves swiftly down the aisle to summon his wife from the corridor.

THE SISTER

> . . . *I'm not saying she was as bad or worse* . . . .
>
> —Carol Walker

Carol, eight months pregnant, is a bright, attentive, good witness who radiates a quality of long-suffering, of remembered concern for her sister, of having been protector and mother to her in times past. She repeats the story of their happy homelife, claiming that she and Terry had "no sibling rivalry," and describes, from a slightly different angle, her sister's troubles at Cornell and her hospitalization in 1971. Carol touches again on the elements of the plaintiff's charges: Terry was depressed and suicidal in 1971, and when the phone calls started coming in 1975, it seemed like the same thing was happening all over again. She concludes her direct examination with a weeping account of visiting her sister in the hospital after she jumped off the roof. She tells again of Terry's pitiful condition and of her efforts to rehabilitate herself.

Maddux proceeds gently with his cross-examination, each question leading the witness to modify or take back some of her claims about the obvious disintegration of her sister in 1975. From asserting that her sister was agitated and depressed in the late summer of that year, Carol changes her judgment to say that Terry seemed vaguely "unhappy." What about, Maddux asks. Her life, Carol answers, her life "in general."

Maddux reminds her that, according to her father's depositional testimony, he had visited Terry three days before she jumped and reported "to you that she was a little nervous but otherwise fine."

Carol responds carefully. "He said that she was having trouble making decisions over certain things but she seemed in better shape than he'd expected, judging from the phone calls."

They review the by-now familiar territory of Terry's hospitalization. Carol is hesitant in her responses.

Maddux asks a final question: "You disagree with your mother, who said she wasn't as bad in 1975 as she was in 1971?" Murphy's objection is overruled. Carol speaks cautiously. "Uh, I'm not saying she was *as* bad or worse. I can't make that discrimination. But it was very eerily similar in enough ways that it made me quite nervous. . . ." Maddux turns away and Murphy stands up and thanks the witness who moves down the aisle relieved to pull free of the web of circumstances that holds everyone else motionless in the courtroom. Judge McGarr calls a ten-minute recess.

THE FATHER

I don't remember. I really don't.

—Mitchell Walker

The recess is at an end and the judge looks down at Maddux, who is waiting for the plaintiff's lawyer to return to the courtroom with his next witness. "Here's your chance to win the case," McGarr says genially. "How's that?" Maddux smiles back at him. "Well, you have no opposition." McGarr sees Murphy at the rear of the courtroom. "Oh, there he is." Laughter ripples across the spectators. "Mr. Murphy, your next witness. . . ."

"I didn't hear what you said," Murphy calls in a prickly voice.

"I didn't see you there," McGarr replies pleasantly. "I told Mr. Maddux this was his chance to win the case in your absence."

"I was conferring with my law student," Murphy pipes. "My law student is a Catholic priest."

"While you're at it," McGarr responds, "you can ask him to pray for you."

Murphy, uneasy and suspicious, replies quickly, as though notching a cause for appeal, "I hope that's not an indication of how our case is proceeding."

Maddux grins and the judge, switching back to his official voice, says, "We'll go to four-thirty and quit for the day."

Murphy calls Mitchell Walker, a tall, slightly bent man of fifty-two whose face, beneath graying red hair, is pouched and drawn. He has large, sad brown eyes. Murphy immediately establishes that Walker was a marine in World War II and asks him to describe what action he saw. Maddux wryly objects to having the witness recount his war stories and the judge tells Murphy to move on. Mr. Walker married Gerda in 1947. "I import textiles," he says.

He echoes the claims of his wife and daughter about the Walkers' close home life. "With my being in the import business, I was offered a lot of free trips through the airlines so we had an opportunity to go to Europe at the cost of the airlines."

Murphy carries him through material with which the jury is now fully familiar: Terry's promise as a student and a human being, the troubling phone calls during her first year at Cornell, her return for treatment by various doctors, and her hospitalization in 1971. Murphy moves on to graduate school in 1975. Did "anything unusual begin happening again?"

"We were informed by Carol that Terry had been making phone calls. She said we shouldn't be concerned because she felt it was different than it was at Cornell. . . . We were informed about it at the end of October." Mr. Walker describes calling his wife from Honolulu on his way home and his decision to stop and see Terry in Chicago on November 12, 1975.

"I went to Terry's apartment," he says in a throaty voice, "and then we went out to breakfast. She was at a clinic as a student therapist and she introduced me to her colleagues and then I left that evening."

Murphy reviews the phone calls Terry made to New York on Friday. Then he asks about the calls on Saturday. Walker explains that he planned to leave Saturday morning for Chicago but that he had been detained by Terry's phone calls. "Terry started calling early that Saturday morning, something about medication. Terry had called Dr. Waxman and also my son-in-law, Lester, and they were thinking that I should get some medication to Terry. It was Mellaril." He procured the medication and flew to Chicago only to discover that Terry was in Northwestern Hospital. He weeps softly as he tells of seeing her briefly in the intensive care unit. Murphy asks if Mrs. Walker flew to Chicago later that night. "Yes," Walker responds hoarsely, "she was with a friend of ours, Jack Konig."

"At any time on the fifteenth or sixteenth did you meet Dr. Sara Charles?"

"Yes, I did. Dr. Charles called the hospital and Jack Konig received a message and Dr. Charles said that she wanted to come to see me. I agreed to it. Had nothing against it. Dr. Charles did come to the hospital." He is filled with sadness as he sets the scene. "Jack Konig met her, brought her over to see me, and introduced her to me."

Murphy's voice hardens. "And who was present at your conversation with Dr. Charles on Sunday morning, November 16?"

"Jack Konig was there."

"And do you recall what, if anything," Murphy asks, "you said to Dr. Charles and what she said to you on that morning?"

"Yes," Walker answers gloomily. "Dr. Charles came, was introduced to me. And she said that Terry loved me. And, uh, I told her that I had come with some medication, with Mellaril." He speaks with an effort. "And I told her that Terry was not sleeping very well, and, uh, she was confused. And why didn't she at least give her some sleeping pills? And Dr. Charles said that she *might* have made a clinical error. Or *did* make a clinical error. I wasn't quite sure. But the *clinical error* I certainly heard."

"Did she, Dr. Charles," Murphy asks, concluding his direct examination, "did Dr. Charles say that she, Dr. Charles, made a clinical error?"

"Yes, she did." Walker seems worn out by painful recollection.

Maddux walks slowly across the space between the defense table and the witness stand. "Mr. Walker," he says brightly, "let's go back to the episode involving your daughter in 1971. You remember that?"

Maddux asks about the incident when Terry stuck her foot out the window. Mr. Walker says that he did not see it, that he heard the scuffle from another room and that he beat Terry afterward "on the behind." Did he then go on a business trip? "Not immediately," Walker says anxiously, "but I went on a business trip in January." The episode with the foot out the window, he recounts uncertainly, was in December. Walker seems spent and unable to concentrate.

Maddux reviews the two incidents as Walker looks at him intently. He cannot say for sure that there was a gap between the two episodes. He cannot remember when they happened. Maddux takes a breath and reconstructs the two episodes once more. There must, Maddux says, have been a gap of time between them.

"Perhaps," Walker responds quietly.

Maddux shifts to 1975, to the business trip just before Terry's jump. Walker had received no phone calls. He was somewhat concerned about his daughter but proceeded with his trip to Hong Kong anyway. Yes, on his way home he stopped off at Chicago to see Terry. That was Wednesday, November 12, 1975.

"You thought she was okay, didn't you?"

Walker speaks very slowly. "Uhh, yes, I thought she was okay. I thought she was okay, but there were certain signs that concerned me slightly."

"You found that she was a little nervous?"

"Yes, I found that she was somewhat nervous." Walker speaks softly. "Yes." He did not feel the need to do anything and returned to New York.

He had no phone calls on Thursday and three on Friday. Maddux asks him if he spoke with Dr. Waxman.

"I don't recall," Walker sighs, "I, no, I did talk to Dr. Waxman." He explains that Terry had called Dr. Waxman that morning. "I believe," he says, warily again, "she did it on her own."

"All right," Maddux responds. "And he told her some things about herself in that conversation. Or were you made aware of that?"

"I don't know what Dr. Waxman told her. I know that Dr. Waxman told me that she should have medication and that somebody should intercede with her psychiatrist."

"Did he tell you that he, Dr. Waxman, told Terry, she's sicker than she thought she was?"

"No, he didn't."

"You were aware that no medicine of any kind was used in 1971 while she was at the hospital, aren't you?"

"No, I'm not aware of it."

"Does that surprise you?"

Walker straightens his shoulders. "I'm not a doctor and wouldn't presume to prescribe medication or to tell a doctor to use medication."

"Whether medicine is needed or not needed, that's something you'd leave up to the doctor, right?"

"Yes, I would," Walker answers hoarsely. He made no effort to contact Dr. Charles, the psychiatrist, on Saturday morning.

"And do you know what Mellaril is?" Maddux asks.

Walker shifts in his chair. "I'm not really sure what it's used for, but it's an antipsychotic, I think."

Maddux suddenly changes the subject. "Mr. Walker, in August of 1975, did you ever have a discussion with your daughter Terry about deducting the expenses of the therapy visits to Dr. Charles from your income tax?"

Walker licks his lips. "Terry paid for the therapy visits. . . ."

"I know that," Maddux responds.

"I had no discussion at all with her about that." He pauses. "I, I don't understand any discussion, but Terry was paying for it. There was no way that I was going to deduct it. I couldn't."

"You never had a discussion with her about that?" Maddux persists calmly.

Walker shakes his head numbly. "I don't remember. I really don't. . . ."

"You don't remember?"

"I don't remember. . . ."

After a few concluding questions Walker leaves the witness stand, stepping carefully around the chairs and tables, and moves to the last row of spectator seats. He bends over his wife, who gazes past him at us as we leave the courtroom for the day.

DAY THREE

_____

The Plaintiff's Strategy

Everybody knows who Ann Landers is.

—Judge J. Frank McGarr

I thought I saw a quotation mark.

—Patrick Murphy

Sara possesses an extraordinarily sensitive unconscious, picking up messages out of the ether all the time. On Wednesday morning she says undramatically, "Murphy is going to call me as a witness this morning." She tells the same thing to Maddux when we arrive at his office around nine-thirty.

Maddux waves his hand good-naturedly. "Call you as an adverse witness? That would really be dumb of him. He won't do that." Tom Boodell agrees that it would be a peculiar strategy.

Sara persists in her conviction, however, and as we stand in the hallway a few minutes before court is to convene, Maddux suddenly turns to her and says, "I think you're right. It's dumb but I think you're right." They can see Murphy standing beside the plaintiff's table surveying a pile of books and notes that he has placed on it. Next to him stands a middle-aged man, short, dark-haired, contained. He is Jerome Goldberg, Murphy's partner.

A number of older men and women have taken seats near me. I can hear them talking as, everything in process around and beyond me, I wait for the day's activities to begin.

"There's a murder on twenty-three," an octagenarian in plaid pants whispers hoarsely to his companion.

"Not much to it as far as I can tell," a plump, grizzled woman says as she wrestles her swollen shopping bag into a comfortable position on her lap.

"Where's Harry?" the first man asks, "golfing again?"

The man next to him nods. "He said he'd be here this afternoon. Says psychiatric malpractice is a very unusual type of trial. . . ."

These are the court buffs. Harry takes a great interest in our case over the next several days. He is a retired businessman who golfs every morning and has his chauffeur drive him to the Federal Courthouse every afternoon. The buffs are part of courthouse culture, free with their speculation, advice, and judgment about trials, judges, and lawyers.

McGarr enters and things settle down. Murphy explains that he is having difficulty scheduling his experts, he may have to go a morning or an afternoon without a witness. "That would be a fairly unhappy development," McGarr observes before he summons the jury.

"Call Dr. Sara Charles as an adverse witness," Murphy says loudly. Sara rises, walks to the stand, and takes the oath.

"Dr. Charles, at one time you wrote an article for a book called the *Ann Landers Encyclopedia.* . . . Is that correct?"

"I presented material for an article."

Murphy has the encyclopedia marked as a plaintiff's exhibit and continues his questioning. The article for which Sara was given credit is entitled "Suicide Among Adults." Murphy reads from it.

"It is stated that 'contrary to popular belief, about seventy percent of persons who threaten suicide actually make the attempt. The warning is a cry for help and not merely a bid for attention.' Is it not a fact that that sentence appears?"

"That sentence appears in the article." Sara answers.

Murphy quotes two more sentences from the article, including one on getting help for suicidal patients. Then he switches to the material to which he has previously referred, Sara's personal notes on Terry Walker's therapy sessions. "In September of 1975, do you recall Terry Walker telling you she wants to get it settled right now and be done with it? And also saying that she might end up screwing herself. Do you recall Terry indicating that to you?"

"I can't say I recall it as you state it," Sara answers, "because I don't know what context you're talking about or whether these were even connected ideas. I wouldn't be able to answer that."

Murphy moves on. "In September of 1975 do you recall Terry Walker telling you that she feared the psychosis?"

"I think," Sara responds, "there's something in my notes that says 'fears the psychosis.' Do you want me to explain what the idea is?"

"Please just try to answer the question," Murphy says angrily. ". . . I'd like you to recall Terry Walker at any time telling you that she feared the psychosis."

"Again, that's a very hard thing to answer because I can't say that she said that to me specifically."

"Do you recall," Murphy presses, "Terry Walker telling you that she felt massive distrust of herself, that she cannot effectively do something, that she feels weak and impotent, and that she does not exist unless she is number one? . . . Did she say that to you?"

"To my knowledge," Sara responds, "she did not say that kind of thing to me. These notes are not quotes. . . . Those are all separate ideas that were communicated one way or another, not necessarily related."

Using quotations from her notes, Murphy is attempting to create the impression that Sara was well-acquainted with Terry's suicidal potential during the time of treatment. It explains the strategy he followed when he took Sara's deposition before the trial. He reviewed her personal notes but merely inquired about spelling and punctuation, and asked her to interpret the words that were illegible to him. Murphy's plan is to construct a context of meaning for them in the courtroom.

Sara recalls four phone calls from Terry in October 1975, the last one coming at one o'clock in the morning, and Murphy rolls on. "I presume you also recall Terry Walker telling you something to the effect that either she would resolve it or she would kill herself, in October 1975?"

"She said something like 'I'll either get through this thing or kill myself.' Yes."

Murphy continues, ". . . in October of seventy-five or the fall of seventy-five saying she feels very anxious and depressed and panicky?"

"I don't know if she said she felt anxious, depressed, and panicky, but I think those words are in my notes. It may be my perception or her own statement."

". . . that she felt like she did the first time she was hospitalized?"

"No." Sara acknowledges that Terry did experience periods of obsessive thinking. And, yes, she did have some panicky feelings.

In November 1975, didn't Terry say, Murphy asks, that she was losing control?

"She had some fears of loss of control in November."

"I have no other questions of Dr. Charles," Murphy says contentedly and sits down.

Maddux walks easily toward the witness stand.

"This article you were asked to refer to. It was in the *Ann Landers Encyclopedia?* Who's Ann Landers?"

"Everybody knows who Ann Landers is," Judge McGarr interjects and there is a rustle of laughter in the courtroom.

Maddux establishes that the volume is not an authoritative medical or psychiatric journal and asks if the article is the same one Sara submitted. No, she replies, she had sent in the notes of the lecture on suicide she gives to first-year medical students at the University of Illinois. Someone else had edited it considerably.

Maddux refers to the statement that Murphy quoted earlier, "Contrary to popular belief, about seventy percent of persons who threaten suicide actually make the attempt." He asks Sara, "Is that an accurate statement?"

"No," she says, nor was it the statement in her lecture notes. "What I had submitted," Sara explains, "was that seventy percent of persons who actually suicide have made a previous attempt." There is no way, she says, to measure the number of people who threaten suicide.

Maddux moves on to Terry Walker. "Did she make a prior attempt?"

"I have no knowledge of a prior attempt at suicide."

"Well, you heard the testimony in this case," Maddux says. "Was there a bona fide attempt at suicide described in the testimony you've heard in this case?"

"I didn't hear any." Sara explains that in a suicide attempt people actually *do* something, they overdose, slash their wrists, they actively try to harm themselves in some way. "Suicide ideas are very, very common ideas. Probably everyone in this room has had a suicidal idea at one time or another in life."

Maddux asks about psychiatric indicators of a potential suicide attempt in a patient.

"The assessment of suicide potential," Sara answers, turning toward the members of the jury, "is a judgment call. What it amounts to is assessing a whole list of possible factors and if the patient weighs more heavily in this direction, the risk is greater. If the patient weighs heavily in this direction, the risk is less. And you have to make a judgment based on weighing a large number of factors."

Promising to explore that later Maddux turns to Sara's personal notes that Murphy brought up in his direct examination.

"A psychiatrist," Sara begins, "deals with very intimate material . . . material that individuals probably reveal to no one else in their lives. So the area of confidentiality is very critical to a patient-therapist relationship. The tradition in psychiatry is to take personal notes, that is, your own little shorthand. There could be anything in those notes: your observations, there may be your ideas, there may be a quote of the patient, hunches you may have, there may be any number of possibilities that relate to therapy with the patient. Generally, I have a session with the patient for forty-five or fifty minutes. Then that patient leaves and I might take two or three minutes just to write ideas down. The idea is that the next time I see the patient it warms up my circuits and I have an idea of the feeling we're working with."

Maddux asks Sara about the notes in September that Murphy cited piecemeal earlier.

"I think it might be helpful if I read the whole note," Sara says, inspecting her handwritten originals. "The whole note says: 'Entire session on theme of "want to get it settled right now and be done with it." Associated later to my comment "it didn't interfere with your functioning I think her more fragile than she feels she is. Then I had a dash, 'settled thing with father but it's still unsettled.' Then I had another dash, 'New York trip.'

Another dash, 'Kevin,' dash, 'need to see him now.' Dash, 'money thing with Arnie.' Dash, 'wanted something then so settled but end up screwing herself she feels.' "

"What does that mean?" Maddux asks.

"She was dealing with a lot of different issues. She had some discussion she was having with her father she had to get settled. There was a relationship with a boyfriend that she wanted to be more settled. She had another boy that she had some differences of opinion with, something about money. What she was communicating to me was there seemed to be many things up in the air and unsettled. The theme of the session, as I said in the beginning, was she wants to get all these things settled and be done with it."

What about Murphy's statement that Terry said she wanted either to solve her problems or kill herself?

"In the fall of the year," Sara responds, "she felt she had many, many decisions to make which were really appropriate for a second-year graduate student. She had to decide to take this course rather than that course. She had to decide on what was going to be the main focus of her research over the years of her graduate study. In other words, the expected kinds of decisions that anyone at that level has to make. And she felt very stressed by having to make these decisions. And in one of the sessions she commented that she wanted to straighten all this out or kill herself. And my response was, you know I really think she could straighten these things out."

"Were there any indications that she would do anything except continue in therapy?"

"No, that's a very common subject that comes up with patients. . . . It's the only time that I remember her mentioning suicide as it relates to herself during the therapy."

"In that entire treatment period," he asks, "that was the only reference?"

"That's the only one that I remember."

Maddux turns to the quote, "fears the psychosis."

"What that really means," Sara answers, "is that even early in the therapy one of the issues Terry wanted to deal with was, what was the first incident, in the first year in college, what was that all about? What kind of experience was that? And one of the questions she had in her mind was 'Was I psychotic or was I not psychotic then?' Apparently nobody ever really talked to her about this. She did not really know. And I think this had really very important implications, particularly given the field she was going into. So for me the shorthand was, one of the issues she discussed was, first of all wondering what that was all about and would that ever happen again to her? So that's my shorthand for that whole issue: 'fears the psychosis.' "

Sara explains the nature of obsessive thinking and acknowledges that Terry sometimes used the word *panicky*.

"Is it a layman's term?" Maddux asks.

"Yes, probably everybody knows what it means to get a little panicky."

Maddux looks up at the judge. "Those are all the questions I have at this time, your honor."

"It'll take me a moment to get my notes straight," Murphy says as he approaches the witness stand.

Murphy inquires about the quotation marks in Sara's notes. "The quotation mark is the little mark you put up there?" he asks. "It usually means someone is saying something, doesn't it?"

"Right," Sara replies. "But you have to understand I've seen a patient for fifty minutes and I do not take any verbatim notes. They're recollections of things. . . ."

Murphy cuts across her answer, "You don't know why you put down quotation marks beside something?"

"Well, they were an expression of something she was saying to me."

"Now, Doctor," Murphy resumes, "I believe you further stated . . . that she talked about a New York trip, problems with a boyfriend, problems with another boyfriend, problems with her father, and this was the theme of the session and these were the things she said she had to get settled. Is that your testimony to Mr. Maddux?"

"Yes."

"Well, Doctor, on that same date it also states that she fears that she might end up screwing herself. Is that one of the things she wants to get settled, too?"

"No," Sara responds, but Murphy cuts her off. "She *didn't* want to get that settled, is that right?"

"Do you want to know what . . .?"

"I just want you to answer my question," Murphy interrupts. "Is not this screwing herself one of the things she wanted to resolve?"

"I can't understand the question," Sara responds.

"Well, then it's my fault," Murphy answers sarcastically. "I'll withdraw the question. Now, Doctor, you do state here one thing I see on this note. It says, 'I think her more fragile than she feels she is.' Did you feel that way about Terry Walker on the fourth of September, Doctor?"

Sara looks at her notes. "You're only reading part of the sentence. . . ."

"Well," Murphy responds, "I'm reading the entire line. It says, 'I think her more fragile than she feels she is.' It appears the entire sentence is in quotation marks. There's a quotation mark right above it. There's a period after it. So I'm reading one typed sentence. 'I think her more fragile than she feels she is.' " Murphy bores in again, "You felt that way about Terry Walker on the fourth of September, isn't that correct, Doctor?"

"Well," Sara answers, "I would have to say that the sentence really begins. . . ." A touch of irritation creeps into Sara's voice, "Listen," she says, "you want to know what the sentence says?"

"You tell me what it says," Murphy responds.

"The sentence says, 'Associated later to my comment, "it didn't interfere with your functioning I think her more fragile than she thinks she is.' That's the whole idea."

Murphy steps closer to the witness stand, "Well, Doctor, maybe. Let me see your original notes here. I may be looking at the wrong ones. Now let's look at this together, Doctor." He bends down like a teacher over a wayward pupil's desk. He places his typewritten notes next to Sara's originals and studies them.

"All right," he says, "it's the same as mine." He steps back, sure that he has things under control now. "Isn't it so that the sentence reads as follows, 'Associated later to my comment—in quotation marks—it didn't interfere with your functioning. Period, end of quotation marks?"

Sara gives a straight line answer, "There's no period and there's no quotation marks."

Murphy hunches his back, "Well, I'm gonna have to look at it again."

"You're gonna have to," Sara responds. Murphy steps forward, picks up Sara's originals and studies them. "I thought I saw a quotation mark," he says. He studies the document intently. "Now, before it," he says, "what are those two lines going up in the air?"

"That's a quotation mark. It never ends."

"Well, it does on my copy, Doctor," Murphy, his face bright pink, growls as he steps back in front of the witness stand still staring at his typed version of her notes.

"But," Sara answers, "those are my originals."

"Okay, let me present this," Murphy says determinedly, "and then try to explain it." He stares down at the note, rehearsing the lines to himself, straining like a shoe salesman for a proper fit, "Associated later to my comment. Associated later to *my* comment. Now, quotes, my comment being. . . ."

"No," Sara cuts in, "that isn't what it means."

Murphy asks her to explain the sentence.

"During the session, one of the issues that we talked about was that a few weeks prior to this I had been away on vacation, which is very frequently a very difficult time for patients who are engaged in psychotherapy. . . . One of the things we talked about was that she had managed that period of time away quite well, and that she functioned quite well. And she wondered if maybe I didn't expect her to do much worse than she did. And so that sentence 'I think her more fragile. . . .' She wondered if I thought that she was more fragile than she felt she was."

"This is part of the quotes, Doctor. You're saying she also said it didn't interfere with *your* functioning?"

"It didn't have anything to do with me."

"You then thought Terry was more fragile in September 1975, than she thought she was?"

"No."

"Do you think she was more fragile on November 15, 1975, when she leapt off the building and crushed her spine than she thought she was, Doctor?" This intensely, angrily.

"I don't know what happened that day," Sara responds.

"Now, Doctor," Murphy says. "You made a statement here that every college student, that most people have suicide, that most people think about suicide, isn't that right?"

"At some time in their life, most people have the idea."

"And do most people actually leap off buildings?"

"No."

Murphy looks through his papers. He reviews Terry's graduate school problems and moves to Sara's comment that she had no knowledge of Terry's having made any suicidal attempts prior to 1975. "Do you recall writing in your notes on the twentieth of December, 'breakdown, first year of college, suicidal, hostile, hospitalized at Cornell.' Do you recall writing that?"

"Yes."

"So, in fact, as early as the twentieth of December, in the third session that Terry came to you, eleven months before the suicidal attempt, you knew that Terry Walker was suicidal in the first year of college? Didn't you?"

"Suicidal does not mean suicidal attempt," Sara answers.

"You're very careful with words that way," Murphy asks bitingly, "aren't you, Doctor?"

"Well," Maddux cuts in, "I have an objection to that, your honor."

"The objection is sustained," McGarr says.

"I know," Murphy says, "you're trying to get something on the difference between what suicidal means and suicidal attempt. . . ."

Maddux objects again and is sustained.

"So, you're admitting she was suicidal in the first year of college, is that right, and you knew it on the twentieth of December 1974?"

"I wrote down that she said she was suicidal."

"And she was hospitalized!" Murphy hammers away. "In a mental health hospital, you knew that on the twentieth of December 1974, didn't you?"

"That is correct."

"Now, Doctor, you said something about the figure seventy percent of those who have attempted it once before, or seventy percent of those who attempt suicide have done it once before."

"No. What I said was that seventy percent of people who actually commit suicide have attempted it previously."

"So on December 20, 1974, you had known that Terry Walker was suicidal and had been hospitalized, isn't that right?"

"Suicidal is different than suicidal attempt."

"I'm sorry, I keep forgetting you're very careful with words." Murphy's sarcasm trails faintly in the air as sulphur from a just-struck match.

"It's a very important issue in psychiatry," Sara adds. Other than getting Sara to agree that it was possible that more people read Ann Landers than Sigmund Freud, nothing new emerges. Murphy seems irritated as he concludes his questioning.

The Plaintiff

It was like a switch that was turned on.

—Terry Walker

Murphy tugs at the vents of his creased summer suit and calls Terry Walker, the plaintiff, to the stand. Terry maneuvers her wheelchair down the aisle to a place in front of the witness stand. Murphy seems tender as he helps her get settled. Terry seems lackluster, dazed, as she is sworn in and repeats her name softly.

Murphy moves quickly to the story, now told a half dozen times by others, of Terry's first-year troubles at Cornell. He asks the plaintiff for her own perception of her emotional problems at that time.

"I first began to have difficulty," Terry answers, "I had broken up with a boyfriend and I was dating someone else, and I became, all of a sudden, very depressed. I thought that everything I was doing was wrong, I couldn't make a decision, I was ruminating, I began attacks of severe insomnia, I wasn't eating, and I lost control." She concludes, "It was a very sudden onset and it was very strange. And I had never experienced anything like that before in my life." Murphy wants a further description of her symptoms.

"Well, I never knew from moment to moment what I was going to do. I thought about killing myself at that point. I would walk up—we have in Cornell things called gorges, they were waterfalls—and I would find myself standing on the gorge and I would say, no, I don't want to do this, and going back to my dorm and trying to see someone that I would get help and control myself."

Terry recounts calls to her sister from Cornell: "I got into this depressed and agitated state that I've been describing and I had to go home."

"What do you mean by *depressed?*" he asks. "We all get depressed sometimes."

"It's not the kind of depression that is experienced momentarily, sometimes day to day, in the course of a normal life. It was a very, very different kind of experience. I thought about killing myself, I was criticizing everything I did, I felt that I couldn't function, I was totally losing control of my life."

"Did this come and go?" Murphy asks.

"Not really," Terry answers. "It was sort of like, it was like a switch that was turned on. And it went that way for several months without any remission and then it stopped." Her voice becomes more dramatic as Terry gives her account of an episode at her parent's apartment. She looked out her bedroom window, she explains, "And I went toward it and I stuck my leg out the window. And I said, I was going to feel this way my whole life and it just kind of descended upon me. I'd never felt this way before, and I thought there was no hope of ever recovering. I thought I had to kill myself." She also describes the incident at her sister's dormitory. She cries as she recalls looking out that window and seeing her mother coming along the street below. "And I opened the window and I thought, I have to jump because I can't stand feeling like this, I was so terrified."

"Then you did go," Murphy asserts, "voluntarily to the Cornell Hospital?"

Maddux cuts in, "I object to the leading form of the question," and Judge McGarr sustains him. He addresses Terry again, "Tell us how you got to the hospital that day. Mr. Maddux doesn't want me to put words in your mouth." Maddux objects again and the placid Judge McGarr betrays annoyance. "Counsel," he says, "it's not necessary to make editorial comments on the progress of the trial. I'll make the ruling. You don't have to explain it."

Terry takes up the story of going to the hospital, of her efforts to break away, of her arrival finally at Cornell at White Plains: ". . . and they took me into the hospital and they said I was going to be on constant observation because I was a high suicidal risk and they weren't going to let any. . . ." Maddux objects to the hearsay nature of the testimony. He is sustained but, within a few questions, Terry claims again that she was suicidal, that she was put in a special room. "There were four of us there, people who were very dangerous to themselves." She cannot remember how long she was on suicide precautions. Probably a couple of weeks.

"March and April were very bad and then I started seeing Dr. Waxman and fairly suddenly I began to feel much better." Murphy looks pleased as Terry reinforces her appreciation of the hospital. "Being in a protected environment where if I couldn't control myself there would be control" was beneficial, "and also being in therapy and able to work out and understand some of these things on a very continuous basis."

Murphy concludes the morning session five minutes ahead of time after the judge discourages him from beginning a new series of questions.

In the afternoon Murphy proposes to show a videotape of Terry Walker's routine activities in support of the damages that he will claim if liability is assessed against Sara. He tells the judge, who wants to preview it before he allows it to be shown to the jury, that it lasts about twenty minutes. Ann Masters, a blond-haired woman in her thirties, supervises the showing of the tape. Maddux's objection recapitulates the nature of the tape, "It was told to you it was twenty minutes. By my calculation it was forty minutes, double that time. I think the prejudice to the defense by the showing of the film is obvious by reason of the lengthy episodes showing only a few activities of this young lady. The typing, the getting in and out of bed assisted and then assisted again; the dropping of an item while she was typing and the difficulty in picking it up; the double exhibition of the method of urination, the method of bathing, the method of using the stool. In short, in this colored rendition there is nothing that could not be demonstrated by word. . . . The showing of this film in my opinion would be prejudicial to the defendant in the overemphasis, the inflammatory emphasis on one aspect of the case. We have implored this jury that they should not use sympathy to decide this case. I do not see how anyone could not be unaffected, sympathywise, by the viewing of this film."

Maddux knows that the judge will admit the film. That is routine in such cases. The surreal quality of the viewing experience is further accented by the sudden announcement that the court must be cleared because of a bomb threat on the building.

When we reassemble several minutes later I watch a broadly smiling Maddux introduce himself to the blond-haired woman who has been in charge of the videotaping. She hands him her card.

Murphy calls Ann Masters to the stand, puts her under oath, and asks her if on June 17, 1980, she made the tape in Terry's apartment. Did the tape truly and accurately reflect Terry's movements? Yes. Were there any changes afterward? No. Murphy asks about her credentials as a maker of videotapes for the legal profession. He suggests that she has shown such tapes at legal seminars and at the Rehabilitation Institute. Any retakes? No. Any editing? No. Ann Masters smiles expectantly as Maddux, the man with whom she had such a pleasant exchange a moment before, approaches her. He is not, however, smiling as he asks, "Just to be clear, you're in the business of making these kinds of films?"

"Yes," she says, still smiling.

"And, in fact, you have a card which says 'Video Service for Lawyers'?" Maddux holds up the card so that the jury can see it. Clearly a business card from which the face of Miss Masters beams. She cautiously agrees.

Murphy hired her for the purpose of making this film for this case? Yes, hesitantly. "It's not for any seminar, or teaching, or anybody else, the Rehabilitation Institute or anyone else, to help Terry Walker out physically. It's simply to show to this jury?" Ann Masters nods and says, "Yes." She is subdued as she leaves the stand to turn on the tape machine. As Maddux sits down next to Sara he whispers, "They don't usually give you their business cards. . . ."

The lights go out and, joined now by the jury, we watch the tape in the strange, close, heavy, cough broken silence. The forty-minute showing still seems an exploitation more than a sympathetic exposition of the life of the plaintiff, a shaming kind of exposure of her awkward intimate moments.

Murphy recalls Terry Walker to the stand and she propels herself back into position in front of the witness stand. Why had she started seeing a psychiatrist after her entrance to graduate school in 1974?

"For several reasons," Terry answers, but she goes into detail about only one, her interest in finding out about her first hospitalization. "I was wondering whether I was psychotic. I was very frightened about how suicidal I had been at that point and I wanted to be as understanding and prepared for it if it ever happened again."

When, Murphy asks, did Terry tell Dr. Charles about her initial hospitalization?

"During the second session."

"And did Dr. Charles get some background from you the first time around?"

"No," Terry answers quickly.

"Did she ever ask you if you'd ever been hospitalized?"

"No."

"Can you recall what you told Dr. Charles about the hospitalization on the second time?"

"I told her I'd been hospitalized for two and a half months
because I had been unable to control myself, I was suicidal, I
was seriously at risk of taking my own life, I was extremely angry,
and I was just crazy."

Terry claims that Dr. Charles did not inquire about any of
this, did not ask permission to look at her hospital records or
to talk to her former therapists. Terry asserts that in the first
six months of therapy she brought up her hospitalization five
or six times. Did Terry express to Dr. Charles the suicidal and
depressed feelings she had had during her first year of college?
"Somewhat. But she never seemed interested in going into it.
. . . I would bring it up and question whether I had been psychotic
and what that was all about. . . . She never asked any further
questions, she never reacted."

The jury members watch Terry closely. Murphy brings Terry
to the fall of 1975 during which, according to his charges, she
disintegrated again, this time with her psychiatrist watching. Terry
continued to have trouble sleeping in September. Did she communicate this to Dr. Charles? "Absolutely," Terry answers. "I was
saying that I had not been sleeping well, that I had not been
eating well. I told her that I was sleeping some nights not at all
and some nights a couple of hours. An average of about four
hours a night then."

"Do you recall," Murphy asks slowly, "in September relaying
these feelings back to how you felt [your] first year [in college]?"

"Let me see," Terry responds. "Definitely. In September, in
the fall of that year, for sure. Maybe October. Yeah, October.
The middle of October."

"And what," Murphy asks a moment later, "did Dr. Charles
say?"

Terry mimics her doctor, projecting haughtiness, disdain, " 'I
won't argue with you about that. I didn't know you then. I'm
the doctor now.' "

Did her feelings persist after she described them to Dr. Charles
in October 1975?

"Persisted and got worse." Terry answers. She slept poorly
in October. She understood that she was feeling the same way
she had in 1971. "The only thing I could do," she says with a

sigh, "was to call Dr. Charles and tell her I was feeling this way, to see if I could have more therapy sessions, and asked her if I could have sleep medication to help me sleep." She did this on more than one occasion between mid-October and November 15. "Mostly," Terry says, "I remember the last time . . . she said to me, 'There's nothing wrong with sleeping only four hours a night and you have to go through anxiety and bear up and then you'll be healthier afterward.' "

"At any time," Murphy asks, "did you indicate to Dr. Charles that suicidal thoughts had occurred to you?"

"Yes, I did," Terry answers flatly. "I told her I was feeling suicidal and didn't understand it and she told me . . . I was feeling that way trying to destroy everything. . . ." She told Dr. Charles this several times during this period, mostly in person.

She was trying hard, Terry says, to be normal. She had acted the same way at Cornell. There were phone calls to the east. She was losing control, Terry explains, "I tried very hard and you get upset when you can't. You give it your best shot and try to hold on but. . . ." She grew worse during the week before she jumped.

After her brother-in-law, Lester Walston, called her therapist, she felt relieved. "I felt that finally Dr. Charles might have been hearing the state I was in. However, she still refused to give me medication for sleep. And I began to feel, well, she says that there is nothing wrong with sleeping four hours a night—while I was going crazy! . . . I finally started saying to myself this woman is not helping me. As a matter of fact, I feel she's destroying me."

Why, Murphy asks, didn't she dismiss Dr. Charles and go elsewhere?

"I really did not have the wherewithal to do that. I had a respect for psychiatry. I thought she was doing what she was supposed to be doing. But I really did not have myself organized enough to make a phone call and switch therapists after I've been involved with her for about ten months at that time. And I didn't think I could just go to another therapist and be able to communicate . . . all that I had worked on in ten months."

Terry acknowledges that her father visited her that fateful week in November 1975. She had been up late the night before and awakened with "a startle" very early the next morning. That was why she had her apartment cleaned when her father came. Nothing had upset her, she reports, about her father's visit. Thursday night she went to a movie with her boyfriend. She did not sleep well Thursday night. On Friday, in her continuing effort to act normally, she carried out her clinical training assignment of interviewing a patient at a Veterans Hospital. In the afternoon she went to pay a traffic ticket but went to the wrong place. "I was very disorganized," Terry says. "It was hard for me to organize myself."

The judge notes that the afternoon has worn on and the trial is dismissed for the day. As Sara and Maddux emerge from the courtroom we catch a glimpse of Murphy, surrounded by aides, crouching beside Terry Walker's wheelchair.

DAY FOUR

The Plaintiff Continued

It made me feel, you know, she really doesn't know what the hell is going on with me.

—Terry Walker

The next morning when we awaken Sara begins to pick up messages from the ether. We are expecting Dr. Edward Wolpert, the chief plaintiff psychiatric expert, to appear after Terry finishes her testimony. As we dress, however, Sara finds that every time she wants to use Wolpert's name, she mentions that of Maddux instead. She pauses and listens for a moment to herself. "There," she observes as she searches for something in her closet. "There I just did it again." She does it, in fact, seven times before we leave to go downtown. "I think that Wolpert is dropping out of the case," she says. "Something like that is going on. That's why Murphy was holding that conference yesterday afternoon." Maddux smiles at her but says nothing when she tells him her hunch in his office.

The trial is delayed while the judge holds status calls on other cases under his jurisdiction. Every trial is clogged with irregular and unpredictable chunks of time spent in the hallways. During these intervals Murphy and his assistants sit with Terry and Mr. Walker in an alcove near the elevators. They are joined this morning by a tall mustachioed man with blown-dry white hair. Jack Konig has flown in from New York to testify for the plaintiff. The court buffs loll in the same area reading the newspapers and exchanging gossip about the various trials that are in session. By this day a steady group of a half dozen is following the proceedings.

When the trial resumes, Terry Walker testifies about the Friday before she jumped. After her second call home in the evening she felt calmer. She told a friend with whom she went to a movie about her dissatisfaction with her psychiatrist. "I thought she was being destructive to me." After her friend left, Terry called home again. Then, after pacing up and down, she slept "for a couple of hours." The next morning she woke up "really in shock" and called Dr. Waxman in New York. "It was the last resort," she says, because she was so distraught and suicidal: "I told him that I felt like for the first time since my hospitalization I was feeling exactly the same way. I was going down a greasy pit trying to hang on and couldn't. And that I felt like a piece of cardboard. And that I hadn't been sleeping for several weeks on end and that I had asked for help and medication for sleep and I had been refused." Did she tell Waxman of her relationship with Dr. Charles? "I told him," she says, "that I kept telling her that I was thinking of killing myself, that I felt like cardboard, and that I felt that she wasn't responding to me at all. . . . I said I was feeling *exactly* the same way I felt before the hospitalization. I was having the same problems."

How did Waxman respond?

"Well, he was taking me seriously. He heard what I was saying. He realized that I was depressed or beyond depression. And I felt, well, now someone believes me at last. Someone is taking it seriously."

"Did he give any advice to you at that time?"

Waxman told her, she relates, "that I should try to get medication, I should call my psychiatrist and tell her again what I was going through and ask her for this medication. Then he said,

'You know, if you want, if you can come home for the weekend, I will see you in consultation.' "

Terry also called her brother-in-law, Lester Walston, who told her she was in a bad state and that she needed medication. She then called Dr. Charles. It was ten or eleven o'clock. "I told her 'I feel like a piece of cardboard, I haven't been sleeping, I'm terror stricken, I've been speaking to my former therapist and my brother-in-law, and they both said I really needed Mellaril' . . . and she said, 'Who told you that?' And I told her the two of them did. And she said, 'Who's the doctor here anyway?' "

A staccato exchange follows between lawyer and witness.

"Did she at that point offer to see you that morning?"

"No, she did not."

"Did she suggest it, about getting together right away?"

"No, she did not!"

"Did she agree that you needed medication?"

"No, she did not."

What then, Murphy asks.

" 'Well,' I said, 'you know, I'm really out of my head and I didn't sleep again last night.' And she said, 'Well, if you insist, I can give you Librium or Valium.' "

"And what did you say?"

"I said *never mind*. Because I knew what I was going through could not be helped with a minor drug. As a matter of fact, it made me feel, you know, she really doesn't know *what the hell is going on with me* if she would suggest something like that!"

"Yes," Terry replies to a question about a suicide plan. "I had been thinking all along that the best way to do it would be just to jump off the roof of the building or out of the window."

After her conversation with Dr. Charles, Terry spent "the whole day" talking with her parents, Lester Walston, and Dr. Waxman. She knew that her father was on his way from New York, but she did not know he was bringing Mellaril. She ran up and down the stairs and finally climbed out of her window onto the fire escape and went up to the roof where she stood thinking. "I'm going through this whole thing over again. I feel I can't bear it. It's unbelievably abnormal. And what can I do? I just have to kill myself. . . . I went and I sat at the edge of the building and I looked down and I said 'I'm never going to feel anything different from this.' And I said, 'Now or never,' and slipped off the roof.''

Murphy leads her through an account of the pain of her hospitalization and rehabilitation experiences and finishes his questioning. Terry looks at Maddux guardedly as he rises from his chair and walks toward her.

The Plaintiff—Cross-Examination

I'm sure it was correct if I gave it then, and now I remember.
                                                    —Terry Walker

Maddux begins by asking Terry about Dr. Waxman, who took care of her at the Cornell Hospital, establishing that Terry had continued in treatment with him for another year and had kept up "checking in" contacts with him after that.

"And," Maddux asks gently, "in all that period of time . . . you never told Dr. Waxman that you had any suicidal thoughts, did you?"

The question disconcerts Terry. "When?" she asks.

"When you were under his care?"

"Are you talking about after I was out of the hospital?"

"Any time."

"Oh, certainly," Terry responds, "when I was in the hospital, yes."

Maddux pauses, looks at her carefully and adds a clause that continues his earlier question, "Or that you were self-destructive, did you?"

Terry speaks softly, "I suppose, yes."

"And Dr. Waxman asked you what you meant when you said 'self-destructive'?"

Terry is wary. "I don't remember the conversation."

Is it because of the length of time, Maddux asks, that she cannot remember? Then back on course, "Didn't you really tell him that what you meant by 'self-destructive' was that you simply weren't doing things that were helpful to yourself? You don't recall telling him that?"

"Sounds like something I might say."

"And at no time," Maddux continues evenly, "did you indicate to Dr. Waxman that you had considered or had thoughts of taking your own life? You didn't tell him that, did you?"

"I think I told him that," she answers. "It was common knowledge that I felt that way when I was in the hospital."

Maddux speaks directly. "First of all, do you remember when your deposition was taken in this case?"

"Remember when it was taken?"

"Yes. Or that it was taken. I can refresh you about the date. . . . We're only talking about the first," Maddux says, "the first day when your deposition was taken on February 18, 1977."

"Yes," she says quietly.

"And you appeared in my office."

"I think so," Terry says. "But I didn't see you."

"Right. One of the lawyers in my office asked you some questions, right?" Terry mumbles acknowledgments to a quick series of inquiries. She was under oath, she swore to tell the truth, there was a court reporter present just as there is in the courtroom now. Questions were asked and she gave some answers. Yes, she remembers that.

"You said that. . . ." and Maddux interrupts himself. "First of all, when you entered that hospital, you were under the care of Dr. Morrow, is that right?"

"He was head of the unit. But he was . . . technically I was under his care. . . ."

"And you never mentioned anything about the subject of suicide with Dr. Morrow, did you?"

"I can't remember really," Terry answers, "because I know it was common knowledge that I was suicidal. That's why I was in the hospital."

"Well, then," Maddux says easily, "let me ask you this question. On page eighteen, weren't you asked this question and didn't you give this answer?" Maddux shifts the folder of sworn deposition testimony in his hands and reads aloud. " 'Question: Do you recall ever discussing your feelings concerning suicide or the subject of suicide with Dr. Morrow? Answer: No. But I want you to understand that he was just the unit head. He was on an administrative level, the doctor in charge, but I was not in therapy with him.' Do you," Maddux asks, "remember that question?"

"Well . . ." Terry's voice trails off. She says again that she was in therapy with Dr. Waxman.

Maddux hefts the binder of testimony. "So the next question

is . . . 'Did you discuss the subject of suicide with Dr. Waxman? Answer: I believe so.' " Maddux looks up at her. "You said that, okay?"

Terry does not disagree.

" 'Question: Do you recall what you said to him on that subject? Answer: I said once that I was self-destructive.' " Maddux looks at her again. "Do you remember saying that?"

"If it says it in the deposition," Terry answers, "I'm sure I said it."

"And then the question went on further. 'Question: Okay, did you say anything more than that in expanding on that concept? Answer: The only thing I remember is during a family conference it was brought up. . . . Question: What did you mean when you used the term self-destructive? Answer: I just meant that I wasn't doing things for my benefit, that many of the things I was doing were not helpful to myself. I wasn't particularly saying that I was going to *kill* myself or anything. Wider implications than that. Question: Are you saying that you were doing things that are not in your own best interest, or were you hurting your career or personal relationships? Answer: I believe so. That really wasn't going on at that point, but I believe so.' " Maddux pauses, then asks her, "Did you give those answers?"

Terry answers in a subdued voice. "If it's from a deposition, I'm sure I did."

"And continuing on," Maddux says, reading from Terry's deposition again, "the question was: 'Did you, at that time—this is while you're under therapy with Dr. Waxman—indicate to the doctor that you considered or had thoughts of taking your own life? Answer: No.' "

Terry mumbles, "Right."

Maddux then asks, "Did you hear that question and give that answer to that question?"

"I'm sure I did," she says softly.

"And you were under oath and you were doing your best to tell the truth, what the facts were, okay?"

Terry does not answer and Maddux places another question, "You were not treated with any drugs at that hospital?"

"Right." She hurriedly agrees that she only had individual and group therapy sessions. Maddux tells her that there were no closed units at the hospital. She insists that there were. Maddux returns to the previous subject. "Now then, you just got through telling us that you never told Dr. Waxman, nor did you remember ever having suicidal thoughts at that time. Right?"

"No, I didn't say that," Terry responds quietly.

"Well, you said in your deposition that you didn't tell Dr. Waxman that you had any suicidal . . ."

Terry breaks in, "I *did* have suicidal feelings!"

"So what you said in your deposition under oath is incorrect? Is that what you're saying?"

Murphy asserts an angry objection. "He's quoted one page out of five hundred pages of deposition. If he wants to refer to that one page, that's fine, I'm sure, your honor, but I object. . . ." The judge responds, "We can't do five hundred pages at a time. . . ." The judge turns toward Terry Walker, "The question is, you had been reminded that in the deposition you made a statement and that statement seemed somewhat inconsistent with the statement you made here yesterday. So the question is, which, to your memory, is correct?"

"Well, there's two questions. One was, did I tell Dr. Waxman that I was feeling suicidal. And one was, uh, was I feeling suicidal."

"No," the judge replies, "the question is what you told Dr. Waxman."

"That's what I asked you," Maddux says. "Was that incorrect— that answer you gave us under oath in your deposition—or is . . .?"

"I'm sure," Terry says softly, "it was correct if I gave it then and now I remember."

Maddux pushes on. "You didn't tell Dr. Waxman or anybody at that hospital about any episodes besides the one that preceded your admission to the hospital, did you?"

"Any other episodes?"

"You never had any similar episodes in your entire life up to that point?"

"Not that severe, no."

"You didn't have any that you really had, did you?"

"I don't know," Terry answers. "Everybody has problems. . . . But you're asking, did I ever go through what I went through during my first year of college before then?"

"Right."

"I'd say no."

"Or anything similar to it?"

"Right."

Terry is uneasy and subdued as Maddux establishes that she never had any trouble in graduate school in the fall of 1975, that she had gone to all her classes and had carried out all her assignments, such as seeing patients at local hospitals as a professionally supervised psychotherapist trainee. She had seen a patient at a Veteran's Hospital the afternoon before she jumped. She usually slept late, she admits, and, yes, she spent Wednesday, November 12, 1975, uneventfully with her father who then went on to New York. That same evening she got a traffic ticket and on Friday, November 14, she went to the wrong office to attempt to pay for the violation.

"Anyway," Maddux says, "you couldn't pay it on that Friday."

"Right."

"So you made a decision to postpone it to the next week and pay it next week?"

"I didn't think that far ahead," Terry answers. Does she remember her depositions? "Uh, huh," she replies.

"On page 322," Maddux says, gazing down at the deposition, "where you said you went . . . to a bookstore to buy a present for a friend: 'I went to try to pay a traffic ticket. . . . I was at the wrong place and they told me where to go and it was open but I didn't want to go all the way down there. I thought I'd do it next week.' Were those questions asked and did you give those answers?"

"Uh, huh."

"So that at that time you had the intention of paying the traffic ticket next week?"

"Uh, huh."

"All right, that's something you planned to do for the next week. That's on Friday before the Saturday, November 15. Right? Is that correct?"

There is a long pause. Finally, Terry raises and lowers her head slowly. "I don't want to be technical," Maddux says, "but, you know, they don't take down the nod of the head. . . . Yes?"

"Okay. Yeah," Terry answers softly. Maddux, noting that she seems tired, says that he will continue his examination in the afternoon.

Maddux refers to Terry's earlier depositions to establish the regularity of her schedule on Thursday and Friday of that November week. She had seen patients on both days. Then he returns to the Saturday morning phone calls. Terry agrees that Dr. Waxman told her that her father was coming to Chicago. "That was the last conversation, when Dr. Waxman told you your father was coming?" Yes. "You worried about your father coming out to Chicago, didn't you?"

"I don't recall that I felt worried about it then," Terry replies steadily. Maddux opens the binder of her previous testimony.

"You were worried about your father coming to Chicago . . ." Maddux pauses as he finds his place in Terry's deposition, "because it meant to you that you had communicated a real emergency. . . ."

"I was not sure it was an emergency."

"And you were frightened?"

"Uh, huh."

"You told us," Maddux says evenly, "that you were worried about this series of phone calls, right? And that you were worried about your father coming out because you had communicated a *real* emergency. And you were frightened about what it meant. And you might really have to go home or do something drastic and you could not remain in Chicago to handle it on your own as you had been doing."

"Well," Terry replies, "I guess I was saying that things were building and building and culminating. . . ."

"It was right after that phone call conference with Dr. Waxman." Maddux addresses Terry with great directness. "And you were informed your father was coming out and you were frightened, as we discussed, and you went to the roof." Maddux waits for her almost silent agreement, then turns away. "No further questions."

Murphy rises to read other sections of her deposition into the record as Terry leaves the area of the witness stand and rides her electric wheelchair swiftly out of the courtroom.

The Best Friend

That's correct. I didn't know I was gonna appear as a witness.
—Jack Konig

Murphy calls Jack Konig, the family friend. The blue-suited, deep-voiced Konig testifies that he greeted Sara when she got off the elevator at the hospital on the day after Terry's leap, that he introduced her to Mr. Walker, that he overheard Sara admit that she had made a "clinical error."

Maddux begins his cross-examination with a few general background questions. Konig is from one "bedroom" community of New York City, Paramus, New Jersey, and works in another, Yonkers, New York. He is executive vice-president of an auto trade association. Konig regards Maddux confidently, "Just ask your question, Counsel, I'll be glad to respond." Well, what about this trade association?

"Independent Dealer Association Committed to Action," the smiling Konig responds, ". . . I.D.A.C.A." It is, he explains, a franchiser of car dealerships.

Maddux establishes that the Konigs and the Walkers are social friends, that they have been to each other's houses often, and then abruptly shifts his tone. Konig had been up until five A.M. after a midnight flight from New York on that Saturday night that he flew with Mrs. Walker to Chicago.

"Where is the hospital located?"

"It's someplace in downtown Chicago. I'm not familiar with Chicago, quite frankly."

"Where was the hotel?"

"Within a few blocks. . . . I couldn't give you the name of the hotel."

"You know what the name of the hospital was?"

"It was something with Northwestern in it. There was a ramp. . . ."

"And do you remember which building you were in?"

"No, sir, I do not," Konig answers quickly.

"Do you know what floor you were on?"

"No, sir."

Maddux sets the scene of Dr. Charles's arrival at the hospital and asks, "The first thing she did was to tell you and Mr. Walker that she made a clinical error?"

"She didn't tell it to me. She told it to Mr. Walker," Konig says. "He asked a question. I didn't, Counsel." Konig then left. "That was enough," he adds, lowering his eyes. Then, looking up again, Konig says, no, he has never discussed the present case with the Walkers. "We don't discuss this as part of our social evenings."

Konig cannot recall when the possibility of his testifying first came up. He cannot even give a ballpark figure. "Within the last year," he finally says.

No one spoke to him about it between 1975 and 1979?

"That's correct. I didn't know I was gonna appear as a witness." No, he did not keep a record, he did not give a statement to any lawyer. The first time he met the Walkers' lawyer was this very morning.

"I have no further questions," Maddux says, turning away from the subdued witness.

I watch the unsmiling Konig walk down the aisle as Murphy noisily insists that he had scheduled him as a witness long before today. I had, in fact, accompanied Sara to the hospital on that grim Sunday, I had stood by the elevator as she had walked across the small reception area to meet Mitchell Walker where they sat down on a small bench. I regret that, by Bill Maddux's decision, I cannot at least do the one small thing of telling the jury that, wherever Konig was that day, he did not meet with Sara and Mitchell Walker at the hospital. I feel impatient as Murphy announces that he will call his experts to the stand tomorrow.

PART II

The Experts

Some Relevant Definitions

Excerpts from *The Diagnostic and Statistical Manual of Mental Disorders*, DSM-III (Third edition), American Psychiatric Association, 1980.

Affective Disorders [p. 205]

The essential feature of this group of disorders is a disturbance of mood, accompanied by a full or partial manic or depressive syndrome, that is not due to any other physical or mental disorder. Mood refers to a prolonged emotion that colors the whole psychic life; it generally involves either depression or elation. The manic and depressive syndromes each consist of characteristic symptoms that tend to occur together.

Major Affective Disorders include Bipolar Disorder and Major Depression, which are distinguished by whether or not there has ever been a manic episode. A category of Manic Disorder is not included in this classification; instead, when there has been one or more manic episode, with or without a history of a major depressive episode, the category Bipolar Disorder is used.

Personality Disorders [p. 305]

Personality *traits* are enduring patterns of perceiving, relating to, and thinking about the environment and oneself, and are exhibited in a wide range of important social and personal contexts. It is only when *personality traits* are inflexible and maladaptive and cause other significant impairment in social or occupational functioning or subjective distress that they constitute *Personality Disorders*. The manifestations of *Personality Disorders* are generally recognizable by adolescence or earlier and continue throughout most of adult life, though they often become less obvious in middle or old age.

301.83 Borderline Personality Disorder [p. 321]

The essential feature is a Personality Disorder in which there is instability in a variety of areas, including interpersonal behavior, mood, and self-image. No single feature is invariably present. Interpersonal relations are often intense and unstable, with marked shifts of attitude over time. Frequently there is impulsive and unpredictable behavior that is potentially physically self-damaging. Mood is often unstable, with marked shifts from normal mood to a dysphoric mood or with inappropriate, intense anger or lack of control of anger. A profound identity disturbance may be manifested by uncertainty about several issues relating to iden-tity, such as self-image, gender identity, or long-term goals or values. There may be problems tolerating being alone, and chronic feelings of emptiness or boredom."

* * *

"The 'switch process' is operationally defined as the events occur-ring at the time of change from depression to mania."

The article further describes 10 episodes (in 8 patients) of spontaneous behavioral switches from depression to mania and 7 episodes of spontaneous switches out of mania into depression. The depressed period was characterized by (1) seclusiveness, (2) non-verbalization, and (3) dozing.

—"The Switch Process in Manic-Depressive Illness" by William Bunney et al.
Archives of General Psychiatry, vol. 27, 1972.

Devising the Case

*That was my question, 'history of previous depression.' And she said no—
and I underlined that three times.*

—Edward Wolpert, M.D.

There can be no medical malpractice trial without the presence of experts qualified to make judgments on the special subject matter of the litigation. While the judge's task is to be the "tryer of law," and the jury's obligation is to be the "tryer of fact," expert witnesses enjoy wider freedom. They may draw inferences as well as conclusions based on the supposed facts of any case. In a medical malpractice case experts who are the defendant's peers testify as to whether there has been a deviation from the accepted standard of medical care in a particular situation. To substantiate malpractice the experts must also testify that the injury in question resulted directly from the alleged deviation. Both the plaintiff and the defendant employ expert witnesses. The jury decides which offers the more credible and compelling testimony.

Dr. Edward Wolpert, a psychoanalyst from the Michael Reese Hospital in Chicago, was retained by Patrick Murphy in March 1977 to serve as an expert witness in behalf of Terry Walker. After interviewing her that April, he began to gather materials to support the case against Sara. When asked, under oath during his deposition, to name authoritative texts or articles in the area of affective disorders, Wolpert replied, "It might be easier if you took the table of contents from my book, *Manic-Depressive Illness— History of a Syndrome.* . . . You could look at my publications and read what I have quoted, the people I have quoted, and that would be a pretty good example. . . ." When asked how Sara had deviated from the accepted standard of medical care, Wolpert replied, "She did not obtain a complete psychiatric history; she did not investigate the previous treatment that the patient received by writing to the appropriate people to have information of that treatment. . . . The consequences of these lacks were that she was not in a position to treat the patient in a way that would have been more correct, which would have included increased sessions at various times in the treatment."

Anything else? he was asked.

"I think that if she had made the correct diagnosis, that she would have addressed the issues differently. But that is a consequence of the fundamental issues I just mentioned." Sara should also have used antidepressants and seen the patient more frequently. Yes, it was Wolpert's opinion that the patient was suffering from a clinical depression, a type of affective disorder, prior to her accident of November 1975. Through two long depositions in the fall of 1978, the expert explained his findings to Tom Boodell and Brian Fetzer, an associate of William Maddux.

Wolpert obtained the records from the hospital in New York where Terry had been hospitalized in 1971. Dr. Waxman, her psychotherapist at the time, had noted in the records her family's contribution to her psychological problems and that her only treatment had been psychotherapy. Terry was thought, in 1971, to have been self-dramatizing and she described herself as "very theatrical." The hospitalization was considered a relief from familial and other life pressures.

Wolpert also entered in his notes on December 19, 1977, an account of a phone call from Dr. Howard Morrow, a supervising psychiatrist at the Cornell Hospital in 1971, who said that he had "no impression of psychosis" in Terry and that he "felt it was a situational reaction." He also said that "she seemed less severely depressed than others" and that she received no medication during her hospitalization. According to his interview notes, Wolpert found recurrent episodes of depression in Terry's life beginning in early childhood. Under oath in his deposition, he explained how he had questioned Terry. He had inquired, he said, about any "history of previous psychological depression, and she said no, and I underlined that three times."

Wolpert described Terry's experience of the "switch process" in moving her into a depressive state at regular intervals. He mentioned an article on the subject by Bunney and spelled that researcher's name for the lawyers who were questioning him. Later, during her direct trial testimony, Terry would describe her alleged depression by saying, "It was like a switch that was turned on." Wolpert explained how he had uncovered the hitherto undetected illness in Terry, "The red flag is that the patient may not say what you need them to say." After explaining the manic-depressive syndrome, Wolpert concluded that Terry suffered from unipolar affective disease "that could develop into a bipolar illness," that is, that she suffered from depression that could turn into alternating periods of mania and depression. He also judged that she suffered from a narcissistic personality disorder.

The first two parts of Wolpert's depositions, 138 pages in all, were spread across our dining room table. Sara, in sweater and slacks, was bent over these materials. After several hours of checking out the references he had made, she looked up, removed her half-glasses, smiled, and pointed to a thick volume open before her. "I read your book," she grinned, recalling a scene from the movie *Patton.* "I read your book, you bastard." And, for one of the few times during those long, grim years, she laughed and we laughed together. "Wolpert's wrong!" she said. "He's not only wrong about me, but he's wrong about the literature."

Scientific research on bipolar depression—swings from extreme highs to extreme lows—shows that the possible pattern of inheritance applies more strongly to bipolar classifications, that is, patients who experience these alternating periods of depression and mania. The evidence is much less clear regarding unipolar depression, that is, patients who suffer only from repeated depression. This is well-documented in the book Wolpert edited. The "switch process" is given a strict operational definition in the very research article by Bunney that Wolpert mentioned in his deposition. Based on a study of eight subjects, it refers only to bipolar manic-depressive patients who constitute a much more homogeneous group than those termed unipolar. Wolpert claimed that Terry had gone through a switch process even though the process, as described in the article he cited, applied only to bipolar patients. Apparently unaware of his mistakes or their implications, he then gave Terry a diagnosis of unipolar depression. Wolpert disagreed with the diagnosis given by Sara and every other expert, including those of the plaintiff, in the case.

Sara met with Thomas Boodell and prepared him to question Wolpert on these scientific issues during his final deposition session in January 1979.

Boodell was received by Wolpert in his hospital office. The lawyer began with a series of technical questions, pressing Dr. Wolpert for examples of research "on patients that have both unipolar and another mental disease, concerning the cause of depression in these patients." Wolpert had given Terry Walker such a double diagnosis. Sara's search of the psychiatric literature had shown that *no* research had as yet untangled the interaction of depression and character problems in the way Wolpert had claimed.

"Wait," Wolpert replied, "rephrase that somehow. I don't understand your question. Could you split the question into two parts, perhaps? It seems to me it is two questions."

"No," Boodell responded. "I think we are dealing with a patient that you have diagnosed as having two problems." Wolpert answered: "I am not aware of anybody, other than the writing that *I* am doing, that talks about patients having both disorders simultaneously."

Boodell turned to the "switch process." The lawyer had read the article by Bunney to which Wolpert had previously referred. The switch, scientifically, referred to a tightly defined phenomenon. The bipolar manic-depressive patients in the research had also all exhibited other significant symptoms: seclusiveness, nonverbalization, and dozing.

"Is it your position, Doctor, that this patient went through a process that can be described as a switch process?"

"Yes," Wolpert answered confidently.

"How is the switch process operationally defined?"

"It is a sudden change."

"From what to what?"

"From any one of the three states I talked about previously to the other one, to another one . . . hypomanic or manic on the one hand, normal, depressed on the other hand."

"Does the switch process as defined in the research papers you mentioned last time—by Bunney and others—or other research papers, apply to unipolar affective disorders as well as bipolar?"

"Yes."

"What articles would you cite as showing that that is so?"

Wolpert hesitated. "To answer you correctly I would have to look it up so I can give you the right reference. I believe it is Bunney, but I would have to look for sure." Wolpert agreed to mail the reference when he found it.

Boodell moved to other aspects of the Bunney article, the list of symptoms reported in the subjects who had experienced the switch.

"Did Miss Walker describe to you any periods of seclusiveness?"

"Yes," Wolpert said slowly, "she talked about not feeling like talking to people or being with people at various times."

"Did she say when these periods occurred?"

"To the best of my memory I don't have down in my mind any specific time that she attributed any of these periods occurring."

"Did she describe any periods of nonverbalization?"

"What do you mean by nonverbalization?"

"The meaning attributed to it in the research articles."

"No," Wolpert replied quickly, "she did not talk of nonverbalization."

"Did she describe to you any periods of dozing?" Boodell asked.

"No," the plaintiff's expert answered quietly and in a few moments the deposition ended.

Marvin Waxman, the New York psychologist who had been Terry Walker's psychotherapist during part of her 1971 treatment, wrote the closing summary on her at the New York Hospital, Cornell Medical Center, Westchester Division. Dated May 24, 1971, it reveals his contemporaneous impressions of the nature and causes of Terry's hospitalization.

> Terry was successfully treated during her three months' stay at New York Hospital basically in psychotherapy and moderate work with the family. At this point Terry is not particularly at home there being a great deal of conflict between her parents and herself and between her parents. However, the problems that exist are out in the open and no longer have the same pathognomonic influence that they once did. . . . She shows a relatively positive and optimistic outlook and has considerable insight into some of the difficulties in the family and her relationship to other people. Hospitalization was completely beneficial in terms of giving her a respite from the pressures that were on her and allow her an opportunity to put together a new view of herself and her relationships to other people. Prognosis for the future is quite good.

In 1977, Waxman remembered her condition quite differently. "My impressions at that point," he said under oath at his deposition, "were that she was susceptible and might be susceptible to recurring depressions. . . . I would see her having a constitutional vulnerability depression. It may be," he said, "a genetic loading, or other family members who had depression, and she specifically is vulnerable to that kind of disorder." Waxman claimed that Terry had a family history of depression, thus offering support for Wolpert's assertions about depression-ridden Walker forebears.

Admitting that, as a psychologist, he was not licensed to prescribe medication, Dr. Waxman recalled discussing the case by phone on November 15, 1975, with the same Dr. Howard Morrow who had been a supervisor in the White Plains Hospital when Terry had been a patient. Waxman talked to him "because I had to know his impressions and also his willingness to give out a prescription."

"So that based upon your recommendation, Dr. Morrow prescribed medication to a patient that he himself had not seen for two and a half to some three years?" asked the lawyer.

"Based on my description. . . . Correct."

"Based upon your telephone conversations with Terry, you described to Dr. Morrow and recommended that he prescribe medication for a patient that you, yourself, had not had any face-to-face contact with or telephone contact with for at least a year prior to that day?"

"I didn't recommend it to him. I discussed it with him and that was the decision he arrived at as making sense."

"So, you are saying today that Dr. Morrow is the one who decided to prescribe the Mellaril."

"Correct."

The case was drawn against Sara, and Edward Wolpert would be the chief expert witness. Now Murphy tells the Walker family what he has apparently known and they have feared for some time. Wolpert will not appear for the plaintiff. A news item had appeared in the *Chicago Sun-Times* for May 31, 1980, under the headline, *Psychiatrist Hit by Suit in Bliss Deaths.*

The story read:

> The psychiatrist who reportedly was treating *Chicago Tribune* reporter George W. Bliss for mental depression in 1978 when Bliss killed his wife and himself was accused Friday of malpractice. Medical malpractice suits against Dr. Edward A. Wolpert were filed in Circuit Court by the children of the couple. . . .
>
> The lawsuits say that during the five months prior to the shooting, Wolpert had been treating Bliss for "agitated, depressive psychosis" and "profound agitated depression." In that period Bliss had returned to work after a seven-month disability leave for illness. On September 11, 1978, the 60-year-old award-win-

ning *Tribune* reporter and former investigator for the Better Government Association fatally shot his wife, Therese, 51, then turned the gun on himself in their Oak Lawn home.

Wolpert is accused of negligence for, among other things, not recommending hospitalization for Bliss and not warning Bliss' wife and other members of the family of his "potential homicidal tendencies."

Not included in the account was the name of the attorney who had filed the suits,* William Maddux.

* This lawsuit is still pending, as of April 1985.

Day Five

Plaintiff's Expert I

I do. . . . She did.

—Marvin Schwarz, M.D.

In court, Murphy calls his first medical expert to the stand. Marvin Schwarz takes the oath, spells his name, and describes his medical career. He has appeared as a psychiatric expert in court "a large number of times . . . many hundreds of times." He interviewed Terry Walker for one hour, he explains, and read other materials, including the hospital summary from Cornell, Dr. Waxman's deposition, and Dr. Charles's notes.

"Doctor," Murphy asks, reading from his yellow pad a phrase that he will use repeatedly during the day, "do you have an opinion based upon reasonable medical certainty as to what Terry's condition was in November of 1975 when she leapt off the roof?"

"I do," Schwarz says gravely. ". . . It is my opinion that at that point she was in a severely regressed psychotic state with very strong affective features. . . . with a severe depression at the same time. . . . but the evidence shows that at that time she was in an acute state of falling apart similar to the one which the hospital records revealed in 1971." Schwarz offers an account of the allegedly suicidal episode that led to Terry's earlier hospitalization. He then gives, in slightly different terminology, the same diagnosis of borderline personality that Sara had given to Terry; he equates Terry's experiences in 1975 with those she had in 1971.

Murphy looks up from his yellow legal pad. "Doctor, as a result of your interview and examination of Terry Walker, as a result of your review of various documents and records and depositions in this matter, do you have an opinion, based upon reasonable medical certitude, whether or not Dr. Sara Charles in the treatment of Terry Walker deviated from the generally accepted standard of care that one would expect from a reasonably competent and careful psychiatrist practicing in Cook County, Illinois?

"I do!"

"And what is that opinion, Doctor?"

"That she did." This exchange will take place many times during this direct examination. Schwarz, after giving his opinion about a psychiatrist's obligations to hospitalize patients, details his case against Sara: ". . . There were marked evidences that the patient was falling apart, the patient was talking about killing herself, there were hospital records that showed what this woman was capable of doing by having done in the past. There was every possible reason to demand that in addition to interpreting what was going on inside the patient's mind . . . to take an active role to protect the patient. I feel that there was an obligation on the part of Dr. Charles to hospitalize the patient immediately . . . and probably use extensive amounts of medication in the acute crisis."

Sara failed, according to Schwarz, by not getting the previous hospital records. If the patient refused to give the hospital records to her, Sara should have hospitalized her. Sara failed in not offering daily visits and in not prescribing medication to Terry. Murphy asks a question, based on a phrase from Sara's personal notes. Does Schwarz have an opinion concerning "November the seventh when Terry Walker called Dr. Charles and said she was 'losing control,' whether or not Dr. Sara Charles deviated from what one would expect from a reasonably competent and careful psychiatrist practicing in Cook County, Illinois, by not at that time instituting additional measures in her therapeutic relationship with Terry Walker?"

"I do. . . . she did. . . . the least she could have done, she should have gone to her home and saw her. Dr. Charles should have called the police and said she had reason to believe that this person was going to kill herself, and the Chicago police would have gone and sat with the girl until Dr. Charles came." Sara failed by not referring Terry, by not certifying her, by not paying attention to her previous hospitalization during which suicidal precautions were taken. Murphy comes to the essential question, "Doctor, do you have a further opinion, again based on reasonable medical certitude, whether or not the actions of Dr. Charles leading up to and including the fifteenth of November was the proximate cause of Terry Walker's attempted suicide?"

"It is my opinion that the actions of Dr. Charles, for not taking action, was the proximate cause since, if she had taken action as a physician should have . . . it would not have happened. . . ." Sara also deviated, according to this expert, by not going to the patient's house. After the Thursday phone call from the brother-in-law, Dr. Walston, Dr. Charles should "have hospitalized her and . . . used extensive amounts of medication." Schwarz does not feel that the Walker family hysteria or Terry's fear of being hospitalized contributed to Terry's decision to leap off the roof.

Murphy asks Schwarz if, on the basis of everything he has read, including Dr. Charles's notes, he can describe the symptoms that Terry manifested throughout the fall of 1975.

"Yes, sir," Schwarz responds. "The key issues were inability to function, panic, fear, calling everybody, running, pleading, going to people in the middle of the night, feelings of depersonalization, fears of the suicide, obsessive characteristics, continuous concern about things, the feeling that she wasn't a person . . . the key issues are that this person—who, according to Dr. Charles's previous notes, was relatively functional, able to attend school, able to deal with people—was moving into herself, withdrawing, and ceasing to function." He clicks off additional symptoms: "Intense anxiety, suicidal preoccupation, feelings of hopelessness, which are crucial." Were these the same as the symptoms of 1971? "According to Terry and according to the history and the material and the records of Cornell, Westchester, yes."

There are a dozen additional questions about Terry's supposed suicidal attempts in 1971 and the drugs that might have been helpful in 1975. The members of the jury remain attentive, impassive, their eyes fixed on Schwarz as Murphy asks his final question. Does Dr. Schwarz have an opinion of "the reason why Terry Walker attempted to take her life by leaping, jumping, or sliding off the roof on the fifteenth of November 1975?"

"Yes, sir," he replies.

"What is the reason?"

"That she was very sick." Murphy lowers his legal pad and turns away.

Plaintiff's Expert I—Cross-Examination

That's an irrational question!

—Marvin Schwarz, M.D.

The afternoon session is delayed as the judge hears a motion on a case involving a large Chicago company. Maddux, eyes glinting merrily, peers through the window of the courtroom door, shakes his head. "There are seven senior partners from a big law firm sitting in pecking order in there. Only one of them will speak but they'll all get paid. That two-minute motion is costing about fifteen hundred dollars." A row of middle-aged, well-tailored lawyers files out of the room and in a few moments Schwarz is back on the stand waiting for Maddux's first question.

"In Waxman's deposition about November 15, about the last conversation in the late afternoon . . . he says that Terry was not suicidal. Do you recall reading that?"

"Would you like to show it to me?" Schwarz asks.

Murphy complains that it is not his recollection, either. Maddux says that he will read it so that everyone can hear.

Murphy picks up his copy of Waxman's deposition. "Page fifty," Maddux tells him and begins to quote the exchange.

" 'Question: Doctor, at the time of the fourth conversation with Terry at approximately four P.M., did you form an opinion or have an impression as to whether or not Terry was suicidal at that time? Answer: Usually someone who is suicidal will be willing to let you know that they are suicidal, and again to my question to her specifically whether she was going to be all right, she said "Yes." So while I felt there was a likelihood of her being suicidal, I did not think it was imminent. Question: You didn't think it was so imminent that you would have to make a telephone call to any type of authorities in Chicago, that you would have to attempt to intervene with Terry, did you? Answer: No, not at that point.' "

Maddux lowers the folder of testimony and looks at Schwarz. "And that was at four P.M. on November 15. Did you read this?" Schwarz says that he did. "Do you agree or disagree?"

"Well, agree with what, sir?" he asks.

"That he says that it wasn't imminent?"

"Was that the question you asked me, sir? Would you repeat your question? He says he thinks she was suicidal. That he said suicide was likely but not imminent. Uh, but he says suicide is likely, you don't have to . . . that's being suicidal."

Maddux continues. "There were many conversations he had with her that day, right? You recall reading that? He didn't feel that there was any necessity to go to any real intervention by the police, as you talked about before."

"I don't see that," Schwarz responds. "I mean the question you're asking me is, was he concerned? It is my feeling . . ."

"Excuse me, Doctor," Maddux interrupts, "I'm not asking you whether he was concerned. I'm saying he didn't—he specifically states in his testimony that you read to form part of your opinion— that he didn't feel that any suicidal tendency was imminent. And that was at four o'clock P.M. on November 15."

After an objection by Murphy, Maddux takes up the questioning again. "In treating patients, you'd agree with the simple proposition that somebody who's on the spot . . . is in a better position to determine physical status, mental status, or any other status of a patient?" Schwarz agrees. "Sure, so in formulating your opinion you quite obviously would look to what Dr. Waxman would have to say, very closely, wouldn't you?"

Yes, Schwarz agrees and Maddux continues. "I take it you agree that at the time of Dr. Waxman's observation, the possibility of suicide was not imminent?"

"The possibility, a likelihood is a possibility. . . . He also said he did not see it as probable. . . . I have taught consistently that one does not need probability to respond to. . . ."

"So I take it," Maddux counters, "that you'd conclude that

Dr. Waxman should have called the police in Chicago and had her picked up?"

"Whether he should or shouldn't, he was not the treating physician."

"He took it upon himself to intervene with the patient, didn't he?"

"Well," Schwarz responds, "my feeling is he should have called Dr. Charles—but then this is again hindsight—or talked to the family and had the family call Dr. Charles, or suggested to Terry that Terry talk to Dr. Charles. But in answer to your original question, you asked me whether or not he saw her as suicidal. I'll repeat my theory that if he saw suicide as likely, that's suicidal. . . ."

"You mentioned one word," Maddux says. "Hindsight. Looking at what Waxman thought and what was going on with hindsight. Actually, everything you do in this case looks at the case with hindsight, doesn't it?"

"That is true, sir."

"And insofar as the observations of a particular patient, being there at the time is much more reliable than trying to pick it up from what people say when a lawsuit is pending later on, isn't it?"

"That is certainly true, sir."

". . . Statements that a person might make to you after the fact—while a lawsuit is pending—wouldn't you tend to discount those statements if they're in conflict with the statements that were made before the episode occurred?"

"If you're saying," the expert responds, "that the examination at the time of a lawsuit has a different purpose than an examination to treat, that is certainly true. . . . I do not want to convey that I or any other psychiatrist operates with certainty in any case."

Maddux nods, he will get back to that later. First he wants to ask Dr. Schwarz about the *Diagnostic and Statistical Manual,* third edition, the recently published handbook of the American Psychiatric Association, which contains the most current terminology to describe the gamut of psychiatric conditions. "I would rather," Schwarz says, "explain atomic physics than explain the DSM series." Maddux allows him to finish his critique of the new *Diagnostic and Statistical Manual,* then presses him on the nature of the borderline condition. Schwarz says that on November 15, 1975, Terry

Walker was suffering from a "borderline schizophrenic character disorder."

Maddux asks if Schwarz means that Terry is schizophrenic.

". . . I think a borderline means, by definition, bordering on what? And what it borders on is schizophrenia. That's what borderline means."

"That's what it means to you?" Maddux asks.

"That's what it means to everyone."

"Is that what it means in the *Diagnostic and Statistical Manual* three?"

"You bet it does," Schwarz answers. "Yes."

Schwarz relies on an older mode of scientific classification because the patient with a borderline character, although capable of brief psychotic episodes, is now thought of as clearly distinct from the schizophrenic patient. It is a crucial point since borderlines can be lucid and rational, if filled with difficulties, most of the time. Schwarz moves on to a discussion of the summary of the 1971 Cornell Hospital record, which, he claims, Sara should have gotten early in her treatment of Terry. On the basis of reading that summary alone, Schwarz declares emphatically, he would have hospitalized the patient in September 1975. Maddux reads part of the Cornell summary of Terry's 1971 hospitalization to Schwarz.

"It goes right on to say 'denies anxiety or suicidal thoughts,' doesn't it?"

"Yes."

"That means that she was asked whether she even thought about suicide and she said no. Right?"

"That's not what it means," Schwarz insists. He, however, acknowledges that Terry Walker was rational at the time that she went to the roof, that intellectually she knew full well what she was doing, that she appreciated the nature and quality of her act. Yes to questions from Maddux on all these. And yes to the fact that even competent, well-trained psychiatrists can do all the right things and still lose patients. Schwarz also agrees that at times patients who are doing quite well can disintegrate quickly if they are subjected to sudden overwhelming stress. After Schwarz acknowledges the role of clinical judgment in the treatment of psychiatric patients, Maddux places a further question. "Would you agree with the proposition that for a . . . borderline character defect patient the ability to function independently, doing their

normal activities in society, is preferable over locking them up
in a hospital with drugging?"

"That's an irrational question!" Schwarz declares. The courtroom shakes into quiet laughter and Maddux himself grins as
he turns away. "No further questions."

Murphy wants to redo some aspects of his direct examination.
He reads excerpts from Sara's notes, prompting Schwarz to say
several times that he would have medicated and hospitalized Terry
Walker on various occasions during the late summer and early
fall of 1975. Murphy also rereads sections of Dr. Waxman's deposition into the record as well as sections of the Cornell Hospital
summary into the record. Maddux "reluctantly" asks some concluding questions to bring Schwarz back into focus and court
adjourns for the afternoon.

The first week is finished. Mitchell Walker stops Maddux as
we are leaving the courtroom. "If I ever get charged with murder,"
he says to our trial lawyer, "I want you to defend me." Then
he turns and walks slowly out the door. Maddux wrinkles his
brow, smiles, and we walk down the hallway past the court buffs
to the elevator.

The first week has finished on a bizarre note. The plaintiff's first
expert has sown as much confusion as he has wisdom with his
testimony. He has, however, confidently accused Sara of medical
malpractice not for one supposed failure of judgment but for a
score of clinical choices and behaviors. In his hindsight reading
of the relevant documents, he has found nothing that she did
right. What effect, I wonder as we are carried on the tide of men
and women walking through the sultry streets toward home, has
Dr. Schwarz had on the members of the jury? They laughed at
his fussy manner, at the jagged flights of his free associations,
but he had been positive in his accusations, he had entertained
no doubts at all about Sara's negligence. Was he so hard to follow
that the only impression he left was one of certainty? There was
no telling from looking at the men and women of the jury as
they left the courtroom.

Schwarz's opinions blink in my head with the glare of a sputter-
ing neon sign. Sara is quiet and thoughtful as we make our way
to the edge of Lake Michigan seeking, along with thousands of
others on this Friday evening, some relief from its light breezes,
some refreshment from its rolling green presence. All I can think

is that anything can happen, that there is no telling how things will come out, that the worst may happen, and that Sara's sense of herself as a conscientious doctor may be forever altered, that, work as hard as we have and will continue to do over the weekend, we are in the grip of a process that may change our lives profoundly.

DAY SIX

Plaintiff's Expert II

How in the world does anyone come to a conclusion?

—Jerome Goldberg

On Monday morning Jerome Goldberg, Murphy's partner, rises and calls the plaintiff's second expert to the stand. Dr. Bernard Rubin, fifty-three, dark-haired, well-tailored, has been a close associate of Goldberg's brother, Arnold, a psychoanalyst with whom he has published a few articles. Rubin has worked with Murphy and Goldberg on revising the Illinois Mental Health Code. Rubin tells the court that he has been an expert witness "about 150 times."

Speaking in a well-modulated voice, the psychiatrist explains that he examined Terry Walker shortly after she filed the lawsuit against Sara. Terry impressed him as "credible and truthful. . . . I think she was a good reporter of her own history." The plaintiff suffers from a "borderline personality disorder," the diagnosis offered by all the experts who remain connected with the case.

Murphy and Goldberg have put aside the depression theory. Claiming that Terry made a bona fide suicide attempt in 1971, Rubin speaks easily and effectively.

Goldberg asks if there is anything in the summary hospital record "that confirms or supports the opinion you've just given that Terry Walker was seriously mentally ill and suicidal in March 1971?"

"From the hospital record," Rubin answers, "the only two things I can tell is that she was seriously ill because she was hospitalized for three months, and hospitalized at a time when the average stay for serious illnesses in most mental hospitals in this country, both in New York and Chicago, is about twenty days.* That meant that they considered this to be a more serious problem that required more continuing and intensive care. The second thing was that she seemed to be better when she was hospitalized."

What about the statements that Terry made on admission to the hospital that "she was being theatrical, that she didn't think she belonged in the hospital, and she didn't intend to kill herself. . . . What," Goldberg asks, "do you consider significant about those things, if they occurred?"

"They are made by some patients who are seriously ill." Rubin's tone is assured. "They sometimes say they don't belong in the hospital, they sometimes say 'What I did was theatrical and I had more control' than they actually did have." Rubin claims that the hospital summary does not really mean what it says. The entire courtroom—from jury members to the cluster of knowing buffs—seems absorbed by this expert's statements.

Goldberg asks Rubin to read one of Sara's personal notes. Maddux objects immediately and Judge McGarr says that Dr. Rubin cannot interpret the notes. The judge also explains the nature of a psychiatrist's notes to the jury members who were absent when they were first discussed and then sends them out while he establishes some ground rules with the lawyers for the continu-

---

* Length of hospital stay for psychiatric patients in 1972 (taken from American Hospital Association Statistics).

	Average total days
all psychiatric hospitals	381.3
nongovernment, not-for-profit hospitals	100.9
nongovernment, for profit hospitals	53.6
local governmental hospitals	511.6
state governmental hospitals	433.1
federal government hospitals	217.7

ation of the examination. Maddux takes the opportunity to tell Goldberg and the judge that limitations must be placed on Rubin's use of his interview with Terry Walker because it took place after the lawsuit was filed. McGarr sustains Maddux's objection. Goldberg is upset. "You're saying that I cannot ask any questions relating to what Terry told him [Rubin] in the interview?" "That is correct," the judge answers and Goldberg asks, "How in the world does anyone come to a conclusion?" Maddux answers, "Frequently it's done by a hypothetical question. . . ."

After a recess, Goldberg moves to the heart of the matter. "Dr. Rubin, as a result of all of the information that you know about this case, do you have any opinion based upon reasonable medical certainty as to whether or not Dr. Sara Charles in her treatment of Terry Walker deviated from the generally accepted standard of care that one would expect from a reasonably competent and careful psychiatrist practicing in Cook County, Illinois?"

Yes, Rubin answers. "She deviated from the minimal standard of care in the final weeks of treatment early November, late October 1975, at the time when Terry was severely depressed, panicky, and suicidal." Sara should have seen Terry more often, she should have offered the opportunity of medication or hospitalization, or both. One would also have to consider the possibility of Sara's deviating by not getting the hospital records from Cornell. The expert feels that the symptoms in 1971 and 1975 were "almost identical." Yes, there was plenty of evidence that Terry was fragmenting in October and November of 1975. Rubin gives particulars: "Terry's statement that she felt like cardboard, the constant phone calls, the reaching out to half a dozen different people to see if somebody would intervene for her, the fact that she was sleepless for at least twenty-four hours or more prior to jumping from the roof of her building, the fact that she was unable to think clearly and felt as if she was going out of control."

He adds a postscript: "In Dr. Charles's deposition and her notes she was told and made note of the fact that Terry was having the problems I've mentioned." Terry was fragmenting as early as November 6, Rubin claims, but she had complained of major symptoms from September on. Rubin charges that Sara wanted to reduce her sessions with Terry on the very day the patient jumped. Sara also deviated by offering Librium to the patient. Rubin would have prescribed an antipsychotic or an antidepressant if he and the patient agreed on it. Terry's suicidal attempt could have been prevented if Sara had followed Rubin's prescriptions for treatment.

Goldberg asks if the expert has "an opinion based on reasonable medical certainty, whether the acts, the omissions, the deviations of Dr. Sara Charles in her treatment of Terry Walker [were] the proximate cause of Terry Walker's injuries as a result of jumping off the roof?"

"Yes," Rubin answers without hesitation.

In a closing exchange, Rubin asserts that Terry not only had suicidal thoughts but also made a suicidal attempt in 1971. Goldberg has no further questions and court adjourns for the morning.

Plaintiff's Expert II—Cross-Examination

I'd be wondering why they were seeing me.
                                        —Bernard Rubin, M.D.

The afternoon is delayed by another status call. A man in his thirties sits quietly with his sad-looking wife and child. He has violated the conditions of his parole and the hearing is to decide whether he is to be sent back to jail. Sheriff's officers, Marlboro men in tight suits, sit around the parolee as though he were high on the most-wanted list. A forlorn scene. Judge McGarr cannot settle the matter today. He apologizes to the officers for the time they have taken to come to court, but he will deal with the matter tomorrow at 1:30. The melancholy group, judgment deferred, departs and the cast of our own trial reassembles in the court. Rubin takes his place again in the witness stand.

Maddux moves close to him and asks if the doctor is familiar with the *Diagnostic and Statistical Manual of Mental Disorders*, third edition. Yes, Rubin knows and uses it and his diagnosis of Terry's borderline condition matches the one that is given in that book. Yes, the borderline differs from the schizophrenic; the borderline and the psychotic are not the same.

"I think," Rubin says, "the borderline distinguishes the borderline personality disorder from the psychosis but does not mean that the borderline person can't be psychotic."

"No," Maddux says, "but if they're psychotic, they're not borderline, right?" Rubin agrees and Maddux continues. "That's not

to say that the borderline couldn't—and that's one of the characteristics of the borderline that he can slip into the psychotic and
have psychotic episodes." "That's correct," Rubin replies and
Maddux adds, "But as you mentioned, I think, they're generally
brief and treatable as opposed . . . to the basically psychotic diagnosed patient." Rubin nods in agreement.

Rubin affirms that psychotherapy is the treatment of choice
for borderline patients and that the establishment of a trusting
relationship is essential because borderline patients, influenced
by earlier experiences, have such difficulty in trusting people. Establishing that trust with the patient, Rubin says, is "the major,
first goal. Absolutely."

"That's not to say," Maddux responds, "that you'd routinely
use drugs on a person who's borderline, would you?"

"On the contrary. I would use less drugs than I would with
psychotic patients. I would have a tendency to start without medication."

Rubin agrees that a doctor tries to keep borderline patients
functioning in their regular lives. "As much as you can, yes."
Trust, he reiterates, is everything. In the context of a trusting
relationship the therapist helps the borderline patient discover
"the underlying causes of their illness . . . it's going to take a
while before the borderline patient is going to trust. . . ."

Doesn't the therapist, Maddux asks, often become the object
of the borderline patient's hostility?"

"Frequently," Rubin responds. "Because . . . borderline patients . . . have a lot of anger. They don't know what to do with
it. It comes out in relation to a variety of circumstances. It frequently comes out in relation to changes or separations. Those
are the most likely times in which you see the anger. . . . Changes
in appointment time, separations in which there are vacations
or unexpected interruptions. . . ."

The psychiatrist agrees that Terry never suffered from an affective disorder. She was never, in other words, psychotically depressed or psychotically manic. Rubin looks attentively toward
Maddux, who leans on the lectern in the middle of the courtroom
well, glancing down at some papers in his right hand.

"Is there significance to the psychiatric examiner that there's
no psychomotor disturbance in a patient?"

"Yes," Rubin answers, explaining the frenzied activity witnessed in the manic stage of manic-depressive illness. What you do in making a diagnosis, the doctor says, is look for a series of things "so you have a pattern."

Maddux continues. "The fact that there is no psychomotor disturbance would lead you to believe that manic-depressive illness or the major affective disorder is not likely?" Rubin agrees again.

Maddux again consults the papers he is holding and asks if the person's ability to respond to the psychiatric examiner is a noteworthy clue.

"It's one of the clues."

"Now, if you ask a patient some series of questions and their talk is spontaneous and it's always coherent, and of normal rate, is that significant to you as one of the clues in trying to assess the mental status of that person?"

"That tells me that they spoke fairly freely and regularly about themselves. . . ."

Maddux raises a question about thought disorder in the assessment of a patient.

"Well," Rubin expands, "thought disorder is usually another way of saying schizophrenia. . . . It's probably likely there's no schizophrenia."

He then agrees that patients usually know if they are depressed, and yes, it is "absolutely" worthwhile to ask patients whether they are depressed or not. And follow-up questions as well. Suppose, Maddux asks, they say they feel neutral? That they have a feeling of emptiness?

"That's a kind of depression," Rubin answers, "it might be a clue that they are suffering from a narcissistic character disorder or borderline character disorder. . . ."

"Is it appropriate," Maddux inquires, checking his paper again, "to ask a patient whether or not they are in a state of anxiety or whether they are anxious?"

"Yes, it's appropriate. . . . and they might tell you directly."

"If they deny again that they're anxious, is that significant in assessing the mental status of a person?"

Rubin hesitates very slightly. He agrees that a patient's denial of anxiety is significant in assessing his or her mental status.

"And in trying to assess the mental status, you're, I take it, vitally interested in knowing whether or not they have suicidal thoughts?"

"Uh, huh."

"And if that same patient we've been talking about denies all the things we've discussed so far, plus they deny they've had any suicidal thoughts, that's of tremendous significance to you, isn't it?"

"Yeah," Rubin answers, "I'd be wondering why they were seeing me."

"Right," Maddux says, "so far you're wondering why you're even seeing this patient?"

"I would wonder what I was seeing [the patient] about. Yes."

Maddux checks off further symptoms—delusions, hallucinations, and compulsive phenomena—listed as not reported. Rubin would still be wondering why he was seeing this patient.

The lawyer quickly reviews responses signifying a patient's proper orientation in time, place, and sense of self-identity as well as the tests for brain damage. "So far in that entire examination," he inquires, "you haven't found anything very disturbing, have you?"

"Not with just that information, no."

Maddux picks up the pace as he asks, "Have you examined the records of Terry Walker . . . from the hospital in New York?"

"I did, yes."

"Now on those records there was no specific diagnosis given of her condition, was there?"

"That's correct."

"And you read the examination that was made of her by the physician who examined her at that hospital?"

"That's right."

Maddux holds up the papers he had read from a few minutes before. "And the exact findings I went over with you are the exact findings of Terry Walker at that time."

Murphy explodes with an objection, claiming that Maddux is "misstating the facts. . . . He didn't read the last three sentences and now he's telling Dr. Rubin that he did, in fact, read the last three sentences."

Maddux glances at Murphy, "I object to this, your honor. He is accusing me of misstating things. And this is not the case." The defense lawyer turns to the judge, "I'll just read it, since he wants me to read it all. I'll give you the rest of it. . . . 'Feels her behavior forced her here. Nevertheless feels she could be let out since she knows how to control herself.' Then there's a physical examination. 'Severe facial acne.' " He looks up at Rubin. "That's not very significant, is it? Acne, on the face?"

"Nothing more than acne," Rubin says quietly.

"Otherwise physically she's within normal limits. Did I misstate anything to you as a result of what I just read here from what we talked about previously?"

"No," Rubin replies. "You haven't misstated anything from what you've read."

Maddux asks Rubin if these are not the examination results found in the Cornell Hospital records. Rubin clears his throat, "That examination was done by a resident, Dr. Kent. I *assume* that he was a resident. . . . I *assume* it was done when she was admitted. . . . I *assume* that they treated her for a mental illness, and I *assume* they kept her there because they felt that she was improving under the treatment and they released her when they felt she was ready."

"Well, Doctor," Maddux says, "I'm not in the area of trying to *assume* things. I only suggest that the *only* examination in these records is that one I read to you. . . . Right?"

Rubin reluctantly agrees.

"And it said," Maddux continues, "she often put her leg out the window but did not resist when pulled back. She insisted that it was all an act and she could stop it at any time she wanted."

"Uh, huh."

Rubin reflects on attention-getting suicidal gestures saying that he does not know any "that are not real." Well, Maddux wants to know, what *does* this entry mean?

". . . I'm only making a guess, there must have been a time when someone talked to her and she said, 'I don't have any suicidal thoughts.' " Such a gesture, he adds, would be serious unless a person were drunk or grandstanding. No, he doesn't think you can grandstand without being drunk.

"What about a person who is theatrical by nature?" Maddux asks.

"The . . . same thing I said."

"You read in this record that she [Terry] complained when she went into the hospital. . . . she talked spontaneously and freely in answer to the questions. And one of the things she said was she was theatrical."

"That was one of the statements she made." Rubin replies

guardedly. He then laughs nervously to a question about a nota-
tion of Dr. Morrow's opinion of Terry that had been in the materials on which he based his own judgment. "I couldn't do anything
with that note, except to confirm Dr. Morrow was the chief of
service at the New York hospital when Terry was a patient on
that service. . . ."

"In other words," Maddux presses, "when he [Dr. Morrow]
said that 'it was a situational reaction, and thinking back, she
was not as severely depressed as others,' that formed no basis
of any of your opinion?"

"I never said it."

Rubin admits that he does not know how many phone calls
Terry made and that he is confused about Dr. Waxman's calls.
Maddux changes the subject, "If you had a patient that you had
been out of touch with—for a matter of two years, would you
consider it good practice on your part to prescribe medicine for
that person?"

"You mean what would I do personally? I would not prescribe
medicine over the phone. That is, to someone I had not seen
for more than six months. . . . I would consider it if the person
were my patient. If the person were not my patient any longer,
I wouldn't prescribe anything over the phone."

"No matter what the period of time was?"

"No matter what the period of time was. That's true. . . . It
would not be my idea of good medical practice." Maddux asks
again and Rubin answers forthrightly, "If you're not the physician
of that person then you're obviously in no position to prescribe
for them. And if you're not treating them, and you don't know
enough about them, it's not a good idea. I would agree with
that."

"Well," Maddux asks, "do you agree with the general proposition that if another therapist, who no longer has that person as
a patient, injects himself in the treatment or the care of a person
with mental disorder, that there can be circumstances envisioned
where that intervention might be harmful to the patient?"

"The intervention of giving them medication? I can't go that
far. . . . Giving medication to someone that you're not the doctor
of is doing something you shouldn't be doing."

Maddux reviews the importance Rubin has previously put on
the relationship between the therapist and the borderline patient.

Rubin agrees again. "Is it important, then," Maddux continues, "for other therapists not to inject themselves with a different attitude or approach to that patient?"

"I think that it's important that they not inject themselves. But if they're terribly concerned, they should call up the doctor who's doing the treating and say, 'I'm terribly concerned and you ought to do something about it.' If you're asking me what I would do if a former patient of mine called me who was in treatment with a new doctor, I'd say, 'I'm going to call your doctor right now and tell them that it's terribly important that they see you.'"

Maddux reviews the appropriateness of psychotherapy as the treatment for borderlines. Referring to Terry Walker, he asks, "And you say that somewhere along the line the treatment should have changed?" Rubin agrees. "And," Maddux returns to the evidence Rubin cited about Terry's fragmentation in the fall of 1975, "and the clues you looked to are the statements that you read and heard about: that she felt out of control, felt like a piece of cardboard, and making all those phone calls?" Yes, Rubin says, and Dr. Charles's statements in her deposition and notes.

"Are you aware," Maddux asks, "from the things you read, that the statement that she feels like a piece of cardboard was made for the first time—at best—on Saturday morning to Dr. Waxman?"

"And in the telephone call to Dr. Charles that same morning."

"No," Maddux says firmly, "you didn't get that . . . from Dr. Charles."

"If she said no," Rubin says, "I can't argue with you."

"You didn't get it from any of the notes of Dr. Charles, either."

"Not the word *cardboard*, no."

"Right. Did you get from Dr. Waxman his feeling that she was not imminently suicidal . . . on the morning of November 15?" Rubin agrees, acknowledging that Terry had a fear of hospitalization and that Terry wanted to function independently. Maddux reviews the events of that Saturday morning. Dr. Waxman told her she was seriously ill? Yes. He told her that her father was coming to Chicago? Yes. That he was bringing medicine? Yes. And after that last phone call Terry went up to the roof and jumped? Yes.

"In other words, she was reaching out for help, somebody

said now here it is, here comes the help and then—and only then—
did she go up to the roof and jump?"

"The help wasn't there," Rubin says. "She needed the help
then. Right then. . . ."

Maddux again shifts the subject and Rubin agrees that borderlines are impulsive, and that some sudden upset can cause them
pain. They then may impulsively "undo" themselves in order to
deal with the pain.

"Right," Maddux rejoins. "So that there's a sharp injection
of a situation that evokes that kind of pain in them, they can
react to that, and it can be a single episode that can occur at
one particular time?"

"That's possible. That's correct."

Maddux next asks whether those who commit suicide are not
rational. No, Rubin says, quoting statistics, many people make
rational decisions to kill themselves. Maddux pursues the subject
in terms of the borderline personality. "You know, we've already
established that the person with a borderline personality disorder
knows the nature and the consequence of their act and they can
intend a certain result by the intentional doing of a particular
act, can't they?"

"Yes."

"Bringing it right down to the question of suicide, a person
with that condition can rationally intend to take their own life?
There's nothing to prevent them from doing that?"

"Using your logic," Rubin responds, "yes."

Rubin agrees that they can be in pain, they can be unhappy
and feel bad about themselves.

"And it could well be," Maddux continues, "that they consciously say, 'Here is the solution to that problem. I'm going to
jump off the roof.' In that sense, can they do that?"

". . . You mean in that sense can they decide to kill themselves? In this way? Yes."

"And fully intend to do it in answer to that problem of the
pain and the unhappiness, and the circumstances, by jumping?"

"Absolutely. That's what suicide is." Rubin says that people
with major affective disorders, people with manic-depressive illness "are just as rationally bent on destroying themselves."

"Okay," Maddux responds. "Then people with mental disorders who are able to know the nature and the consequence of

their act, for whatever reason they might do it, have that ability to intentionally take their own lives. And know that they're going to take their own lives by an act they're going to commit?"

"That's right."

Maddux turns away, changing the subject to reveal in a few quick questions that Rubin operated under false assumption about the circumstances of Terry's 1971 hospitalization. Maddux shifts ground again, drawing from Rubin the sources for his conclusion that Terry had not slept for twenty-four hours before her jump. Terry herself, the expert replies, was the first source, ". . . and the fact that she complained of being sleepless to Dr. Charles in Dr. Charles's notes, as well as, in what she told me, with the activity that went on between the fourteenth and fifteenth there was barely any time to sleep at all."

Maddux reminds Rubin that, in fact, Dr. Charles's notes show that Terry reported that she had slept seven hours on the night of November 14. Rubin does not remember that but admits, "If someone sleeps seven hours through a night, they've had a night's sleep."

Maddux turns away, his questioning ended. The judge calls a brief recess, and as I head out to the corridor, a friendly court buff falls into step with me. "What did you think of the expert?" I ask. He raises his eyebrows and shrugs as he lights his cigarette and shuffles away.

Back at the plaintiff's table, Murphy and Goldberg look through their papers together. Maddux lights a cigarette, inhales deeply, and sums up the day. "You know," he says, "I went golfing this weekend. On the first nine, I shot a forty-five." His reference is to Goldberg's direct examination of Rubin. Maddux draws on his cigarette again, "But on the back nine, I shot a thirty-eight."

After the recess Murphy takes over the redirect examination. Rubin repeats some of his original charges against Sara but will not change on a key professional principle. Rubin would have called the treating physician even if the patient had not wanted him to do so. Murphy says that Terry Walker had been under suicidal precautions at the Cornell Hospital.

Maddux rises again and asks Rubin directly about the hospital records. "Is there one word anywhere about suicidal precautions, whether she was on suicidal precautions?"

"I didn't know whether she was or she wasn't," Rubin responds. "I *assumed* that when the attorney told me that there were

suicidal precautions, that there were suicidal precautions. . . ."
Maddux squares his shoulders, looks directly at Rubin. Did the
expert read Dr. Waxman's deposition where he said there were
no locked wards at Cornell? Rubin lowers his glance and does
not answer as Maddux adds a second part to his question. Does
Dr. Rubin remember reading Terry Walker's depositional account
of why she jumped? Rubin raises his glance, he does not agree
with Terry's explanation of her reasons for jumping. "I think
differently about it," he says softly. Maddux surveys him briefly.
"I have no further questions."

Murphy reviews some questions with Rubin and the examination, and the afternoon, come to an end. Rubin leaves the courtroom, moving, without a sideways glance, through the clusters
of people in the hallway.

DAY SEVEN

Defendant's Expert

They begin to behave toward you . . . very much like they have behaved toward everybody else in their life.

—Leroy Levitt, M.D.

Murphy discusses how he can present his documentation of damages to the jury. These include the cost of Terry Walker's hospitalization and treatment as well as projected costs for her care throughout the rest of her life. A written statement is agreed upon. The judge refuses to accept the *Ann Landers Encyclopedia* into evidence and Maddux summarizes a motion he will put into writing for a directed verdict in favor of the defendant. A directed verdict is obtainable when the issues in law are so clear that there is no issue of fact for the jury to decide.

In malpractice cases, as in all negligence cases, Maddux argues, the experts discuss whether the defendant failed to meet the proper standards of care. But the plaintiff is bound by standards of care as well, and those demand that she exercise proper care for herself and be free of any contributory negligence in her own regard. "Any negligence in the slightest degree," Maddux says, citing the then applicable Illinois law, "requires that the case not be submitted to the jury."

"In this case," he says, "the plaintiff is not excused by any rule of law from the requirement that she use ordinary care for her own safety. . . . It may be the private belief of a physician that there must be something wrong with a person who would attempt this, yet the testimony is clear that she was rational, in the ordinary understanding of the term 'rational.' Both of the plaintiff's experts agree that she knew the nature and the quality of her act and that she was capable of forming and making a conscious decision to do or not to do any particular act. . . . She intended to take her own life. She consciously came to the decision and intended to take her own life. She is not excused under the law. On that basis, the defendant feels she is entitled to a directed verdict." Nonetheless, the judge, claiming that there is no testimony regarding the diminishment of her volition due to mental illness, refuses the motion.

Murphy reads the statement about damages to the jurors and rests his case. "All right," McGarr says to the jury members, ". . . it now becomes the opportunity of the defendant to present whatever evidence the defendant thinks is appropriate to your decision in this case." He swings his head back toward Maddux, "Counsel?" he asks expectantly as the lawyer steps quietly to the center of the courtroom's well. "Call Dr. Leroy Levitt," he says matter-of-factly.

Levitt, a psychiatrist and psychoanalyst, is vice-president for medical affairs at Mount Sinai Hospital Medical Center and president of the Chicago Board of Health. In addition to his other professional experiences, he served as director of the Illinois Department of Mental Health from 1973 to 1977. At sixty-two, Levitt is short, trim, well-tailored, dark-haired.

Does Levitt have an opinion on whether Dr. Charles "used the care and skill required of a reasonably well-qualified psychiatrist in treating Terry Walker?" Did Dr. Charles by any "act or omission" cause or contribute to the injury suffered by the plaintiff?

Levitt, who says that he has served as an expert about half a dozen times, does have an opinion. "I feel that Dr. Charles comported herself in an ethical, highly professional, highly skilled fashion in the care and treatment of Terry Walker. . . . I could not identify in any of the information available to me that Dr. Charles omitted anything, overlooked anything, or did not take into consideration, in her professional management of the patient, anything that would have contributed to the unfortunate event of November 15, 1975."

Yes, the expert agrees, Terry is a borderline. "It's a personality disorder," Levitt says, "which means there are relatively durable ways of behavior." Borderlines have a great deal of difficulty in their interpersonal relationships, he explains, they have trouble with being alone and with managing their anger; their attitudes are unstable. They are "splitters," as we all are at birth. We begin life thinking of our parents as only good and resist thinking of them as bad. We learn, as we grow up, to combine these attributes in our judgment of people; we learn to appreciate persons, not as all good or all bad, but as mixtures of these qualities. But the borderline cannot do that. "They view things as either good or they're bad . . . the mood is so changeable and variable. . . . They will split you. They will think you're the greatest person in the world and the next day they say, 'I think I should find another doctor!'" If you examine their life history you can see how their developmental flaw displays itself all through their lives. Borderlines may be living and working like anybody else while their inner lives are chaotic in "the matter of anger and trust and instability of feelings, and of not wanting to be alone. . . ."

Because of the borderline's central difficulties with trust, the expert notes, the therapist's role is very difficult. "One of the first things you've got to do is to try very tenderly and very slowly and very cautiously to develop a relationship of trust." Levitt brings up the term "transference." "It means what it says. It's the guts of treatment. As you work with a patient they begin to behave toward you . . . very much like they have behaved toward everybody else in their life. They view you as they have viewed their mother or their father . . . they bring those things into the transference relationship." The work of therapy with the borderline, whose foundation may take more than a year to establish, depends on being able to observe how patients treat you like other persons in their lives, and, by interpretation, "to show them they're acting in a way that's not appropriate in the here and now," so that ". . . the patient develops some insight, some understanding . . . then behavior begins to change."

Murphy objects, claiming that Maddux is "asking leading quesions the way I was." Judge McGarr overrules him. Dr. Levitt speaks of the borderline's rage rising from the early years of life when the person has "feelings that are not addressed and taken care of . . . particularly by the mother." This experience of abandonment, of being neglected, generates in the borderline "a very profound set of impulses and angers." Borderline patients may act out in many ways that are harmful to them, Levitt explains, adding that suicidal ideation is common among them, as it is among people in general. One must rely on clinical judgment to determine the real nature of their suicidal talk. Borderlines may make suicidal gestures that are manipulative in intent. They have "a great tendency to exploit other people. . . . Therapists are constantly manipulated . . . and you have to have the . . . courage to be able to put that in its proper setting and to understand it in the light of all the things that you're dealing with with that patient. . . . One swallow does not make a summer."

Levitt says that drugs are overused in the treatment of patients because they may dull them so that they do not deal with their basic conflicts. Hospitalization should be used carefully because it is "an interruption in the usual life events and [is] . . . sometimes due to the patient's manipulation." There is very little question, he says, that "the borderline patient is best treated in the office setting" from which he or she can inspect their outside lives. Levitt would not seek hospital records that were several years old because "if the patient's really going to trust you. . . . like the surgeon wants to keep the surgical field clean, the psychiatrist wants to keep the transference potential clean." The expert would rather not have that record from the past interfere with the developing relationship. "I'd rather not have that and trust the patient to tell me about what happened to them." After all, the borderline patient is not illogical or incoherent, the borderline patient can give the psychiatrist an accurate life history.

It is noontime and Judge McGarr, checking his watch as he lays his legal tablet aside, recesses court until 2:15. Dr. Levitt leaves the courtroom alone, and as I wait for Sara and Maddux to follow him, I strain to catch the comments of the trio of court buffs who edge past me. Their words are lost in the hubbub of the marbled corridor. We head to Maddux's office, as we have on most days of the trial, for a fast-food lunch brought by the lawyer's daughter. We munch our sandwiches absently as we review the progress of the trial.

We walk back afterward through the Loop streets, and as the elevator doors begin to close in the Federal Building, Patrick Murphy shoulders through them to join us. As we rise up toward the twenty-fifth floor the plaintiff's lawyer speaks to Bill Maddux: "I worked on this building when it was being built."

"Did you now?"

"Yeah," Murphy says, "I was the first one up on every floor, the first worker up on the steel. . . ."

The doors slide open on the courtroom floor. The court buffs sit in the quadrant of mote-filled summer light that floods the nearby alcove. Lawyers from around the city who have heard about the case have also begun to stop in to watch the proceedings. Two of them, in dark business suits despite the heat, chat gravely outside the courtroom. "Very unusual," one says, "a psychiatric malpractice case. . . ."

Before the jury comes in, Murphy asks the judge for permission to subpoena Dr. Lucia Tower and Dr. Arnold Tobin, who served as defense experts during the period of discovery. Their testimony, Murphy contends, will support his case. Tobin, he says, "testified [in his deposition] three times that Terry was a suicide risk. . . . Dr. Tower was Dr. Charles's therapist for forty-six sessions immediately after this occurred." Maddux argues against the appropriateness of Murphy's summoning witnesses whom he himself may not choose to use, but the judge grants Murphy's request. After the jury members return, Dr. Levitt retakes the stand.

From reviewing Dr. Charles's notes, Levitt feels that she took a good history during her early sessions with Terry Walker. He has also seen the Cornell Hospital records; there is nothing in them, in his opinion, that suggests that Dr. Charles should have treated Terry any differently than she did. They confirm Dr. Charles's approach. As to the treatment: "The flow of things all the way through . . . fit into what one would expect of the ups and downs—and the general indecision, the impulsive kind of behavior that I described before. . . ." Phone calls from borderline patients are "not unusual at all." You would expect them "as the patient begins to get some insight, which makes them somewhat anxious because it's different from their prior behavior." Frequent phone calls would not mean that the borderline was out of control or psychotic; they mean that "they're reacting in terms of their character formation." Murphy interrupts several times, claiming that Dr. Levitt never interviewed the plaintiff.

McGarr, noting that the expert is only giving his opinion, overrules him.

Levitt reviews elements of Terry's development in terms of her relationship to her parents and describes the contents of the therapy sessions in the fall of 1975 as about what one would expect in dealing with such a patient. "She started," Levitt says reflectively, "to develop a relationship with Dr. Charles and that made her anxious. She felt different than she felt before . . . and that's an advance in treatment." Levitt saw no evidence of Terry's fragmenting or decompensating into a deepening depression during that fall.

Maddux, standing back slightly to allow the jurors to focus on his witness, asks if, on the basis of the materials he has analyzed, Dr. Levitt has an opinion about what caused Terry Walker to jump off the roof on that day. Levitt reconstructs the days prior to November 15. On that Saturday morning, "Dr. Waxman . . . did something which to me is quite unconscionable. He reacted strongly to Terry's anxiety on the phone. He said what I think . . . tilted the balance of things at that moment—and undermined a year and a half of treatment—by saying, 'you are sicker than you think you are.' . . . Remember, here's a person who can really pour it on, who can tear your heart out—and I don't mean that in an accusatory way, I'm not making a moral judgment on Terry. . . . Terry had the capacity to do that and Dr. Waxman reacted to it, said 'you're sicker than you think, we've got to do something.' " Dr. Levitt draws a breath. "He then did what I can't conceive of anybody else doing—involving a host of other people, getting a doctor who hasn't seen Terry in four years . . . doesn't call Dr. Charles . . . he gets hold of [Dr.] Morrow . . . who, God help me, writes a prescription for somebody he hasn't seen in *four years* . . . that he never wrote a prescription for before . . . without knowing anything about her clinical condition, prescribing a very potent antipsychotic drug . . . and phones it in. . . . And everybody's energized to fly out. Nobody calls Dr. Charles, nobody alerts anybody to it. They're just going to fly out and do what the worst thing there was to do to Terry, that is, to come and get her and take her to a hospital on the basis of what Waxman says to her, undermining the transference relationship with Dr. Charles. I think that the incident of the phone call she suddenly made to Dr. Marvin Waxman—and what he said and the prospect then of what would happen—just ripped

away at her defenses . . . and were the precipitating cause fo
the tragedy that then ensued. . . ." As Levitt speaks, Murph
rapidly takes notes, tearing the sheets from his pad and scatterin;
them on the table before him.

There was, in Dr. Levitt's opinion, no error of omission o
commission on Dr. Charles's part. Maddux asks if the decisio
to jump by a borderline patient like Terry Walker is considere
rational, intentional conduct. "Yes," Levitt responds softly. "
think that borderline people, particularly as I've come to under
stand Terry through the record, I think they're certainly capabl
of making rational, logical decisions about many things. . . .'

"Thank you, Doctor," Maddux says. "Those are all the ques
tions I have."

Murphy wants to know if Dr. Levitt talked to Dr. Lucia Tower
whom he describes as "Dr. Charles's therapist." Maddux objects.
Dr. Tower was *never* a therapist for Dr. Charles. Judge McGarr
after sustaining him, cautions the jury "not to accept the statements of [the plaintiff's] counsel." Dr. Levitt is an expert on what
happened before the jump, not about what occurred afterward.
Murphy persists in developing this accusation, linking Dr.
Charles's alleged admission of making a "clinical error" with feelings of guilt that led her to seek treatment from Dr. Tower. Once
again the judge blocks him from pursuing anything that took place
after Terry's jump. Murphy criticizes Levitt for not examining
Terry Walker in person. The judge says, after Maddux's objection,
that Dr. Levitt had no obligation to examine the plaintiff, and
that, in fact, he had no choice in the matter.

The plaintiff's lawyer asks the expert whether, when he was
director of the Illinois Department of Mental Health, there were
borderline patients in the state mental hospitals. "Very few, but
some," Levitt replies.

"And you didn't keep patients in your mental health hospitals
who didn't belong there, did you, Doctor?"

"Oh, yes, we did," Levitt answers. "As you well know. . . .
There were patients who had no place to go and they stayed in
the hospital."

The judge interrupts. An emergency requires his attention.
It is shortly after four and nobody in the room complains about
getting out of court early.

DAY EIGHT

Defendant's Expert Continued

Are you ridiculing me, Mr. Murphy?

—Leroy Levitt, M.D.

The heavy rain that accompanied the nighttime storm has not lifted the siege of summer weather and Murphy's caramel colored summer suit is as creased as his brow as he renews his questioning of Dr. Levitt the next morning. The attorney accuses the expert of allowing experimentation with drugs on back ward patients when he was head of the Illinois Department of Mental Health. Levitt denies the implications of the question but Murphy, asserting the relevance of his questions, claims that "The doctor made comments that he would not use the drug. . . . I'm just bringing out the fact that he thinks enough of drugs to let them be used for experimental purposes on hapless, back ward patients. . . ." Maddux objects and the judge sustains him, warning Murphy about using phrases such as "hapless" patients. Murphy claims that Levitt authorized such experimentation, letting a shocking impression hang invisibly in the air: The Jewish Dr. Levitt used

Nazi-like techniques. He shouts, across Maddux's objection, "I'm going into *drugs, drugs, drugs, drugs!*" The judge again sustains Maddux's objections to this line of questioning as irrelevant, but the courtroom reverberates to the sharp exchange.

Murphy shifts to Levitt's position as president of the Chicago Board of Health. It is nothing, Murphy says, but a political appointment. The plaintiff's attorney works his way to the issue of suicide. "Doctor," Murphy asks, "I presume that you don't worry too much about clinical judgment when, in fact, a patient may be suicidal. Would that be correct?" No, Levitt answers, that would not be correct, but he does agree that patients pretend at times that they are going to commit suicide. And, yes, the doctor may not be as concerned if he thinks they are pretending.

"And so," Murphy says, "if Terry Walker fell off the roof or jumped off the roof that day, that was a pretend suicide?"

Levitt studies the lawyer for a moment. "Are you ridiculing me, Mr. Murphy?"

"No," Murphy rejoins quickly. ". . . You're indicating—since your whole testimony seems to be geared to Dr. Charles—you're saying Dr. Charles shouldn't be concerned with [pretend suicides]." Maddux's objection is sustained and Murphy turns to Sara's psychiatric notes. What about these, he asks, " 'Fears the psychosis,' on October 2; 'didn't get drawn into her panic,' on October 8; 'feels massive distrust of herself.' " Murphy draws a breath, " 'feels weak, impotent, and does not exist unless she is number one.' " Murphy looks directly at Levitt. "Very serious statement. . . . Right, Doctor?"

"No, sir," Levitt responds. ". . . You cannot take that out of the treatment context . . . you cannot treat that apart from the whole picture of what's happening with the patient."

"So we can't treat it apart from . . . on the floor screaming 'Doctor, I feel like a vegetable' . . . from the window, hospitalized . . . for three months! Nor can we separate it from the patient who told Dr. Charles that she was feeling hostile and suicidal in 1971! Nor can we separate it from the patient who said she feared the psychosis nor from the patient who Dr. Charles felt was more fragile than she felt she was! Nor from the patient who felt obsessiveness and anxiety! In other words, Doctor. . . ."

Maddux objects. Murphy glaring at him, shouts, *"I'm talking!"*

"Let me interrupt," McGarr says, ". . . that is not a question and can never become one. The objection is sustained."

Undeterred, Murphy presses the doctor with another series of questions on the theme that Dr. Charles should have treated the whole person and not "a label like borderline. She should have been treating a human being like Terry Walker, isn't that right?" The judge sustains Maddux's objection. It "is inappropriate to argue in the examination of a witness."

"Yet another swallow," Murphy continues, referring to Levitt's earlier comparison, "we're up to eight or nine now. Do eight or nine swallows make a summer?"

"We had about two, Mr. Murphy," Levitt responds.

"How many swallows make a summer?" Murphy asks. Maddux objects, as he has before, that such questions get nowhere.

"I don't know," McGarr says into the shooting gallery atmosphere of the courtroom, "whether this case sounds more like it's being tried in Capistrano or whether we're all candidates for degrees in ornithology, but I think the swallow analogy has kind of outlived its usefulness."

"I'm sorry I brought it up, Judge," Levitt says.

"I'm sure you are," the judge responds as laughter erupts in the courtroom. "So am I."

"Doctor," Murphy says, "what about robins in springtime?" He shifts, after another objection is sustained, back to the notes. " 'Crisis state increasing.' Are we worried about that, Doctor? 'In present situation, felt crisis state increasing re: research topic for course. Invested a great deal in decision.' . . . Isn't it a fact that Terry Walker was focusing on these school subjects, was focusing on her boyfriend, but, in fact, was really falling apart all over the place?"

"That's your assumption, Mr. Murphy," Levitt replies. "I didn't see that."

". . . So you're disregarding Miss Walker's point of view and accepting only Dr. Charles's?"

"No," Levitt answers, "I didn't say that, either. I'm simply giving you my opinion from what I know of such patients and what I have read in the record and in the process notes."

After another intense exchange, Murphy concludes his cross-examination. Sara will be called to testify at two o'clock.

PART III

The Defendant

DAY EIGHT CONTINUED

The Defendant

You pay attention to what they say, you respect them, you communicate in many different ways that you are a person to whom they can entrust whatever it is that's of concern to them.

—Sara Charles, M.D.

At two o'clock Murphy tells Judge McGarr that he cannot find Dr. Tobin to serve him with a subpoena. "We've been lying in wait for him. . . ."

Maddux glances at Murphy. McGarr, adjusting the collar of his robes, looks down at both lawyers. "I am not," he says, "going to hold defense counsel either directly or indirectly responsible for helping you serve Dr. Tobin." He signals the bailiff to bring in the jury and nods toward Maddux. Murphy flips a yellow pad out of his briefcase onto the desk in front of him. Maddux calls Sara to the stand.

Sara, wearing a light summerweight suit, takes her place on the witness stand. Maddux reviews her training and credentials. Yes, she says, after explaining her experience and present position, she is a board certified psychiatrist. Murphy hurriedly writes notes on his pad, noisily tearing off the pages. A few minutes later, the judge asks him to remove a supply of sheets so that he does not interfere with the examination. "These are all notes for my cross . . . ," Murphy says, pulling a thick wad of papers free from their cardboard backing. Terry Walker rides her chair smoothly into the empty space at the plaintiff's table for the first time since she completed her testimony.

The courtroom settles down. The plaintiff and the defendant sit not much farther apart than they did during their therapy sessions five years ago. Terry stares at Sara as she answers her lawyer's preliminary questions. Maddux brings up Terry's first session on December 9, 1974. "Did you," he asks, "get a history?" Sara begins to speak of their first meetings and of how, with delicacy, a history is elicited.

Therapy Session—December 9, 1974

"My father," Terry said, shaking her head, *"he's a businessman who travels a lot.* Things have never quite worked out for him." She spoke affectionately. "I feel sorry for him. He means well, but things just don't work out. And he did respond to me. Sometimes he'd make lots of money and things would go well for us. Then sometimes he didn't. I remember once when he bought a big boat and kept it in Long Island Sound. And my mother hated it, wouldn't put her foot in it. They had lots of trouble getting along. He was always placating her. He'd work for something and then she wouldn't go along with it. He always gave in, he had to. Peace at any price. So he got rid of the boat. That was typical. I feel bad for him, I really do. He's never seemed to get what he wanted. And he's had troubles, troubles with deals, troubles with partners. He wasn't a good judge of other men. Once he had to go into bankruptcy because of a partner. . . ."

Affection drained out of her voice. "My mother had her own problems. My mother's hysterical. She was never close to us, never. She hated it when my father was away, she hated it." Terry frowned as she continued. "When I turned twelve, she told my father, 'Now you can take over. I've done my part. You take over raising the girls now.' She was like that, always complaining about being left with the kids while my father was away on business.

She was at home, she didn't work. I don't know what she did. She didn't seem to have any friends. Maybe because she wasn't friendly. We never had other kids over. She never cooked for us. Almost every night we'd go out to some little restaurant or other to eat." Terry drew a breath, her eyes glinting. "She wanted her way, that's what she wanted, in everything she did. I remember coming home from college and I wanted to stop and see an aunt of mine who lived near LaGuardia Airport. But my mother had a fit, insisted that I come home first. Then *she'd* go with me to visit my aunt. It was typical. . . ."

Terry spoke next of her older sister Carol, a teacher, married to a doctor in Boston. Frustrated, Terry thought, not really fulfilled. Carol seemed depressed, but no, she wasn't getting any treatment. She had always told Terry what to do, she had filled the role of mother by giving her exact advice on any question Terry had in life. "Like when I was in high school, I asked her about having sex with boys. She'd tell me what to do about it. She was always definite. . . ."

Terry shook her head, setting her stringy hair swaying, as Dr. Charles systematically asked about her own life, about Arnie, about her school career, about each incident and person about whom Terry had spoken strongly.

How, Terry wondered, did you get along with a man? Having a man in your life was important, but she wasn't sure she loved Arnie anymore. She had never enjoyed sex, it had never been a big deal. That's the way a lot of life was. The documentary of Terry's life continued to unreel. There were blurred spots, sections where she couldn't make things out clearly. She was frustrated by the pressure of doing things solely to get the approval of others, confused by the dizzying self-examination that always followed.

"Did I go to please somebody else, to give in to some man's whim? I'm not liberated enough. Maybe I'm being used. . . ." The cycle of thought, like clothes in a dryer, tumbled over and over. She worried subjects to death, she was just never sure. . . .

Studying, Terry said in answer to Dr. Charles's question, was her strong point and she enjoyed succeeding in her school subjects. That got her some of the attention she craved but could not quite find in her relationships with others. The psychiatrist watched Terry closely. The young woman's inner life seemed filled with the ordinary furniture of human existence and yet empty at the same time.

"I had a poor adjustment in my first year of college," Terry said carefully. It was hard getting used to being away from home. The kind of trouble lots of people have. She went to the College Health Service to talk about it. "I went to see a psychologist a few times. And I saw a social worker in my second year for a while." There was no more to it than that.

Terry returned to her present situation. She was sharing an apartment on Dearborn Street with two young men, friends of Arnie's. That was the relationship she wanted to figure out, that she had to settle somehow in the months that stretched across the calendar before his arrival.

December 16, 1974

Terry Walker called and arranged to see Dr. Charles a week later. She had visited one of the other doctors on the list, another woman, but she had seemed too young. Dr. Charles seemed right for Terry, she had a dynamic psychoanalytic orientation that appealed to her. Yes, she was the therapist she would like. If the doctor had time. They arranged to meet weekly for an hour.

"I want to pay for this myself," Terry said. "I'm on a grant at the university so I have some support. And I've saved some money. . . ."

This would probably be long-term therapy, Dr. Charles explained, acknowledging that many college and graduate students tried to pay for their own treatment in order to stake out an area of true independence in their lives.

"Yes," Terry said, "I know that. And I don't want to take any money from my father. I want this to be my own."

Dr. Charles agreed to a reduced rate. It was settled then. Terry slouched more comfortably in her chair. The rest of her life opened up before her, a question mark dancing across its surface. She wanted to be a professional person, but it was hard to imagine actually being a clinical psychologist. Terry mentioned her uncertainty about relationships, speaking in an emotionally defused and theoretical way. Relating to men was a problem. How could she go so far as sexual intimacy with them and then later on not like them? And Arnie *was* coming. She had to make decisions about that. They would talk about that at their next meeting. Terry was going home for the Christmas holidays right after it.

December 20, 1974

Terry Walker watched Dr. Charles cautiously. What did the psychiatrist really think of her and of the way she had projected her life on the screen of recollection? Terry wanted, she explained, to be a good client, a "perfect client." As a graduate student in psychology, she knew that the word *client* connoted a role less grave than the word *patient.* She *would* be the perfect client, she would do everything right in therapy, and her new psychiatrist would then like and approve of her. "I've been talking," Terry said, "and I don't know what *you* think about *me.*"

"Why do you think that is so important to you?" Dr. Charles responded.

Terry shifted in her chair, bit her lip. "I thought you might think I was silly." She paused. Should she come right out and say it? "I wasn't sure you'd accept me."

This was a big concern, the doctor observed, that had suddenly seemed to become urgent. What made it that way?

"Well," Terry answered, "I wondered if you felt that I trapped you into taking me on. I mean . . ." She pursed the line of her lips. "Suppose I've only told you what I wanted to, suppose I didn't tell you some things I thought were really bad so that you didn't know anything about them? Maybe you wouldn't accept me if, if. . . ."

"You seem uncomfortable about something you've held back. You don't seem sure of what I'll think about you if you tell me."

"Yes, yes," Terry responded. "I didn't tell you everything about when I was in college." Now she wanted to rush it, get it in before the year expired, like a film just making the deadline for awards. Terry could let go, get it out, and then duck under the shield of the Christmas holidays.

"If I told you I was hospitalized in my first year of college, I thought you might not be willing to see me, that you wouldn't have anything to do with me, that you wouldn't accept me."

Dr. Charles understood that patients often brought up highly significant material at the very end of their sessions or at other times when immediate follow-up was either difficult or impossible

"I'd like you to tell me about that, Terry."

"It was a bad time. I was very angry . . . at my parents, I think. For not understanding me. I was angry at them for running my life—but not *really* paying attention to me. . . ." Terry hesitated, pulling back from the subject.

"Are you saying," Dr. Charles asked, "that going to the hospital had something to do with your anger?"

"I guess so," Terry answered. "I mean, I wanted their attention and I got it the only way I felt I could. I'd scream and yell, I'd call them up, I'd say I was thinking of killing myself. . . ."

"Your behavior—is that what you're telling me? What you did as a result of being angry, that's what got you into the hospital?"

"It was all very confusing. . . ."

"Tell me about when you were in the hospital," the doctor urged. Where had Terry been hospitalized? At Cornell in White Plains, New York. How long had she been there? Three months.

"Terry," Dr. Charles said, "the fact that you needed to keep this information back before I accepted you as a patient indicates how really important this experience is. I know it's hard to talk about, I understand that. But if I'm going to help you, I do have to know about it."

Terry nodded. She had been treated only with psychotherapy. By a psychologist, not a psychiatrist. No, she had not received any medication at all during her stay there. The psychiatrist, sensing Terry's uneasiness about this episode, would not press her for everything. Not yet. "Terry," Dr. Charles said, "I may want to get the records of that hospital stay sometime."

Terry lowered her eyes, nodded her head. She had revealed as much as she could for one day. And the time was almost up.

The psychiatrist studied her new patient. Terry Walker had long-term problems. Only the surface showed now, its sparkling mica as old and hard as the rock of which it was a part. The first thing was to establish a relationship with this young woman to make some real contact with her so that she could lower her defenses and begin to explore herself more deeply. Terry would tell her the rest of the story of her hospitalization when she felt more sure of herself.

January 7, 1975

Terry Walker was right on time for her first appointment in the new year. But the holidays into which she had moved so swiftly had turned out to be oppressive.

"I feel my mother's always hated me," Terry said, bristling as she brought up the subject, "I'm sure of that. I call her the 'Guilt Machine.' She's a master of it. That's how she works on me. I go home, I mean, she pressured me to come home for the holidays, like you'd be doing the worst thing in the world if you didn't show up. Then it's hell when you get there."

Terry snapped her head back angrily. "Like the High Holy Days last year. She'd say, 'All right, so don't come. But remember this is probably the last year your grandmother is alive at the Holy Days.' *That's* my mother. . . ."

Terry unreeled more of her life, flashing just the surface on the wall, the emotions as flat as the pictures. Frame after frame, home movies of a hovering, angry mother, flipped by.

"My mother told me once that she had an abortion when I was three years old. She said she did it because she knew that I would never be able to tolerate a younger sibling. . . ."

Had Terry, filled with rumination, trapped Dr. Charles into seeing her? Had she in some way manipulated the fee arrangement as well? Such self-questioning fed on itself, producing not understanding but rather the peculiar gratification of indecision, the strange but familiar comfort—for it made her anxious—of being off balance, of keeping everyone around her off balance, too. Terry adjusted by constantly resetting the scales in which she weighed people and events. No wonder she felt in midair, numb, demanding that people be there whenever she needed them. Will *you* be there, Doctor, when I need you? There, Doctor, how do you like me, now?

January 14, 1975

Dr. Charles greeted Terry as she arrived for her appointment almost aggressively on time, as if staking out a territorial claim to her hour and ready to fight off poachers. The psychiatrist could feel Terry's intensity, always challenging, always demanding, as the young woman reviewed the arrangements for therapy and spoke again of wanting to be the "perfect client." Being first in her class, being regarded as the best by her superiors and supervisors—these were the landfalls she sought.

"I don't know why you won't see me twice a week," Terry snapped. "Now that I'm started, I want to work hard at this, I want to straighten things out in my life. You know that *I need* this extra time," Terry insisted. "You know I need two hours a week. Why won't you give it to me?"

"We've discussed all this in detail," Dr. Charles responded. "We've cleared these issues up already. The fact—reality—is that I don't have an extra hour available right now."

"*You* know that I need it!"

"Your feeling is that you want to get this done immediately, get it accomplished overnight," the doctor answered. "And you're frustrated if you can't get it done the way you want it. But therapy doesn't work that way." Terry's glare faded. She settled down and began to reflect on the kinds of demands she made on herself and others. They were similar to the ones she had just made on Dr. Charles. But the doctor had not rejected her, had not made the exchange between them into a tug of war. Maybe there were other ways to do things than the way she was used to.

January 21, 1975

"*I had this dream,*" *Terry said anxiously.* "I was on my way for a session with you, I was late. Then I got to the elevator and it didn't work. . . ."

"What feelings do you associate with that?"

"Well, here I am and I want to get to work at myself. I want to understand why I do things." She slashed the air with a gesture, "And *you,* I happen to know, you—who say you only have time to see me once a week—I know that you've agreed to see another student from the university in an evaluation session. I know about it because I know the girl!"

Terry's accusation was a cross-section, Dr. Charles understood, of the style Terry had learned long ago, it was the only way Terry knew of relating to other people. Arguing with her was not the way to establish a relationship. Giving in to Terry was not the way, either; that was just repeating the behavior of so many others. Terry could not stand anyone else in competition with her, certainly not another student getting an hour of the doctor's time. The psychiatrist recognized the omnipotence that flowed through Terry. It would be a long time before the patient would be willing to look at it herself.

Terry spoke of her habitual way of analyzing things, of going over and over them, until, like rugs under heavy traffic, the fibers thinned and splayed apart. After a while, dizzied by obsessions, she didn't know what she felt. But she had talked to Arnie. Arnie, laying the groundwork ahead of time, had asked her, "Will you keep on going to therapy even after I come to Chicago?" What was she going to do about him, or about her career? What *was* she going to do about herself?

January 28, 1975

Terry, on time, was less combative. No need this week for the immediate arm wrestle with the psychiatrist. No need to reject her interpretations out of hand. There was something in the things Dr. Charles said. Terry *was* more comfortable with people when she was angry at them. There were feelings she could talk about.

"I've met this other person. His name is Kevin. He's in the same program with me." They were in the same group and he was fun to be with. Not Jewish, her mother would cluck in disapproval. No, he wasn't Jewish, but Terry enjoyed herself when she was with him. She had been ruminating about this relationship, analyzing it in her familiar style. What did it mean? And what did it mean about Arnie?

"I mean, God, it makes me wonder about men. Getting into a relationship with a man means something I don't like. It means getting dependent on him. That means you can't stand alone.

"If you're dependent on a man, you can't *ever* stand alone. And then if he leaves you, you're abandoned, and you can't do anything, you can't function at all." She paused. "That's the way it is with my mother. She's totally, I mean *completely,* dependent on my father. It seems to me that if he ever left her, she'd kill herself. She almost killed herself when her own father died. The only reason she didn't was that she was pregnant with me. It could not have been a happy time for her." Memory had pierced a sachet of sadness that had not, as she supposed, dried out long ago. The scent of depression from another time hung in the air. "And Arnie is coming in four or five months. That's all the independence I've got. Just four or five months." Terry shook her head. "And I'm not sure what I want to do about him . . . or myself."

Dr. Charles sat for a moment after Terry left, reflecting about her before she made her usual brief notes about the session. What was the best way to think about Terry? There was plenty of evidence of family disruption—problems in the relationship of mother and father. Terry desperately needed to look "good" in the eyes of others and so she held back what she saw as the "bad" aspects of her personality. How flooded with need she was! To be understood instantly, yet always feeling that nobody understood her, to manipulate others according to her designs. . . . Terry kept herself together through the intellectual strengths that insulated her from emotion. Terry had persistent difficulties in relating to men. The meaning of her hospitalization would have to be explored. Her mental status showed no evidence of gross psychopathology. There was no evidence of psychosis. All the data so far pointed to long-term characterological difficulties.

In response to Maddux's question, Sara explains that children who receive mixed parental messages of approbation and disapproval for trying to assert themselves come to mistrust themselves; such children are made to feel bad for wanting a healthy adventure in independence. The mother feels abandoned by the child who tries to stand on her own. "So the mother," Sara says, "in some way feels down. Children notice this. So what do they do? They go back to mother. They go back and try to calm and reassure mother but they end up being dependent. . . . If they stay in mother's orbit and all their friends are growing up, they become enraged . . . so the idea of being independent and being dependent in relationships is a constant theme in these kinds of patients. . . ."

After a five-minute recess, Murphy speaks urgently to the judge. He wants to raise "a matter, your honor, that is—I may be wrong—but I saw Mr. Maddux talking to Dr. Charles in the hall when I walked by. It seemed they were talking about her testimony. It was always my understanding that once a witness took the stand, there was to be no communication between her and her counsel concerning the testimony. I hope I'm wrong, but I'd ask the court to direct counsel and Dr. Charles not to speak to each other further."

The judge looks toward Maddux who frowns at the plaintiff's

awyer. "It's a constitutional right for any party—if he or she wants—to consult with their attorney at any stage of the proceedings, whether they're on the stand or not on the stand. I refuse to let him know what we are discussing or how. . . ."

"I'm not interested in what they're discussing," Murphy says. "I just think that once she's under oath and on the stand, you can't take. . . ."

Judge McGarr, hesitant about making a ruling, says that they will discuss it at four-thirty after the jury is excused.

Maddux returns to his questioning of Sara, glancing now and then at a set of her psychiatric notes that he holds in his hand. What, he wants to know, is the meaning of the note, made in February, "Needs to be in control for she doesn't trust herself—keeps thinking she might screw herself and be sorry for it."

February 1975

Terry was perplexed, angry, on the verge of tears. She had just had a blow-up with a woman psychologist who supervised her clinical training. The episode was like a cavity that could not be filled in. "This isn't the first time I've had problems with women psychologists. I had a bad experience with a woman psychologist I worked with when I was doing research in Boston. She was pregnant and I did most of the work." Terry shook her head angrily. "I did so much of the work that she told me that when our article came out, I would be listed as first author. And then when it came out it didn't happen that way. I was second author. . . ."

Women! Mothers and supervisors! She had trouble with all the women whose support she needed. "Like my parents," Terry said, hunching forward in her chair. "Sometimes they would respond and sometimes they wouldn't. I was never sure what was coming. It was, well, it was just unpredictable." She sighed. "It isn't just women relating to men, it's women relating to women, too. That doesn't work, either."

Terry fingered the zipper on the flap of her coat, which hung over the arm of her chair. She began to cry, "That's why I need them—I need my supervisor, I need *you*—to be consistent with me, to give consistency to me." She sobbed. "I'm lucky to have found this relationship, I'm grateful to be here." Terry looked away, feeling depleted. Dependence and independence, liking and disliking, idealization and devaluation: sharp taloned twins rode in her soul all the time. "Now," she said, her tone pushy, demanding, "I think I should get my sessions twice a week with you. You owe it to me, so I can be sure that I can trust you. I wonder if it's really your time schedule. I think sometimes you think twice a week would be too much for me. . . ."

"You know, Terry," Dr. Charles responded, "I would expect that you would have some difficulty trusting me since you've given me many examples of the same difficulty you've had with others." Terry sat erect as Dr. Charles continued her mild interpretation of Terry's problems in trusting people. "Your idea of trust," the doctor said, feeling her way along the resistant wall of Terry's omnipotence, "seems to involve the notion that you have to know everything the person is thinking. You want to know everything about their motivation. Then you decide whether they're trustworthy or not." Terry's distorted notion of trust had nothing to do with believing in others; it only demanded that others be absolutely predictable, that they be reliable and consistent, that they "freeze" in place in relationship to her.

Terry drew back. That was not true, no, she was not that way at all. In the next session she discussed how upset the psychiatrist had made her by this observation. "But," she added, "it's probably true, it really is. I've just got troubles in that whole area. With men, with women, with everybody. I wonder about Kevin, for example, and the therapy group we're running together. And I wonder if our relationship will upset our supervisor. I'm just unsure of all these areas." Terry bit her lip and talked about her dreams of not coming for therapy, the dreams in which it was so difficult to get to her treatment sessions. She wanted to fight it. . . .

"But now that I've really been mad at you, I feel more comfortable with you. I feel better this way than when I feel warm toward somebody. . . ."

A moment later, Terry threw down a fresh challenge: "You used the wrong pronoun!"

Dr. Charles, aware that Terry was not yet ready to look observantly at these volcanic feelings and their deep and early source in her life, did not respond. A doctor did not help a patient by letting the fire and ash of such primitive emotions settle on her. The task was to be patient, to be consistent, to remain separate from all the other confounded relationships in Terry's life. Then a real relationship could begin between them and Terry could start to redefine trust in her life.

"You know," Terry said thoughtfully, "I expected to talk just about my inner feelings, not about my relationships with others. I thought that would be a waste of time." She paused. "But I know it's not . . . my problem is really in sorting out all my relationships." Tears welled in her eyes. "My family, they don't trust anybody. They were always after us. Don't trust anybody outside the family, you can only rely on your own. If other people seem interested, it's only a fluke, it's nothing. They really don't care about you and they end up hurting you." The young woman reached for a Kleenex and dabbed absently at her cheek. "They just don't have it. But I've been trying to do what they said, I've been trusting only the family, I haven't been trusting anybody else." She could not quite fit together the pieces she had spread out before her. The family trusts nobody. "The family tells me to trust them. But they are unpredictable, they're always unpredictable. That was the catch in everything. . . .

"So," Terry continued, "if I rely on others, they'll screw me. And if I rely on myself, I might not act for my own good, either. I'm in the middle." Trying to understand this central conflict was like climbing a steep, craggy mountain in the dark. One step after the other, as the pebbles rolled loose around her.

"It's like Arnie. Should I say okay? It's okay, Arnie, if you come and live with me. But if he does, he might overwhelm me. And if I don't let him come, I'm not being trustworthy. If I can't control things, I might screw myself, and then later I'll be sorry for it. . . ."

"That notion is really a verbalization," Sara tell Maddux, "of that very basic conflict . . . if she makes a decision on her own, or asserts herself in some way, she's going to get cut off. She's going to get punished, she's going to be made to feel guilty. That's her way of verbalizing it, 'If I try and do something, I'll end up screwing myself.' In other words, I'm bound to make the wrong decision. . . ."

The afternoon session has ended and the expressionless jurors file out. Murphy is on his feet with his complaint again. There is no rule, McGarr says, that prohibits a client from conferring with counsel in the middle of testimony. "One of the privileges still in existence," Maddux adds, "is that between a lawyer and a client. I don't think any lawyer has a right to even question the communications that go on between us. . . ."

"My view," Murphy responds, "is that I should be able to inquire . . . I think the jury has a right to know that after every session counsel goes out and talks to his client and tells her what to say. . . ."

"Your leaping to the conclusion that counsel was telling his witness what to say," McGarr says, "is rather breathtaking. . . ."

"The evidence is very thin. That's why he's leaping, your honor," Maddux says, shaking his head. Murphy's objection dissolves as he speaks about Dr. Tobin, whom he may call to the stand the next day. Maddux objects and the judge reserves his ruling until the morning. Then McGarr inquires about jury instructions, which are prepared by each lawyer and submitted to the judge in every trial. The judge, in a discussion with the lawyers, decides which ones he will read to the jury before they go out for their deliberations. Maddux's are ready. Murphy suggests that maybe Maddux could give him a copy of the one Maddux prepared because he's sure he would agree with most of them. The judge looks quizzically at Murphy. "I'm not going to tell Mr. Maddux to do that," he says, as court ends for the day.

DAY NINE

_____

The Defendant Continued

*The borderline creates a kind of a "storm" around them and gets everybody
into the wind of the storm.*

—Sara Charles, M. D.

man we have never seen before—fortyish, a light veil of perspira-
on on his forehead, in a crisp seersucker suit—stands in the
allway outside the courtroom. William Fleming represents the
ompany that carries Sara's malpractice insurance. No need to
et excited, he seems to say to Bill Maddux, who regards him
tonily. Just want to see how the trial is going, you know, a little
noral support. He chucks Maddux on the shoulder. It is not a
vell-received gesture. Maddux moves into the courtroom with
ara while Fleming, smiling nervously, lights a thin cigar and
urries toward the pay phone halfway down the hall.

Fleming has been sent to observe the trial. Does the insurance
ompany want to get this off their hands and off their books even
t the last minute? Murphy called Maddux at his office earlier
hat morning to inquire about the limits of Sara's insurance policy.

Maddux, knowing that Sara would rather lose than settle, had ignored him. Fleming returns, wiping his brow, to sit restlessly behind the court buffs as Sara retakes the stand. Is he afraid we are going to lose? Or is he afraid we are going to win?

Maddux resumes his questioning of Sara, circling slowly back away from the witness stand, sitting down finally in the first row of the spectator seats so that every eye in the courtroom is focused on the witness as she continues her testimony about her treatment sessions with Terry Walker.

March 1975

In March the signs of a therapeutic relationship, as small and uncertain as those of spring itself, began to manifest themselves. Terry, tense, coiled to strike before someone else struck her, tested Dr. Charles constantly. She worked out of the angry, dependent style she had learned in dealing with her mother—and had extended to her sister—provoking the psychiatrist with inexhaustible strategies of demand. She wanted two sessions a week. Why wouldn't Dr. Charles give them to her? She was envious of those, like her new friend Kevin, who were in psychoanalysis, because they got to talk about themselves every day with their therapists. Here, Doctor, is my situation with Arnie. You don't think I can work it out, do you? You think I'll fail. Then it will be all my fault again, won't it? You're not good enough to me, Doctor.

The therapist could identify Terry's reactions to her as the same ones she had toward her mother and other significant people in her life. There was nothing constructive going on in treatment if these transference feelings did not appear. Therapists were lightning rods for these fiery emotional bolts from their patients; it was in remaining a separate person, in not taking on the dominating role of mother, in being a consistent and trustworthy adult, that the psychiatrist slowly and patiently built a bridge of relationship with a patient.

Was trust, Maddux asks, important in dealing with her? "What you do," Sara answers, "is set an exact time when you are going to meet each other. You set an exact time of how long you are going to see each other. You try to be consistent and trustworthy and honest with the patient. You pay attention to what they say, you respect them, you communicate in many different ways that

ou are a person to whom they can entrust whatever it is that's
f concern to them. What you find in a developing therapy is
hat the person begins to give you more and more of what's really
oing on with them. . . ."

"Was there any evidence," Maddux asks, "during the course
f time you saw her that she began to trust you?" Maddux reviews
he months of therapy, noting the various minor crises that Sara
ad helped Terry work through. He asks specifically about a note
ara made on October 1, 1975. "Feels better. Phone call important
ecause it helped her trust me. Actually it reinforced the healthy
ather than the sick side. . . ." What did that mean?

Terry, Sara explains, had been seeing her twice a week since
xtra time had become available in May. Near the end of Septem-
er, Terry had to make a choice about an important graduate
ourse that was scheduled during the time of one of her therapy
essions. They had discussed it and Sara said that, although she
id not have any extra time, she might be able to have another
atient change appointment slots with Terry. When Terry called,
ara said the change could be made and Terry had to make up
er own mind about whether or not she wanted to follow through.
he decided to go ahead with the change: ". . . she came into
hat session and she said she really felt better. Terry said having
hat phone call was very important because she felt she could
rust me . . . I had given her the data, I had talked to the other
patient, and if she thought it was important for her career to
take those courses that I was willing to make an adaptation to
that. . . . What she's saying is 'Okay, we got through that one.
That worked and I feel pretty good about that.'"

But Murphy has made much of the word *panic*, which appears
in the notes the next day. Can the doctor explain it? The entry
reads "Feels more secure in herself. . . . Some reassurance for
first time if I don't get drawn into her panic (her mother and
sister always used to)—some separateness there."

Terry, Sara recounts, had told her that "when she has to make
a decision she tends to get a lot of people involved. Some people
have written about this in terms of a 'storm'; that the borderline
creates a kind of a 'storm' around them and gets everybody into
the wind of the storm. And she is saying that we dealt with it. I
answered her phone calls, but we tried to deal with it in a calm
way—let's look at the facts of the situation, what are your options?
She made the decision and that was a good experience for her.

In the past, people would get drawn into it and somehow it was harder to make the decision than ever."

"So," Maddux asks, "would the role of therapy be to try to decrease that kind of panic and make the decision-making process easier for the person?"

"I think," Sara answers, "that the *only* way you can decrease that kind of panic is by responding, each time it comes up, in a consistent manner. . . . As someone is able to make their own decisions they begin to rely on their own strength to deal with it the next time it comes up."

Panic appears one more time in her notes, Sara explains, referring to the anxiety Terry felt as she began to make more truly independent decisions in her life. That didn't mean she was out of control. It signified that she was beginning to trust herself, and that, because this was new for her, she found it a little frightening. The price of building a healthy relationship is the experience of freedom from old constraints, from the defective but familiar ways in which she had dealt with things in the past. These were signs of trust developing, of Terry's healthy self beginning to awaken.

Fleming, his suit turning lumpy, stands nervously in the hallway during a brief recess. "Great day," he says to me. "Great day. Yessir." He jingles the coins in his pants pocket. "Just a couple of calls I have to make." A coach's chuck to my shoulder. A knowing wink. "Things are going great. Nothing to worry about. Great day. Great day for a barbecue outdoors." A sidling step away, then a hurried passage toward the phone. What the hell is he up to anyway? One of the regular court buffs approaches me solemnly. He hesitates, tugs at his lip. "That doctor," he says in measured tones, "is a hell of a good witness." In another moment we all herd back into the courtroom to listen to Maddux's continuing examination of Sara.

July 1975

Terry worked through several decisions that made her feel better. On June first she had moved into her own apartment, to live alone for the first time in her life. She had handled Arnie's pressure by making the transition to independent living. Arnie had been disappointed and they had broken up. The experience of being on er own had been exhilarating. She made her own schedule, she could grow plants that she liked, she was free of the constant expectation of others. Terry also resolved her uncertainty about the choice of summer clinical psychology clerkships. Some of her familiar obsessiveness had surfaced again, but she had managed her way through to a selection that was working out well.

"Now," she said, "I've got to make up my mind about going on a camping trip with Kevin." What to do about men? Such questions would never go away. And summer brought up echoes of its own. Terry had been sent away to camp every summer since she was four years old. It was the thing to do in her New York neighborhood. Even if her parents were low on money they would scrimp and save to send her and Carol away to the Catskills in the summer.

"If I spend time camping with Kevin, well, I don't know what will happen. I have these fantasies. I can just hear what my mother would say. 'You go away with a man for a few weeks, and you'll pay for it. You'll pay for it by going crazy.'" Terry shook the image out of her head. "And my father, he'd say, 'Just don't get me involved.'" She shook her head again and rubbed her jaw with her hand.

"The trouble is, what will Kevin think of me? If I refuse to go, will he leave me or stop dating me?" Terry furrowed her brow. There was more to it than that. If she went away, she would be giving in again; doing what *he* wanted more than what *she* wanted. And when people were alone together for a while, they began to tell each other things about themselves. Terry would tell Kevin about what happened to her in the first year of college. That she had been hospitalized. Kevin had a brother who had been hospitalized. But still! What would he think of her? She had told Arnie of it and he seemed to act differently toward her afterward.

As the trust between them deepened, Terry continued to explore aspects of her earlier hospitalization with Dr. Charles. It was never an easy subject to talk about. Terry still did not understand it completely. And here it was again. "I was always told by my parents never to talk about it. '*You*,' they'd say, '*you're* the *crazy* one. You're the *different one* in the family. Tell a man about it and he'll never marry you. Go ahead, see what happens. You want to be alone, an old maid, all your life?'"

What had the hospitalization meant anyway? And what did it

mean when she exploded in anger as she had that very day a
an airlines clerk who had called to tell her that the schedule
had changed and her flight would be at a different hour than
she had planned? "Why did I get so angry?" Terry asked anx
iously. "Why do things have to be so black and white?" She swal
lowed and looked directly at Dr. Charles. "If I get so angry abou
things over which I have no control, what does it mean abou
me? It's like I missed something when I was growing up. Maybe
that's part of what I was doing back in the first year of college. . . ,"

Terry shifted in her chair. This hard, honest look at herself,
this was something all new. . . .

"Maybe when I don't get enough attention—like with my
mother and father—I go to extremes. Only when I go to extremes
do people pay attention to me." Terry began to weep softly. "So
when I got so angry at my mother and father, I had to go a
long way to get their attention. Maybe that's part of what the
hospitalization was." Terry took a deep breath, edging tears away
with the side of her hand. Her words broke apart on a rack of
sobs. "I—always—had—to—fight—to—be—loved."

She coughed, pulled herself together, looked at Dr. Charles.
She hadn't resolved her conflict about camping with Kevin.
"Maybe that's what I do all the time. I get involved with a man—
like my father—who seems to be strong and independent. A man
who is attractive but not affectionate. And the only way I can
get that affection is by getting angry. That's what I did the first
year of college. I got *angry* and people paid attention. . . ."

Terry was upset, unstrung by a call from her father. "He wants me,"
she said angrily, "to add up everything I've paid to you, make a
list of it, and send it to him. Then he's going to deduct it from
his taxes. . . ." How could her father do this? How could he
do it now, of all times? And not even seem to know what it meant
to her.

"Maybe I can't really be independent," Terry sobbed, "maybe
there's no way I can get free." Maybe it was all a cruel hoax,
this idea of getting away from her family's demands.

"And my father . . ." Terry paused, a catch of affection in
her voice, "*he's* given me so much. I'll feel guilty if *I* don't give
this to him. . . ." Terry frowned. "But if I do give it to him,
then I'll feel guilty about that, too. . . ."

The courtroom is utterly silent as Sara finishes her account of how Terry's father had continued to pressure his daughter into the fall for a statement for his taxes. That was one of the things Terry had been so anxious "to get settled and be done with." The mother had pressed for Terry's return for the Holy Days in September. *This* year might be grandmother's last, Terry, how could you stay away? Carol had visited her in the summer and Terry had felt a surge of the old competitive tension with her. You're the one who was crazy, Terry, and now you're the one who is the psychologist. . . .

Maddux brings up a November 7 note, quoted often by Murphy as proof of Sara's negligence, about Terry's "losing control." This had come after Terry had successfully weathered a crisis about going away on a weekend with Kevin. She had called several times, something as Sara explains, very characteristic of borderline patients. Such calls were part of the "storm" they generated around themselves. In early November, after the weekend had been canceled, Terry settled down, moving her concern to the choice of a dissertation topic. Freedom remained novel for Terry as she moved through the normal struggles of building a new life and career a thousand miles from home.

On November 6, 1975, Sara had to cancel her morning patients, Terry among them, because of illness. But Sara had not been able to reach a patient coming in from out of state, so she got out of bed in the afternoon and went to the office to see him. Terry called while she was there and became angry when Sara answered the phone herself. "Again," Sara says, "the issue of control . . . it touches on the issue of trust. Was I really honest? I had said I was sick and here I am in the office seeing someone." Terry accepted Sara's suggestion to come in the next morning to discuss the incident. The November 7 note about losing control had reference to two issues.

"The issue of control of me in a psychological sense. . . . If I said I was out of the office and sick, I ought to be out of the office and sick. And that's a reasonable expectation. That exceptions occur was very hard for her to deal with. . . . There was also the issue of the feeling that her rage was so much—you get frightened when you get so angry—I think people often use that term, a fear of losing control . . . that's a very common way of saying . . . I almost lost my cool."

The doctor and the patient had gone on to discuss the issue

of internal and external controls. "Part of development," Sara explains, "is processing and controlling, modulating your own internal environment."

"Did that," Maddux asks, "have anything to do with the concept of not being able to function?"

"No."

They are in the week of the Saturday on which Terry jumped. Maddux asks about a note made on Wednesday, November 12, the day Terry's father had visited her on his way back to New York. This is the centerpiece of Murphy's charges that Terry was openly suicidal for several days before November 15. What about that session, Maddux asks, and what about that phrase "Destructive behavior when left to her own devices" in your personal notes?

"That," Sara says, "was the week after I was sick. . . . She had seen her father, came down to see me, and was going back to be with her father. We dealt mostly in this session with the impact on her of making decisions that reflected her own independence. And I have a note here, '*Destructive behavior when left to her own devices.*'"

"What does that mean?" Maddux asks. The jury members watch Sara intently. The clerk stamps a document in the otherwise hushed courtroom.

"That was related to a specific issue. She told me she either had or was considering going off the birth control pill that she had been on. And it related to her relationship to Kevin. . . . They were getting farther apart. . . . And we spent a good deal of the session talking about the effect that would or could have on someone who was in graduate school, had certain ambitions, had a certain time schedule—we talked about it in terms of the impact it could have on someone's life." Sara pauses, "In other words, if by chance someone off of birth control pills got pregnant, that could interrupt a lot of her plans. And that was what the issue was about. . . ."

Murphy whispers a question to Terry Walker. She merely nods and he pulls his head slowly away.

"Well," Maddux asks, "did that in any way have any reference to destructive behavior in the form of taking one's life?"

"No, it was destructive behavior in terms of disrupting one's life. . . . and her observations about that. . . ."

"Well, on November 12 was she suicidal?"

"No."

Maddux refers to Dr. Walston's call. Yes, Sara remembers it. He had been inquiring, she says, "quite appropriately . . . as you expect a well-trained doctor to do in a family." Terry had called them five times in recent weeks, Walston had said, between midnight and five A.M. He had raised the issue of an antidepressant drug. Sara told him that "there wasn't any reason for an antidepressant. . . . but that I would talk to Terry that morning about his phone call and his concerns and also about the phone calls she'd been making."

They had discussed the phone calls at her appointment on the thirteenth. They had examined "what kind of response she was looking for from these people by engaging them in this particular way." Terry was separating somewhat from Kevin, Sara explains, and she was calling to test her strengths in other relationships. "The borderline patient has periods when they don't deal with being alone very well. They can have rapid changes of feeling states. Ten minutes before they may have no intention of calling someone and ten minutes later they're on the phone."

Isn't one of the goals of therapy, Maddux asks, to get them to control this kind of impulsive behavior?

"One of the things you do," Sara says, turning toward the jury members who have heard so much about Terry's phone calls in the last two weeks, ". . . is you try to understand the patient's perception of why they're making these calls. The other thing you do is to try to get them to stop that kind of behavior, to control it as much as possible."

"There's a note," Maddux says, " *'trying to get someone close that will help her function.'* What does that mean?"

"She was making the point that here she is out in Chicago, she's getting into a relationship with a new therapist that she's . . . not entirely comfortable with in terms of trustworthiness. And she had a boyfriend—I think she's probably always had a boyfriend, someone that she could have close to her—and he was withdrawing . . . but they were still seeing each other somewhat. And she was cognizant of the fact that it was important for her to have someone. And it related in part to . . . can *I* be that person? Am I trustworthy?"

Otherwise, Terry was going to class and leading a normal social life. She gave no signs of being suicidal.

The next time Sara heard from her was on Saturday morning, November 15.

* * *

The jurors lean forward as the lawyer asks Sara about the phone call she received from Terry on that Saturday morning.

"I was out shopping," Sara explains, "and I returned home and . . . I always call my answering service to see if there are any calls. And there had been . . . one . . . from Terry. And I returned the call. So it might have been ten—between ten and eleven."

"And what," Maddux asks, "was the purpose of that call? Why'd she call you?"

"She called me, as she said, first of all, she wanted some medication for sleep. . . ."

November 15, 1975

Terry's voice was metallic, ungiving. "I want to talk to you about some medication for sleep."

Terry's tone was familiar but the subject was new. She had never before complained about problems with sleep.

"What time did you go to bed last night?" the psychiatrist asked.

"Midnight. One o'clock."

"Did you get to sleep right away?"

"Not right away. In a half hour or so."

"What time did you get up this morning?"

"About eight or eight-thirty."

"Well, it sounds like you had six or seven hours of sleep." Terry had had a reasonable night's sleep and she had never requested sleep medication before. What was behind this request? "Do you," she asked, "have any particular drug in mind?"

"Mellaril," Terry snapped.

"What do you know about Mellaril, Terry?"

Terry hesitated, did not answer.

"Did you hear about Mellaril from your brother-in-law, Dr. Walston?"

"Yes, he recommended it."

"You know, Terry, Mellaril is an antipsychotic drug. It's not a sleeping medication. I don't see any indications that the use of this drug should come up at all for you." Terry mumbled a response as the psychiatrist continued. "I think you have been anxious. You've talked about that in connection with some of the decisions you've been dealing with. I'd be glad to write you— or call in—a prescription for some Librium. I think that would help you settle down a bit."

"I don't want that," Terry answered. "I'm not interested in that." She paused and changed the subject. "I've been thinking of going home to New York this weekend." She had, in fact, already talked for almost an hour with her former therapist, the psychologist Waxman. She had talked to her parents. They had all invited her back to New York that weekend. But she did not speak about that now.

"You say," Dr. Charles responded, "you're thinking of going east. Is there some reason that's come up all of a sudden?"

"Well, I've been thinking about all these decisions I've had to make. And I thought maybe it would be good for me to have a change for a few days."

"Well, there's certainly no reason for you not to go to New York if you want to," the doctor answered, "but you don't sound decided. Do you have other plans for the weekend?"

"Yes, I have some studying to do and I'm meeting a friend this afternoon at four o'clock. I have lots to do. But I'm not sure; I may still go to New York . . ." Terry paused again. "I've just been so introspective lately; I'm wondering if maybe I should decrease our sessions from two to one a week for a while."

"Well, I'd be glad to talk to you about that. But I don't think it's the sort of thing that we ought to settle on the phone. How about coming in for an extra session first thing on Monday morning and we can talk about it?"

"Well, I may go to New York. . . ."

"I'll put you down for ten o'clock Monday morning. If you can't make it, just give me a call."

"When you asked her about Mellaril," Maddux asks, "did she mention anything about Dr. Waxman?"

"No," Sara answers. "I knew that she had a former therapist because . . . she had told me before that she had contacted him when she was in New York in September. But I don't believe I knew his name. And I knew nothing of his involvement in the events of November 15."

"Well," Maddux inquires, leaning forward, "at the time when you talked with her on the phone, was Terry Walker psychotic?"

"No."

"Was she suicidal?"

"No." Terry had plans for the weekend, things to do, not the kinds of plans made by self-destructive people who are contemplating suicide.

"Did you have any further contact with Terry Walker after that phone call on Saturday morning?"

"I had no further contact until Sunday afternoon."

Did Sara receive calls from anybody else? Dr. Walston? No. Dr. Waxman? No. Her parents? No. Sister? No. Friends? No.

"Did you know anything at all about what went on after that phone call? Any firsthand knowledge on the day in question?"

"No."

"Well," Maddux says, shifting his weight from one foot to the other, "is it a good practice for a psychologist to tell Terry Walker . . . that she was sicker than she thought she was?"

"I don't think a doctor ever tells patients that they're sicker than they think they are." The plaintiff watches the psychiatrist closely from her wheelchair. "What you always do with a patient," Sara continues, "is to strengthen the healthy, strong parts of them rather than to emphasize the sicker, weaker parts. One of the basic orientations toward therapy is always supporting what we call healthy defenses. We support those; we encourage those. We don't attempt to break down people's defenses."

"Why, then, did Terry start calling New York that morning?" Maddux asks. It was characteristic of Terry, Sara explains, to involve others in her decision making. "That's what she had done all her life." It is the kind of thing borderlines do. "Getting people involved, getting a lot of input into the decision-making process, whatever the decision is all about, getting them to take over." That was the way it had always been with Terry and her family. "And yet," Sara adds, "part of her doesn't want that . . . because another part of her wants to be independent."

Then, Maddux interjects, a psychologist should understand

this pattern. Absolutely. A psychologist should know enough not to tell her that she was sicker than she thought she was. "There's a communication in that," Sara says, "which confirms all the worst things she thinks about herself. . . ."

Sara explains how she had consulted afterward with Dr. Lucia Tower, a psychoanalyst in Chicago, reviewing each session of her treatment of Terry Walker, trying to understand it as deeply as possible. She had done this with her patients for years as a way of continuing to educate herself as a psychiatrist. Sara had intensely studied her relationship with Terry because she had not learned about all the things that had happened—the roles that others filled on that day—until after the lawsuit had been filed. She had learned about the extent of Dr. Waxman's involvement only after she had read the depositions that had been taken long after that November day.

"I felt," she says, "that I in some way had been left outside of something. And, as I say, I never really knew many of the events of November 15 until years later. And that somehow I had believed in her, I had believed the things she told me about herself were what were really going on in herself. I believed that we were working very hard. I believed that we had really begun to trust each other. . . ."

Murphy is on his feet as the noon recess nears. "I'm asking the court," he says, "to direct the witness not to talk to her lawyer about her testimony during the lunch hour. . . . If Dr. Charles's testimony is in any way different from what she said this morning, I would ask leave to point out where. . . ."

Maddux reminds the judge that a client may consult her lawyer at any time and the judge, perplexed by Murphy, says, "I will *not* instruct her *not* to discuss her testimony. . . ."

Sara and I stand together for a moment outside the courtroom itself. Murphy rounds the corner, a short, balding man at his side. He is defense expert Dr. Arnold Tobin, whom Murphy has subpoenaed to testify in the case. Maddux shakes his head. "He'll never call him," he says as he pushes through the doors. I glance at Tobin, who seems a reluctant presence, "I'll call you, Doctor," Murphy says to him. "I may not need you until next week." Tobin turns and heads for the elevators and Murphy, eyes down, brushes past me and into the courtroom.

Judge McGarr holds another melancholy status call on pending cases and the afternoon session begins shortly after two o'clock. Murphy, yellow legal sheets cascading familiarly out of his right hand, asks, "How many times do these words appear?" referring once more to Sara's notes, "fragile, very anxious, panic, massive distrust, fears the psychosis, vulnerable and afraid, phone calls, depressed, losing control, destructive behavior if left to herself. . . ."

Murphy steps closer to the witness stand. "Doctor," he asks, "you've done a lot of thinking since you've testified this morning?"

Sara looks puzzled. "I had lunch."

"You may have spoken with some people?"

"I went to lunch with my husband."

Murphy inches closer. "Doctor, do you realize that you made a big mistake when you testified this morning?"

Sara looks carefully at the attorney, "No."

"Did anyone tell you that?" Puzzlement again wrinkling her forehead, Sara says no.

Murphy reviews Sara's morning testimony about not knowing the name or the true extent of psychologist Waxman's involvement in the events of November 15 until she had read the complaint and depositions taken in the case. He speaks harshly, "You didn't know his name so you went to see Dr. Tower forty-four times to get Dr. Waxman's name. Is that right, Doctor? . . . You told the jury you went to see Dr. Tower because you didn't know Dr. Waxman's name. You said that!" Murphy, ignoring the judge's admonitions, thrusts his head to within a foot of Sara's face. "You said this morning, according to what I put down—*before* you had a chance to talk to anyone who may have said you made a *big* mistake." He heaves forward another inch, shouting, "'Cause Murphy's got you now!"

McGarr half rises in consternation from his chair. "Counsel, that statement . . . that comment in front of the jury . . . the jury is instructed to disregard it. Ask questions, stop making speeches." Murphy insists that somehow Sara has deceived the court in saying that she did not know of Dr. Waxman's involvement in the case until after the complaint had been filed and depositions taken from the principals.

Maddux immediately objects and, after Murphy repeats his charge, the judge excuses the jury. Murphy speaks intently, "We're exactly at the point I *knew* we'd be when we recessed this morning.

. . . This morning she testified—it's written down twice . . ." he brandishes his own notes again, "that she had to see Dr. Tower, for, among other reasons, because she didn't know what happened on the fifteenth." Murphy waves an arm toward Tom Boodell, sitting next to me in the rear, "I looked at Mr. Boodell who put his hands to his head. . . ."

Maddux groans and the startled spectators look around in puzzlement. Sara watches Murphy closely as he claims that Maddux took her to lunch and had her change her testimony.

"I'm not going to allow this time after time," McGarr says, ". . . This argument, 'my notes say this,' isn't really very helpful. We can't impeach this witness with *your* notes, counsel."

But Murphy repeats his contention. McGarr intervenes again, ". . . You don't find all these sinister implications . . . because I don't think the circumstances are justified, principally, because they suggest that Mr. Maddux was involved in getting her to change her testimony. And that's an unfair accusation." Maddux reminds the judge that there has been no change in testimony but, after the jury returns, Murphy raises his charges again. He quotes Sara's notes and from some literature on the borderline patient. He accuses Maddux of having looked at the books that he had collected on the plaintiff's table. McGarr reproves him again. Quizzical looks above hunched shoulders throughout the courtroom. The plaintiff's attorney sees something clearly, but nobody else does. Murphy cannot let go of his conviction that Sara and Maddux have conspired to trick the court.

The judge's next announcement seems apiece with the afternoon's unusual atmosphere. McGarr explains that at four o'clock a congressman from Washington is waiting to see him. "He may be here to discuss a raise." He smiles as he dismisses the court for the day.

Excerpts from Ethical Principles
for Psychiatrists and Psychologists

Excerpts from *Principles of Medical Ethics with Annotations Especially Applicable to Psychotherapy* (American Psychiatric Association, 1978)

Section 1, Annotation 4:

The principal objective of the medical profession is to render service to humanity with full respect for the dignity of man. Physicians should merit the confidence of patients entrusted to their care, rendering to each a full measure of service and devotion.

Physicians generally agree that the doctor-patient relationship is such a vital factor in effective treatment of the patient that preservation of optimal conditions for development of a sound working relationship between a doctor and his/her patient should take precedence over all other considerations.

Section 6, Annotation 4:

A physician should not dispose of his services under terms or conditions which tend to interfere with or impair the free and complete exercise of his medical judgment and strive or tend to cause a deterioration of the quality of medical care.

In relationships between psychiatrists and practicing licensed psychologists, the physician should not delegate to the psychologist, or, in fact, to any nonmedical person any matter requiring the exercise of professional medical judgment.

Excerpt from *Ethical Standards of Psychologists* (American Psychological Association, 1979 revision)

Principle 7. Professional Relationships

Paragraph b. Psychologists know and take into account the traditions and practice of other professional groups with which they work and cooperate fully with members of such groups. If a consumer is receiving services from another professional, psychologists do not offer their services directly to the consumer without first informing the professional person already involved so that the risk of confusion and conflict can be avoided.

DAY TEN

The Defendant Continued

All Terry's efforts to become an independent, functioning, decision-making person were wiped away. . . .

—Sara Charles, M.D.

This morning should bring the end of the trial, with closing arguments and jury instructions in the afternoon. The deliberations of the solemn men and women who have sat attentively through the trial will then begin. As we wait in the corridor, Maddux says that a jury is right in over 90 percent of its judgments. A judge alone is right about half as many times. There is a full complement of court buffs on hand as we enter the room.

Murphy concludes his cross-examination with a question he repeats three times. Does Sara deny admitting that she made a clinical error to the man who identified himself as Jack Konig? Yes, Sara answers firmly each time he raises the question. Murphy cites words and phrases from Sara's psychiatric notes again but asks no further questions. Maddux rises for redirect examination. The defense lawyer asks what Sara learned, after the suit was filed, from reading the depositions of Terry Walker and Dr. Waxman about their phone conversations on November 15, 1975.

". . . Their phone calls were, first of all, very lengthy phone calls, as I remember, a half an hour to forty-five minutes. . . there was some communication to Terry that, first of all, maybe her psychotherapist wasn't the right one for her, that maybe she should stop seeing me, that maybe she was sicker than she thought she was. In other words, a number of communications that made her doubt herself more and more as she talked. . . . All Terry's efforts to become an independent, functioning, decision-making person were wiped away. . . ."

November 15, 1975

Terry awakened at about eight o'clock. She could almost touch that familiar pressure from the East Coast. Come home, sleep in your own bed, come back to us. Maybe you could talk to Dr. Waxman. Tell him how you're doing. . . .

Terry paced up and down. She and Dr. Charles had gotten through some difficult times. Maybe, now that Kevin was pulling away, maybe her psychiatrist *was* the one who could help her function on her own. She had faced up to a number of small crises in the last few months. The world hadn't ended. Maybe she could make a life for herself, maybe she could trust people outside the family circle after all.

Terry picked up the phone. She had not planned to. It was then that she heard the phone ringing a third of the way across the country. Dr. Waxman answered. Maybe she shouldn't talk to him now. She lowered the phone toward its cradle, but she could hear the psychologist's voice, thin and filtered, the familiar voice of a man who had gotten to know her family well during Terry's hospitalization in 1971. She raised the phone and began to speak.

"You sound depressed," Waxman said. "You sound quite depressed."

Yes, that was it, that was why she called. She *was* depressed. "Yes, yes, I've been having a terrible time with . . . my . . . therapist. *She* won't pay any attention to me. I've been crying a lot, I've been pacing up and down. . . ." But why had she suddenly started complaining about her psychiatrist?

"Maybe I should talk to your therapist," Waxman proposed.

"No," Terry answered swiftly. "No, I *don't* want you to do that."

"Well, you seem to think she's being destructive toward you. You're upset. This is serious."

"No, I don't want you to speak to her. I'm trying to decide whether I should come to New York for the weekend. My parents want me to come home for the weekend. And I don't know, I just don't know what to do."

The psychologist who had treated her at Cornell Hospital was reassuring.

God, the *hospital.* What's happening anyway? "My brother-in-law called. I've been talking to them. He thinks I need medication. . . ."

"From the way you sound to me, I think he's right. Isn't your psychiatrist giving you any medication?"

"No."

"Terry, this *is* serious. Maybe you should consider not going to her anymore. You might just take that time away from her and look for somebody else. Or at least you shouldn't be so involved with her for a while."

"You mean stop seeing her?"

"Yes, take the hour away. And I think, from the way you sound, that you are in *great* need of medication. If your therapist won't give it to you, you really ought to get it from someone else. This is very serious."

"I don't know. . . ."

"Look, why don't you come home this weekend? You can have a consultation with me. I could see you tomorrow morning. . . ."

Terry mumbled about being uncertain about the trip.

"Listen, Terry, you could come home and we could all put our heads together. But you *do* need medication. You need something strong, something like Mellaril. Do you think you can get your doctor to give it to you? If she won't, you really should get it from somebody else. . . ."

Terry felt dizzy. Waxman thought she was really in trouble, that she needed a powerful medication. She would call Dr. Charles. She was firm about one thing, Waxman was not to call her psychiatrist, not at all.

An hour passed. Terry had talked to Dr. Charles who told her there was no evidence that she needed an antipsychotic drug.

Terry had refused the offer of Librium but she would take up the doctor's offer of a Monday morning appointment. Unless she went to New York. Maybe she should go home after all. And see Dr. Waxman. Waxman said she was in real need of Mellaril. If Dr. Charles wouldn't give it to her, then she *should* turn elsewhere. Yes, Waxman was right. Maybe she should get out of treatment with Dr. Charles. She called Waxman again.

"Yes, Terry, I think you're severely depressed. You're not going through a normal depression. It's more severe than that." This was definitely the time to think of going to another therapist. He would speak both to her parents and to her brother-in-law, Dr. Walston. Mellaril was what Terry needed, Mellaril and a new therapist.

"I don't know what to do," Terry replied, confused, hesitant, close to being overwhelmed. "I don't want to be a bad patient."

"Look, Terry, maybe you really ought to come home. You sound in bad shape to me. You're running in circles."

"You mean this isn't normal, what I'm going through?"

"Oh, no, this isn't normal at all. You're severely depressed. You're not going through something normal at all. And I've got to talk to your family, to your brother-in-law, so we can do something about this. . . ."

By the time she heard again from Waxman, he had told her father that some intervention between Terry and her psychiatrist was absolutely essential. The psychologist would work out a plan. He spoke by phone with Dr. Walston in Boston and they agreed on the need for Mellaril. Waxman then contacted Dr. Howard Morrow who had been head of the unit at Cornell Hospital in White Plains when Terry was a patient there. Morrow had never treated Terry directly, and drugs had never been prescribed for her during hospitalization. But the intervention was required, Waxman explained, and if Morrow would phone in a prescription for Mellaril to a drugstore near the Walker home, Terry's father would pick it up and fly it out to Chicago. What did Morrow think? The matter was settled, the prescription called in. Mr. Walker picked it up and headed for LaGuardia Airport.

Terry spoke to Waxman again. He did not tell her of the makeshift plan he had constructed and set into motion. There was plenty of time for her father to get to Chicago with the Mellaril. "I'm worried about what's happening," Terry said, "about whether there will be any repercussions in my graduate program." She was not to worry, Waxman said, everything would be all right. Terry certainly wasn't suicidal. She didn't mention anything like that at all. Waxman wanted to buy a little time—and Terry seemed calm again—just time enough for Mr. Walker to get himself and the Mellaril to Chicago.

Waxman's phone rang at five minutes to four. It was Terry. She was upset again. "I don't know whether to come to New York or not," she said. "I just don't know. . . ."

Mr. Walker was on his way already. It didn't make sense for Terry to wrestle with a decision about coming to New York herself.

"Terry, I want to tell you something," Waxman said. "You've really been running in circles. You're in bad shape and you need medication. We've talked about that. I've got it all arranged."

"What do you mean?" Terry asked uncertainly.

"Your father's on his way out to Chicago . . ."

"My father's coming?" Her voice trailed off.

"Yes, yes, your father's on his way. And when he gets there you can figure everything out. . . . Do you hear me?"

"Yes," Terry answered absently. Her father was coming. Again.

"Terry, are you all right?"

"Yes," she answered flatly.

"Look, Terry, I want to know if you're okay. Will you be okay until your father gets there?"

"Yes." Terry seemed quiet, glum, drifting away from the conversation. The psychologist hung up, satisfied that she was all right.

Terry stared down at the phone. What in God's name was happening? Why had she started this whole thing? She hung up the phone and stood absolutely still. My God. My father's coming to get me, to take me out of school. It's the same thing all over again. They'll put me in the hospital. She felt a quiver of fear run through her body.

Terry felt a surge of panic. Dislodge the first stone and the whole mountain comes tumbling down on you.

She opened the window and climbed out on the fire escape. She had blown up a real emergency this time. She had gotten everybody to listen this time. Waxman said she wasn't getting anywhere with her doctor, that she was sicker than she thought, that she needed strong medication. . . .

Terry stepped onto the roof and looked up at the gray November sky. She made a half circle and sat sideways on the parapet. Four stories below the last yellow autumnal leaves, clotted and worn, lay in the gutters of Dearborn Street. It would soon be dark.

Terry shivered as she gazed down. What had she started? Had there ever really been a chance for freedom? Terry, this isn't normal. You're seriously depressed. You need Mellaril. Take the hour away from her. Come home, sleep in your own bed.

She would have to go home this time or do something drastic. The little life she had carved out and the way she had been able to handle it on her own, that was all over. Come home. You're seriously depressed. The hospital again . . .

Terry slipped off the roof in a crazy, splay-legged descent, falling swiftly, the charcoal sky and the bonelike tree limbs swirling about her, falling down, down, falling freely for the last time. . . .

The jurors are frozen in concentration as Sara describes the psychologist's interventions. His suggestions by long distance phone could, Sara says, "be interpreted as a major stress. . . . Terry had decided on her own therapist, taken some pains to choose a person she thought she could work with. And here she was being told, by long distance, 'You made a bad decision.' " Murphy objects strongly but is overruled as Maddux asks Sara about Terry's own explanation for her leap.

"One of the things she told me," Sara says, "was she thought she had jumped because she thought her family was going to come and take her out of school. . . . School was very important to her. It was one of the ways she was developing and maturing and making progress in her own life. I think school was extremely important to her."

Could Terry's condition have changed rapidly during the hours after she had spoken to Sara on the morning of November 15, 1975? Maddux asks.

"I think there's no question it can occur that rapidly. . . . These people are not able to modulate their internal feelings. They can have a stress they can't process very well . . . I think certainly in fifteen, twenty minutes."

"Less than an hour?" Maddux asks.

"I would think so."

"No further questions," Maddux says, the spell of intense concentration that has settled on the court unbroken, as he turns away.

After a recess Murphy again questions Sara from her personal psychiatric notes. Then Sara is excused.

"Is there any rebuttal testimony from the plaintiff?" Judge McGarr asks. Murphy huddles with Terry Walker, stands and asks for another recess. He wants to reflect on whether or not to put Terry back on the stand. He speaks to her again. She sits unmoving, unresponsive to his whispered words, his gesturing hands. The court is called to order and Murphy stands, head down, eyes averted. There will be no rebuttal, he says and sits down.

McGarr turns to the members of the jury, who have barely changed their positions all morning long. "We have completed the presentation of the evidence in the case. As in any other trial the things that remain to be done are these: The attorneys and I confer as to the legal instructions concerning the law you are to apply, which I give you." McGarr speaks mellifluously, dispassionately. "When the process is completed we have the closing arguments, in which the lawyers will argue to you what they think the evidence means and what inferences you should draw from it, and what verdict you should return. I then instruct you in the law and then you retire to deliberate. . . . Come back at two and we'll start the final stages of the case."

Closing Arguments

You are not partisans, you're not for either side. You're the judges, judges of the facts. Your sole interest and your duty is to ascertain the truth from the evidence of the case.

—Judge J. Frank McGarr

There are no spectator seats left after everyone crowds into the courtroom. Several lawyers have come and Maddux has allowed his office staff to attend as well. What have these quiet, intense jurors made of the proceedings? Will concern for the shattered young woman caught forever in the iron jaws of a wheelchair move them to find in her favor?

Maddux and Sara sit quietly at the defendant's table while Murphy bends close to Terry Walker. Her father, alone of her

family, sits across the aisle from me. We all rise as the judge
enters. McGarr looks puzzled as he sees the jam-packed court
He thinks that a new pool of prospective jurors has mistakenly
come into his courtroom. "Take your cards and go downstairs,"
he says. Maddux explains that they are spectators here for the
final arguments. McGarr signals for the jury members to be
brought in and he explains that all parties have agreed to allow
the two alternate jurors to join their six fellows in the deliberations. There are time limits to the closing arguments, he says
and then nods to Murphy, "Go ahead, Counsel."

Murphy stands up, gestures toward Terry as he begins to speak
The case involves "two decent women, one of whom made an
error, and the other who has suffered because of an error made
by the first party. At the beginning of the case I told you I was
going to make a contract. . . . I was going to show you that Dr.
Charles either did not take an adequate history . . . or if she
did have an adequate history, that she simply failed to act on
what she knew. We told you that we would show you that a lot
of things went on in this therapy. Terry Walker became worse
and worse. And that's reflected in Dr. Charles's notes." The attorney reviews his arguments about these notes, claiming that in
and by themselves, they support his case. He is not asking for
sympathy, he just wants the jurors to understand that the notes
can be perceived in different ways.

Terry was, Murphy now says, a borderline personality. He
reviews her 1971 hospitalization, claiming that she was then on
suicide precautions, and circles back to insist that Dr. Charles's
notes show that Terry was deteriorating during the period of
treatment. "She didn't pay any attention to her notes, she just
made a serious, grievous error. . . ." He quotes from the notes
again, cites the opinions of his experts. Murphy again criticizes
defense expert Levitt as a political appointee who "approved the
use of experimental drugs in patients" when he was head of the
Illinois Department of Mental Health. He recites from Sara's notes
once more and describes again the telephone call from Dr. Walston. "She *knew* what Walston said. What more do we need?"

Sara should have increased her visits with Terry, she should
have hospitalized her. Why, Murphy asks, did Terry jump off the
roof? "Terry Walker jumped because she was going down the
slippery, slimy . . . slope of insanity." He lists the people Terry
called during the days before her leap. None of them had the

obligation to stop her. "The obligation is on the person she paid . . . to do it! And that person did not do it!"

Murphy mentions Jack Konig. The jurors will remember that when Dr. Charles gave her testimony she looked at Maddux and at them. "Three times Mr. Maddux asked her the question, 'Did you tell Mr. Konig and Mr. Walker that you made a clinical error?' *Three times* she looked at the floor and said, 'No.' She did not look at you! And this morning I asked her *three more times!* She looked off in this direction." He flicks his left hand, bears down. "She did not look at you on any one of the six occasions. You go back and talk among yourselves. *You* decide if any of those six times Dr. Charles looked at you in response to those two questions. *She never did.* And that's precisely why I asked her again today. *Three* times. . . ." Murphy seems tired, flat, drained, as he urges the jurors to "go back in the jury room without prejudice, without sympathy, and come back with a verdict on behalf of Terry Walker." He turns back, "Thank you very much."

Maddux walks across the well of the court. He explains to the jury that Murphy, in his coming rebuttal comments, must limit himself to what Maddux now discusses. He will not talk about damages because, in the absence of liability, there will be no reason for the members of the jury to consider damages against Dr. Charles. This is the time to speak about proof. "Who has the burden of proof?" he asks, sweeping the eight jurors with his eyes. "Whose is it? It is the person who brings the action. . . . What we mean, under the law, by burden of proof is that the propositions which you must prove is more probably true than not true." He pauses, steps closer to the jury box. "Think of it in terms of symbolism. You've all seen the statute of Lady Justice. That's symbolic of what we mean by the burden of proof and what happens in a court of law." He extends his hands, open palms up, at the level of his chest. "You recall seeing the statue. She is blindfolded, has a sword in one hand and scales in the other hand. And the blindfold is because—as we talked about a good deal here—sympathy, prejudice, and other emotions, and human feelings shouldn't be used in deciding a case like this. . . ." He raises his open hands a fraction of an inch as he continues. "One side of the scales represents the plaintiff, the other side the defendant. When they start, the scales are even. And unless the plaintiff tips that scale in their favor" Maddux lowers his right hand slightly "they have not sustained the burden of proof. That is done only if they tip in favor of the plaintiff by the evidence that's produced in court. Not by argument, not speculation, guess, or conjecture—but by evidence." He drops his hands slowly to his sides and stands back.

He reminds the jurors that during his opening statement Murphy had challenged Maddux to write down the items he pledged himself to prove, and to hold him to it. Because of the lack of substance, the defense attorney had a hard time making any notes. "Except . . ." and Maddux raises his hand "I did hear it said—specifically, pointedly, and clearly—that it would be proved to you, ladies and gentlemen, that the plaintiff, at the time she was being treated by Dr. Charles, was psychotic and manic-depressive. . . ."

Murphy interrupts, claiming that he never said such things. "The objection is noted," McGarr says, and Maddux observes that in the testimony of every expert and witness Murphy has developed no "evidence that the plaintiff was at anytime psychotic." Maddux scans the jury box slowly. "The contract was breached. That was *never* proved. So, what's next?"

He moves halfway back toward the defense table, explaining once more the distinction between a psychotic and a person with a borderline personality disorder. Terry was the latter; she was not slipping down any slope of craziness. Psychotherapy is the proper treatment for someone suffering such a developmental problem. The experience of this treatment causes them anger and frustration and a number of other emotions. "But it does not mean that they are psychotic. It does mean, as Dr. Schwarz and Dr. Rubin agreed, that she knows the nature and quality of her act. . . . she may be more influenced by impulse, anxiety, and feelings that she's not worth much . . . but it does not mean that she doesn't know what she's doing and can't control what she's doing."

Murphy objects, claiming that there is no evidence that Terry could control herself. The jury will make up its own mind about that, Judge McGarr says, and Maddux picks up his argument. The plaintiff must, according to the law, prove four things. If she fails to prove even one of these, then the conditions for sustaining the burden of proof have not been met. "The plaintiff has to prove that she was using ordinary care for her own safety at the time of her injury. She has to prove the defendant, Dr.

Charles, was negligent, as defined in the instructions relating to the duty of the physician. She must prove that she, herself, was free of any negligence. She must prove that Dr. Charles was solely negligent—and that the negligence of Dr. Charles alone was what we call the proximate cause of her injury."

Murphy objects again, denying that the judge will read such an instruction. "The jury will hear the instruction when I read it," McGarr says. Maddux explains the concept of "ordinary care"—the obligation everyone shares to watch out for their own safety. To excuse Terry from the obligation of using ordinary care, the plaintiff's lawyer must prove "that her mental condition was such that there was an inability—or a disability, a lack of power—to use ordinary care. *That,* ladies and gentlemen, was the plaintiff's burden of proof. During the course of the examination of the psychiatrists . . . there *was not one* question asked of the plaintiff about that topic. *I* asked the only questions. It is not *my* burden of proof. It is that of the plaintiff. If I were the plaintiff, I would establish that by the very presence here of. . . ."

Murphy objects again and Maddux counters with his own objection to the continuing interruptions. The judge overrules the objection. "What this really means," the defense lawyer continues, "is that it isn't fair, right, or just for me to collect damages for injuries that I caused myself, from somebody else. . . ." He moves on to the argument for Dr. Charles's supposed negligence, saying that no proof of it has been introduced into the courtroom. "The only evidence of any erratic behavior on the part of this young woman were these phone calls. But that's it." What would happen, Maddux asks, if, as the plaintiff's experts have suggested, Dr. Charles had had the police pick Terry up and lock her in a hospital? 'Another psychiatrist examines her and says, 'What's going on?' Well, she's been making phone calls for these past couple of weeks.' They'd let her right out." Maddux circles around until he faces the jurors directly again.

"You're asked to believe that she was so nonfunctioning . . . that she wasn't psychotic, but that she was the same as psychotic. And in that last week, for example, what was going on?" Maddux speaks of Dr. Charles's personal notes. "You'll see that there was an intensity that developed in the fall of 1975 because Terry was beginning to react to the treatment. Read the notes and see if they paint the picture of a horror story of somebody who is in serious mental difficulty." He sweeps the air with a gesture.

"Would anybody get back on the stand and rebut what was said?"
He pauses and outlines Terry's activities during the week before
she jumped. Going to class, doing interviews in a psychiatric hospital. Wednesday, her father came, and found her a little nervous
but otherwise all right. "Thursday night she goes to the movies,
out on a date, normal behavior after that. Friday, interviews a
patient in a mental hospital. Goes to pay a traffic ticket, goes to
the wrong place, do it next week. Out to dinner with a girlfriend
and to the movies. Got home, called the parents at midnight.
That is absolutely inconsistent with this frenetic, breaking down,
minimally functioning, psychotic picture that people want you
to believe."

Maddux speaks more intensely, "And the proof of that is demonstrated by the people you *didn't* hear from the witness stand.
You *didn't* hear from the boyfriend who was in close contact with
her, you *didn't* hear it from the girlfriend. You *didn't* hear it from
her supervisors—psychologists in the clinic where she was supervised. You *didn't* hear it from any of her social friends, school
friends, or anybody else that anything wrong was going on. Because there *wasn't* anything wrong going on." Maddux takes a
breath. When an expert such as Rubin says that Terry could be
falling apart without anybody else knowing it, "I don't buy that
for a minute. Nor does anybody else."

Murphy objects. "All the books say the opposite!"

"Counsel," Judge McGarr says, "*that* is an inappropriate objection. Stop interrupting Counsel's argument."

Maddux reminds the jury that most of the time in the trial
has been spent on Terry's hospitalization in 1971. The plaintiff
has charged that Dr. Charles was negligent in not getting the
records of that experience. "When you examine those records,
what do you find? She went to that hospital in New York complaining that she was theatrical. Standing by the window: putting her
leg out the window." That was not a true suicide attempt and
has no relevance to the present case. The jury will be able to
examine the hospital records and see for themselves.

Maddux reviews the testimony of the experts, concluding by
proposing to explain "what really happened." Dr. Charles made
no errors. "There was an error made by the plaintiff, at the instiga-
tion of Waxman and her family." During treatment, Terry learned
that she could not manipulate and control Dr. Charles. "So she
started calling her family . . . [to] get in control of them. And

what happened? They responded. The brother-in-law at Harvard jumped in and suggested that maybe she needs medicine. He talked that over with Dr. Charles. Dr. Charles doesn't think she needs an antipsychotic drug. She's not psychotic, she never was psychotic. And she was all right. What Dr. Waxman did when he was called on a Saturday morning—he had not had this girl in treatment for several years—he told her exactly what she should not have heard. . . . He told her, 'You're sick, and you're sicker than you think you are.' And that wasn't good medicine. That is *not* what she needed. She wanted her independence; she was in therapy. When she acted up on it before, they drugged her and put her in the hospital. This time when she acted up, they responded. The last of these *four* phone calls with Dr. Waxman—alone and not involved with Dr. Charles at all—he told her 'Your father is coming from New York and he's got the medicine.' If she was crying out for help, looking for somebody to hear her, it is amazing that at this point she would walk up to the roof and jump. You would think she'd be relieved if that was what was really going on." Maddux stands for a moment in the veil of quiet that has descended on the room. "What that did to her, as she told me, after that phone call, 'I had communicated an emergency. My father was on the way from New York, I decided I was going to have to do something drastic and went on the roof and I jumped.' Terry told the same thing to her mother afterward. She thought school and independence was gone. Back to New York, in the hospital. And she jumped." Maddux reminds the jury that all this occurred several hours after Terry's last conversation with Dr. Charles. "Has the plaintiff sustained [the] burden of proof? They have not. Dr. Charles's treatment . . . was not the cause of [Terry's] injury. The cause of her injury was her own conduct instigated by Dr. Waxman. It *is* a tragedy, but it is *not* the fault of Dr. Charles." Maddux thanks the jury for their attention and takes his seat next to Sara as Murphy stands up for the five minutes of rebuttal allowed to the plaintiff.

Murphy raises the issue of damages, calculating the costs of hospitalization and continued care for Terry at three-quarters of a million dollars. Maddux objects that this is not proper rebuttal material but the judge allows him to go on. Murphy continues, 'You've got to decide about pain and anguish and suffering. What it's like to be disfigured and what it's like not to experience sex, what Terry has to live like for the rest of her life." He gestures toward the plaintiff. "You saw the movies. . . ." He charges again that Dr. Charles never understood what was going on, that she made a clinical error, that her notes prove that Terry Walker was falling apart under her care. "Would that she had been put in a hospital in 1975! If she were, she would not be the helpless vegetable in a wheelchair today, unable to go through all the experiences you and I can concerning sex, going to the bathroom by herself, getting up, going for a walk on the beach—as Dr Charles can, as you and I can." He derides the idea that a border line could fall apart in four to five hours. "The evidence here is more like three to four months." He thanks the jury for their time. "We are asking for the only verdict which is reasonable in this case. And that is one for a substantial amount of damages for Terry Walker." He remains standing for a second or two and then sits down.

There is a brief interval of silence that is broken by the creak of the judge's chair. McGarr clears his throat. "Thank you, Counsel." The jurors focus tightly on McGarr, as he begins his instructions.

Their duty is to determine the facts without letting sympathy or prejudice influence them. McGarr has not meant, he says, by anything he has said or done, to express preference for either side in this case. "You are the sole and exclusive judges of the facts. . . . You have a right to consider all the evidence in the light of your own observation and experience in the affairs of life." The judge clears his throat again. "Or, to put it much more simply, you have a right to use your common sense." They are also to judge the credibility of the various witnesses, taking into account their ability and opportunity to observe, their manner their interest, biases, and their reasonableness. They are to consider the facts, whatever their source, in determining whether a proposition has been proved. Circumstantial evidence may prove a fact. If it is shown that a witness has said something during the trial that is at variance with statements given earlier, the juror can take that into account in judging the witnesses' credibility. "When I say that the party has the burden of proof on any subject . . . I mean that you must be persuaded, considering all the evidence in the case, that the proposition . . . is more probably true than not true."

A doctor who practices in a particular specialty must "possess and apply the knowledge and use the skill and care which reasonably well-qualified specialists in the same field, practicing in the same locality, ordinarily would use in similar cases and circumstances. The failure of a doctor to do this is a form of negligence which we call malpractice." McGarr explains that the jurors can only make a determination on this from the evidence given by expert witnesses. They are not to follow anything else, not their own knowledge "of a friend who is ill, or doctor you know, or anything of that sort."

The plaintiff, the judge explains, must prove each of the four propositions to which Maddux referred in his closing argument: that she was using ordinary care for her own safety, "taking into consideration the nature and severity of any mental illness that you may decide the plaintiff was afflicted with." Secondly, she must prove that the defendant acted in the negligent ways charged. The plaintiff must also prove that she was injured and that the negligence of the defendant was the proximate cause of these injuries. "If you find from your consideration of all the evidence," McGarr says solemnly, "that each of these propositions has been proved, then your verdict should be for the plaintiff. If, on the other hand, you find from your consideration of all the evidence that any one of the propositions has not been proved, then your verdict should be for the defendant."

McGarr describes ordinary care as it was then understood in Illinois law, as that which "a reasonably careful person would use under the circumstances similar to those shown by the evidence in this case. The law does not say how a reasonably careful person would act under every circumstance. That is for you to decide." Negligence, he adds, means "the failure to do something that a reasonably careful person would do—under circumstances similar to those shown in this case." Again, in this case, that is for the jury to decide.

McGarr reviews the damages that may be assessed if the jury concludes that the defendant is liable in the case. Then he speaks to the jurors in more paternal tones. "The verdict must represent the considered judgment of each juror. In order to return a verdict it is necessary that each juror agree. Your verdict, in other words, must be unanimous." He urges them to be impartial but not to hesitate to reexamine their views if they become convinced that it is erroneous. But they are not to give up their honest convictions because of the opinions of their fellow jurors, or just to reach a verdict. "You are not partisans, you're not for either side. You're the judges, judges of the facts. Your sole interest and your duty is to ascertain the truth from the evidence of the case."

Their first task, McGarr says, is to elect "a foreperson" to preside over their deliberations. The exhibits will be brought to them, as will two verdict forms, one for the plaintiff and one for the defendant. Each juror must sign the form that represents their judgment in the case. "You will retire to commence your deliberations at this time. We do not expect to keep you into the evening hours so, if you have not reached a verdict, you will come back on Monday. Don't worry about time. The important thing is to do a thorough, good, and conscientious job. . . ." The marshal will assist them. If they have any questions they should submit them to McGarr in writing.

It is a solemn moment as the jurors file out of the courtroom and we are left, as we started, plaintiff and defendant waiting for an end to the waiting. The judge calls the attorneys forward, showing them the jury forms that will be used, asking them to get their exhibits together so that the marshal can bring them into the jury room. It is twenty minutes to four. "I suggest we confer about five o'clock. . . . If we don't have a verdict then, we'll decide what to do. . . ."

Terry Walker rides her wheelchair out of the courtroom and down the hallway to the elevators while her father, flanked by Murphy and his partner, Jerome Goldberg, takes a seat in the nearby alcove. The area is crowded with spectators talking among themselves about the possible outcome of the trial. Maddux lights a cigarette and glances at his watch. He must fly to Canada later that evening for a seminar on trial law. He speaks quietly to Tom Boodell. "If you don't have a verdict by Monday, ask for a mistrial. . . ."

The jurors sit around the table in the room set aside for their deliberations. They elect Thomas Scarborough, a dark-haired, husky man in his thirties who is an executive with the International Harvester Company, as foreman. "Well," he says, glancing around at the men and women with whom he has served for ten days, "before we begin our deliberations, I think it would be helpful if we had a show of hands so we can see where we stand. . . ."

Out in the courtroom two platoons of lawyers have infiltrated the small space at the end of the trial. McGarr listens patiently as the spokesman for one group requests a temporary restraining order in a case between the Pullman Company and the J. J. McDermott Company. "When this lawsuit was filed on the ninth of July. . . ."

The court buffs keep their distance as the minutes slowly tick off. Murphy and Goldberg walk down the hallway, leaving Mr. Walker sitting alone. An hour passes.

Suddenly a woman assistant of the judge breaks through the people clustered around us. "They've reached a verdict," she says excitedly. We rise, take a deep breath, and walk back toward the courtroom for the last time. We must still wait for several minutes until the Pullman case lawyers leave and we can walk in. McGarr sits solemnly at his high desk. He reviews some technical matters with the lawyers and everyone moves into position. Murphy and Goldberg stand at the plaintiff's table. Terry will not be present for the verdict. Maddux and Sara are in their places and the jurors, still poker faced, follow the marshal into the room.

"Please be seated," McGarr says. "I apologize for keeping you waiting in the jury room. I was in the middle of another hearing and I wasn't able to cut it short. Do I understand that you've reached a verdict?"

"We have," Tom Scarborough replies.

"Has the appropriate verdict form been signed?"

"Yes, sir." Scarborough hands the signed verdict to the marshal who hands it to Judge McGarr. He glances at it and hands it down to the clerk. "Would you read that, please?" It is ten minutes after five.

The clerk reads in automatic, unemotional tones: "76 C 3782. Verdict. We the jury find for the defendant and against the plaintiff."

Goldberg touches a hand of consolation to Murphy's back. Maddux beams as I step past him to embrace Sara. We hold each other for a long moment.

When Thomas Scarborough, in his first act as foreman, asked his fellow jurors for a show of hands he discovered that they were already unanimously agreed in their decision.

Patrick Murphy made a motion for a new trial on July 28, 1980. It was denied by Judge McGarr on July 30, 1980. There was no appeal.

* * *

What determines the plaintiff's probability of winning a judgment?

An award was more likely if the injury was permanent rather than temporary, and the probability was highest if the injury was fatal. The evidence seems to support the allegation that courts relax the negligence standard in cases of severe injury. However, this is merely a possible, not a necessary, conclusion; evidence from a study of injuries affirms that the more severe the injury, the more likely it was due to negligence instead of normal risk. The courts may simply be reflecting that fact.

> —"The Resolution of Medical Malpractice Claims,"
> by Patricia Munch Danzon and Lee A. Lillard.
> The Institute of Civil Justice,
> The Rand Corporation, 1982

Going Home

As we held each other I realized what we might have lost had the verdict, for whatever reason, gone the other way. I remembered how Sara, on one difficult day during the years of preparation and waiting, had looked up from reviewing the accusations that had been made against her and said softly, "If I am found guilty of malpractice over this, I will never practice medicine again." She had said it again as we lunched alone on the last day of the trial.

What hung in the balance, I painfully realized, was Sara's whole sense of herself as physician, her identification with the profession at which she worked so conscientiously. I knew better than anyone her intense concern for her patients, her untiring efforts to place their welfare ahead of everything else. Found negligent, she would never be the same again—and maybe we wouldn't, either—for charges of professional malpractice aim finally at the soul and spirit.

Sara went back to work the following Monday morning. Some colleagues asked her if she had been away on vacation. Slowly, the pace of ordinary life picked up again. Our troubles were small compared to those borne by so many others. But we know the cost, the effort, the stress of ordeal by trial and we understand, as we never otherwise could, how and why this kind of experience has so profoundly changed the lives of so many other people.

This experience is draining the vitality of American doctors and subtly affecting everybody's health care. There are, as we have come to feel, no real winners in the crisis of malpractice litigation. That is why we wrote this book; the first sections tell our story, the next section involves every American.

PART IV

The Patients

UNDERSTANDING THE MALPRACTICE LITIGATION CRISIS

The decision of the jury brought to an end almost five intense years of engagement with the legal system. To pass through the long months of preparation for trial for medical negligence resembles being swept up by a powerful current that carries you where it will and finally deposits you, slightly disoriented but substantially the same, back at the point where it first took possession of you. Nothing has changed. Or has it? I was grateful for the opportunity to have my case heard in court before a jury of average Americans, and the experience gave me a deepened faith in the jury system and in the tight, highly disciplined court procedures. Those who find themselves falsely accused in any circumstances have a much better chance of getting at the truth by this route than through any of the other approaches, such as settlements or arbitration panels, which have been suggested as substitutes for trial by jury. The adversarial style and the court rules, such as those about evidence and testimony, are evolutionary products that fit the human pursuit of justice and truth very well. I believe that if more people, including accused doctors, saw their cases to trial and won them, fewer nuisance or frivolous suits would be initiated in the first place. In law, as in war, there is no substitute for victory.

I experienced, however, no sense of victory after the trial. I am not sure that other persons who receive a favorable verdict after a long and emotionally draining effort to defend themselves and their reputations experience anything resembling that. There is always too much sadness and disruption for everyone concerned on both sides of the case. I had wanted to have the truth emerge. That is different from wanting to defeat someone else. There had been too much pain for everybody to want any feeling of triumph. It is difficult to make sense of such an involvement, to see it whole, or to view it in a larger perspective of events, or to know whether one has grown or diminished because of it. What, a person must ask, is the point of this? Is there something to learn? Or is it just one of those things that must be put behind oneself in order to get on with life?

What was the impact on the profession I knew best, medicine, and on those who practiced it? Were there side effects that were not immediately obvious, especially since it was clear to me from my own experience and from what I had learned about that of others, that doctors accused of medical negligence did not talk much to anybody, least of all their colleagues, about the nature of their experience? How many doctors were being accused of malpractice and had their reactions been in anyway similar to my own? Who were they and how were they coping with the stress of a phenomenon that could so powerfully invade one's personal life and professional practice? How was it affecting patient care?

The number of suits alleging medical negligence, I learned, was increasing steadily. Did this indicate a massive failure of medicine, as some claimed, or an explosion of litigation that had taken on a life and momentum of its own, as others insisted? Was the malpractice phenomenon a function of other dynamics in the nation's cultural life, its generation-long conflict with authority, for example, or had it all happened randomly through a strange, unpredictable, and perhaps even unrelated series of circumstances? Was medicine—or any other profession—improving because of the intense scrutiny of procedures that accompanies the growing consciousness of litigation for professional negligence? These are only some of the issues, I discovered after the trial, about which little, if any, data existed. I decided to tell the story of my own experience and to try to find the answers to these questions at the same time.

S.C.C.

THE SCOPE OF
MALPRACTICE LITIGATION

The Facts

How extensive is medical malpractice litigation? Not even the American Medical Association has a ready or accurate answer. Dr. James Todd, an Executive Vice-President of the AMA, suggests that in any given year, one in four physicians can expect to be sued. ("MD's hit, attorneys defend tort system, contingency fees," *American Medical News*, 25 [1982]:3). Yet no nationwide tracking system exists to follow trends in litigation, jury verdicts, or awards in medical malpractice cases.

Surveys of physicians indicate to some degree the extent of the problem. Seventy-three percent of obstetrician-gynecologists have had at least one professional liability claim filed against them ("Professional Liability Insurance and Its Effect: Report of a Survey of ACOG's Membership," *American College of Obstetricians and Gynecologists*, November 1985). The average incidence of claims increased significantly across all specialties, from 3.0 claims per hundred physicians prior to 1980 to 8.6 claims per hundred physicians during the years 1980 to 1984. (American Medical Association, Chicago, *Socioeconomic Monitoring System Report* 4 [March

1985]: 2). A 1984 study by the AMA Task Force on Professional Liability and Insurance revealed that obstetrician-gynecologists and general surgeons, including orthopedic surgeons and neurosurgeons, generated more suits than doctors in other specialties; in 19 of 30 reporting MD-owned insurance companies, these physicians had an average 34.5 percent of all claims, although comprising only 19 percent of all policy-holders (American Medical Association, "Professional Liability in the '80's," *Report 1* [October 1984]: 11). Those practicing in the Midwest have experienced a greater percentage increase (225.3 percent) in claims incidence from 1979 to 1983 than have doctors in other regions of the country ("Professional Liability in the '80's," *op. cit.,* p. 12).

Insurance companies have also attempted to monitor the trends in medical liability. Claims reached 16 to 20 per hundred physicians in 1983–84, quadrupling the number of claims reported in the late 1970's and early 1980's by the St. Paul Insurance Companies ("Malpractice: Balancing the Issues," *Ambulatory Care* [June 1985]: 9). An AMACO analysis in September 1984 of reports from 23 physician-owned insurance companies revealed that incidence more than doubled in the past five years, rising from a national average of 12.2 to 20.3 claims per physician. For these companies, 91 claims or suits are filed every working day ("Professional Liability in the '80's," *op. cit.,* p. 10). The physician-owned insurance company in Illinois, the Illinois State Medical Inter-Insurance Exchange (ISMIE) reported for the year 1984–85 2,647 suits against its 9,348 insureds. The most extensive analysis to date is the study published in 1980 by the National Association of Insurance Commissioners. This survey analyzed over 71,000 malpractice insurance closed claims—that is, claims that had been disposed of by having the claim dropped, settled, or tried to verdict—from 128 malpractice insurers. Although this study provides one of the first glimpses of the magnitude and extent of malpractice claims, it includes only those closed between 1975 and 1978. It is limited because it does not include open claims still in process against hospitals and doctors, because a number of insurers did not participate, and because some claims for compensation were closed without legal action against the doctor or hospital. Absolute incidences of malpractice litigation, therefore, are not included, but important data regarding the types of injuries precipitating claims and amounts of indemnity paid are cited. For example, the study notes that physicians who include minor surgery in their practices account for the most paid claims and the largest percentage of indemnity paid for physician defendants, but in terms of average claim size, neurosurgeons and anesthesiologists had the most expensive claims (*Closed Claim Study*, Brookfield, Wis.: National Association of Insurance Commissioners, 1980).

Accurate data are available from the private reporting services that gather information regarding legal actions and are subscribed to by many in the legal profession and insurance industry. These are usually located only within or close to large urban areas, such as Chicago and San Francisco, and report only for these regions. *The Cook County Jury Verdict Reporter (CCJVR),* for example, is a private, weekly subscription newsletter that lists suits filed, names of participants, and trial data on all cases in Cook and the surrounding eight counties in northern Illinois. From 1980 to 1984 inclusive, in an area where approximately 19,761 physicians practice, there were 9,873 doctors (with allowances for repeated suits in some instances) named in malpractice complaints.' ("Index of Medical Malpractice Suits," *Cook County Jury Verdict Reporter,* 1980–84).

In this jurisdiction in 1985, 4,488 physicians were named as defendants, and the total number of suits filed (3,166) represented a 54.7 percent increase over the number of suits filed in 1984 ("Index of Medical Malpractice Suits," *Cook County Jury Verdict Reporter,* 1985). Although this information pertains only to a large urban area, and data are available indicating that the most powerful predictor of claim frequency and severity is urbanization (P. M. Danzon, *The Frequency and Severity of Medical Malpractice Claims,* Rand Report R-2870, Institute of Civil Justice, Santa Monica, Calif.: Rand Corporation, 1982), there does appear, nonetheless, to be a progressive increase in the number of suits alleging medical negligence filed against doctors.

The Disposition of Claims

Once a claim is filed, what happens to it? Information about this aspect of malpractice litigation is also somewhat sketchy, but the sources cited previously give some impressions regarding this process. A Rand study, which used as its base closed claim data from 1974 to 1976, found that 43 percent of claims were dropped without payment, 51 percent were settled out of court by payment to the plaintiff, and 7 percent were litigated to verdict with the plaintiff winning approximately one in four cases (P. M. Danzon and L. Lillard, *The Resolution of Medical Malpractice Claims*, Rand Report R-2793, Institute of Civil Justice, Santa Monica, Calif.: Rand Corporation, 1982, p. 4). There may be some slight shifts discernible as more is learned about trends in malpractice litigation. In the closed claim study that analyzed data for the years 1975 to 1978, 62.3 percent were closed without payment to the claimant. According to this same study, in 1975 only 7 percent of claims were disposed of in court, but three years later, 18 percent of cases went to trial. In 1975, plaintiffs won two out of ten cases, and in 1978, only one in ten cases (*Closed Claim Study*, pp. 161–162 and 21). In civil litigation in general, plaintiffs have become increasingly successful over the last twenty years, winning about 51 percent of all trials (M. A. Peterson and G. L. Priest, *The Civil Jury*, Rand Report R-2881, Institute of Civil Justice, Santa Monica, Calif.: Rand Corporation, 1982). In medical malpractice cases, however, defendant physicians have tended to win over two-thirds of the cases. In one jurisdiction in 1983, defendant physicians won 81.7 percent of their trials ("1983 Calendar Year Summary and Index of Malpractice Trials," *Cook County Jury Verdict Reporter*, Chicago: 1984).

A radical shift in this trend occurred in 1984 within this jurisdiction. For the first time in history, defendant physicians won less than 70 percent of their trials: of the sixty doctors who went to trial, only 57.6 percent were judged not negligent. It has been suggested that this change is attributable to an Illinois law, effective as of September 1979, which was strongly supported by trial attorneys and which changed the tort basis for compensation from contributory negligence to comparative negligence. In contributory negligence, if a plaintiff contributes toward the proximate cause of the injury in question, no compensation is granted. Comparative negligence introduces more liberal rules for assessing degrees of liability. The lag time between the filing of a suit and the trial date in this jurisdiction may explain the delay of its impact until five years after its effective date: in 1984 there is not only an increase in the number of verdicts against physicians but in the amount of money awarded as well. In 1985 this reversed back to the original trend. Seventy-seven percent of the MD/DO's who went to trial were found not guilty of malpractice.

The Illinois State Medical Inter-Insurance Exchange, which

provides liability insurance for approximately 55 percent to 60 percent of Illinois physicians, reported data on its ten-year history as of December 31, 1985. Eighty-two percent of the 6,868 closed claims (most claimed through negligence charges) have been resolved without indemnity payments (no payment to the plaintiff), and of the 236 cases that went to trial, 173 (73 percent) resulted in a verdict favorable to the defendant with 8 (3 percent) resulting in a hung jury. Even though no indemnity was paid in 82 percent of the claims, expense payments (legal fees, photocopying, etc.) amounted to $18,253,949.54. Expense payments for open cases/claims is reported to be over $28 million dollars (ISMIE Loss Analysis, Claim and Suit Status by Policy Year, *12/31/85 Report*).

Claims that are either settled or adjudicated by trial have, however, resulted in escalating monetary awards. Between 1975 and 1978, the average award per paid claim increased 70 percent from $26,565 to $45,187, with inflation contributing only 28 percent to the increase. Indemnity payments, defined as total dollar losses paid by insurance companies under the terms of their policies, of $50,000 or more, increased as a percentage of all reported incidents from 13 percent in 1975 to 20 percent in 1978 with awards of $1 million or more increasing from five in 1975 to twenty-three in 1978 (*Closed Claim Study*, p. 18). Dollar amounts of awards are not always available because in states such as California the judge may seal that information and insurance companies may not always report the amount of an award in the usual surveys. Nonetheless, *The Jury Verdict Research Report* listed forty-five awards of over a million dollars in 1982 compared to fourteen in 1979 (J. Lipman, "Huge Malpractice Suits, Premiums Threaten Insurers and Health Care," *Wall Street Journal*, September 21, 1983). In 1984, in the Cook County jurisdiction, the total awards in medical malpractice trials alone amounted to $45,040,367, compared to $59,182,093 for the fourteen previous years (1970–1983 inclusive) ("1984 Calendar Year Summary and Index of Malpractice Trials," 1985). This means that 43.2 percent of the verdict awards in medical malpractice trials in Cook County over a fifteen-year period was awarded in the one year, 1984. In 1985, medical malpractice trial awards amounted to $38,722,530. The main reason for the large amounts assessed in the past two years is the inclusion in these trials of two record awards against drug manufacturers (1985 Calendar Year Summary and Index of Malpractice Trials, *Cook*

County Jury Verdict Report, 1986). Nationally, one of every five jury awards in 1984 in U.S. malpractice litigation resulted in a verdict award of one million dollars or more (Leslie Hertzog, "The Malpractice Mess," *Newsweek,* February 17, 1986, p. 75).

Some discussion has centered on the seemingly uneven distribution of indemnity dollars among plaintiffs. In the Rand study, the mean court award was $102,000, and the top 5 percent of claims in terms of dollar payment received 49 percent of all dollars paid. Their analysis revealed that the uneven distribution of dollars parallels the uneven distribution of injury severity (P. M. Danzon and L. Lillard, R-2793, pp. 23–24).

In their continuing study of civil jury verdicts in Cook County between 1959 and 1979, Rand Corporation researchers have noted some trends that merit reflection. One report suggests that Cook County juries may have increasingly invoked two tiers of justice, with higher judgments awarded against "deep pocket" defendants, such as those involving work injury, product liability, malpractice and street hazards. (M. A. Peterson, "Compensation of Injuries," *Rand Report R-3011,* Institute of Civil Justice, Rand Corporation, Santa Monica, California, 1984, p. x). In addition, jurors seemed more sympathetic to plaintiffs injured by medical malpractice than by other sources. Observed medical malpractice awards were larger (five times those in injury-on-property cases) but not, apparently, because malpractice plaintiffs claimed particularly severe injuries. With the same injury, a malpractice plaintiff received an award five times the size of an award to an injury-on-property plaintiff, and almost twice as large as the award to a work injury or product liability plaintiff. (A. Chin and M. Peterson, "Deep Pockets, Empty Pockets," *Rand Report R-3249,* Institute of Civil Justice, Santa Monica, Calif.: Rand Corporation, 1985, p. 54).

Both the number of malpractice suits filed against physicians, therefore, and the dollar amount of awards, including those taken to trial and those settled out of court, indicate that the future trend is toward an increase rather than a diminution of medical malpractice litigation.

MEDICAL NEGLIGENCE: A PROTEAN CONCEPT

The concept of medical negligence resembles a simple cottage that has been burdened with so many additions that its original lines can no longer be perceived clearly. The foundation may remain at the intersection of the expanded wings and dormers, but the structure is fundamentally different; it is roomier, may be entered in new ways, and enjoys increased market value. As with the cottage transformed into a mansion, the idea of medical negligence retains its original blueprint lines, they have just been obscured by the broad strokes of later, more ambitious and innovative architects. Indeed, trial lawyers would like this new design to be granted landmark status.

As has been explained earlier, medical negligence is a civil or tort action, a concept that, something like supply-side economics or relativity, remains unclear even though it is explained many times. The construct, however, is deeply rooted in American law and its application has changed along with the nation's social philosophy and its economic and territorial expansion. From being the means through which persons adjusted claims for such faults as trespass, tort has become the action through which people seek recompense for alleged wrongs in settings ranging from industry to health care.

Applied to medicine, negligence is a tort in which the accusation most often made is that a physician, by omission or commission, departed from the standard of care owed to a patient, thereby directly causing an injury for which, through the legal action of a malpractice suit, the patient seeks recompense. As noted previously, only experts in the same field may describe the required standard of care or make a judgment as to whether or not the accused person departed from it. Jurors, in effect, decide which experts and which witnesses to believe.

Medical Negligence: A Protean Concept

The public's impression is that malpractice actions refer to bad medicine, which, after generations of conspiratorial silence on the part of the medical establishment, is finally being brought to light through legal advocacy with the cooperation of physicians who are willing to testify against their errant colleagues. There is some feeling that for too long doctors have made unchecked mistakes and that they are finally being forced to answer for them. Fair or not, that is the imaginative construction of the malpractice situation held by many citizens. Like the cottage that becomes a castle, however, the notion has been so greatly expanded that its once crisp, defining lines have been permanently blurred.

Some misunderstanding may arise from a difference of opinion on the fundamental purpose of tort actions alleging negligence. There is a popular perception, for example, that the intent of this law is to enforce the accepted standard of medical care on physicians, thereby protecting the public from "malpractitioners" and assuring high quality medical care. The Association of Trial Lawyers of America appears to espouse this interpretation that "the cause of malpractice litigation is medical negligence." (Thomas G. Goddard, "The American Medical Association is Wrong—There Is No Medical Malpractice Insurance Crisis," Association of Trial Lawyers of America, 1985, p. 6). They contend that the current system of tort law punishes incompetent physicians effectively, while at the same time serving as a deterrent to bad medical practice. Critics of this stance suggest, in contrast, that the direct intention of tort law is not to discipline erring doctors but to provide a means of obtaining compensation for injury. As a side effect, it may have some impact on practice. The accusation of negligence, however, is an indispensable legal initiative in a process that leads to compensation.

This latter interpretation is supported by current data that suggest most malpractice claims do *not* involve true negligence.

- As noted previously, data document that over a ten-year period 82 percent of closed claims resulted in *no* payment to the plaintiff. (ISMIE Loss Analysis Report, December 31, 1985). This is the clearest available factual evidence that the greater number of already closed claims alleging malpractice were unfounded.

- The doctors' insurance company in New Jersey reports that only 509 (7 percent) of its 7,079 physicians were found to have had a fully chargeable claim (American Medical Association, "AMA Response to the Association of Trial Lawyers of America Statements Regarding the Professional Liability Crisis," August 1985).

- Nor is the problem the so-called repeated offenders, that is, bad doctors repeatedly getting into trouble. The same New Jersey Company found that of all its insureds, only 45—less than 0.5 percent—qualified for the surcharge which the company assesses based on claim involvement.

- The Governor's Task Force on Medical Malpractice in Florida reported that only 70 (4 percent) of 1,728 physicians studied had more than two paid claims (AMA, "Response to the ATLA," *op. cit.*, p. 15).

Ironically, then, allegations of negligence are not at all the same as genuine medical negligence. This is clear from what lawyers say—and from what they do—in dealing with these cases. Paradoxically, a plaintiff's lawyer may charge that a doctor has been negligent and, in the same breath, disavow the notion that the accused person is a bad doctor. Such lawyers readily tell doctors that they should not take negligence charges personally, that tort actions are not indictments of physicians' integrity, they are simply means of securing recompense in specific situations for their legal clients. Trial lawyers, no matter how dramatically they make a case against physicians in court, do not seek to have the latter's licenses taken away or have them barred from practice. Their commitments end with the resolution of the tort action.

The law is, ironically enough, also often used to defend doctors in actions brought against them by peers. When on occasion a hospital, medical society, or national medical organization has taken steps to discipline, by denial of staff privileges or withdrawal of society membership, a physician judged professionally incompetent, such actions have often been severely hampered by lawsuits or other mechanisms that plead physician hardship ("American Surgical Association Statement on Professional Liability," *NEJM* 295 [1976]:1292–1296).

This suggests that the legal profession's concept of malpractice is not cut and dried: Lawyers do not perceive it along with the public as an essentially moral issue. It is useful to understand that malpractice litigation has *no* effect in itself on a physician who may be practicing bad medicine; such litigation neither seeks nor delivers protection to the public from a specific and genuinely malpracticing physician.

Some authors have suggested that the malpractice system may be understood as a mechanism for signaling the potentially negligent doctor. These same authors argue, however, that malpractice insurance, as it is currently administered, effectively insulates the malpracticing doctor from the damages award and, therefore, from the malpractice signal (W. B. Schwartz and N. K. Komesar, "Doctors, Damages and Deterrence," *NEJM* 298 [1978]: 1282–1289). It literally insures that such questionable physicians may, with increased premium costs, continue to practice their specialty. The current purpose of malpractice litigation is to obtain compensation for a patient who suffers a mishap, not to reform medicine or punish doctors who are associated with such incidents. The discipline of such doctors is an issue quite distinct from the intention of malpractice litigation. It is the responsibility of the individual state rather than tort law to insure the quality of medical practice within its bounds. This is accomplished by duly regulated boards who license and monitor the professional conduct of those physicians subject to its jurisdiction.

Medical Negligence and Adverse Outcome

Chicago trial attorney Patrick J. Navin introduced the idea of medical negligence to a group of medical students by saying ". . . a lawsuit, from time to time, goes with the territory. . . . And mishaps, unexpected results, can and do occur and may result in the filing of a lawsuit" (Address in Realities of Medicine course, University of Illinois at Chicago, September 1982). The concept of medical negligence must be distinguished in health care from that of the adverse outcome. Physicians may make proper decisions, following and even surpassing the demands of the accepted standards of care, and still be confronted with less than perfect outcomes in their patients. That some patients do not recover fully, that some infants are not absolutely perfect specimens, that operations may succeed and yet patients die: These are the realities of that geography of the human condition called medicine.

Some lawyers identify any bad medical outcome with medical negligence. This broadened concept of medical negligence has gained increasing acceptance among other advocates who contend that any person who suffers any mishap whatsoever while in the health care universe should receive recompense for it. One prominent personal injury lawyer has told physicians that adverse outcomes are "unconscionable," and Philip Corboy, well-known Chicago trial lawyer, contends that medical malpractice actions are merely ways of seeking a "second opinion" on what went wrong after a patient has had a less than desirable result (*Chicago Tribune*, November 28, 1982).

Presently, the principal means of recovering insurance fund compensation after medical mishap necessitates, as has been observed, the filing of a tort action alleging medical negligence. As will be discussed later, such a notion of medical malpractice moves well beyond the notion of fault; an untoward incident of any kind, whether related to fault, chance, or fate, justifies the tort action. Whether a doctor leaves a sponge inside the chest wall or a patient rolls out of bed, suffers from refusing to take medicine, or develops side effects from a properly prescribed medication, make no difference: They all come within the definition of medical mishap and they have come to be viewed as compensable through tort law.

Such use of the concept of negligence seems rational to Americans who have changed their philosophical expectations about medicine in recent years. Technological advances in health care have been enormous influences in transforming the nature and practice of medicine. They have also increased costs, contributed to some extent to its depersonalization, and, at the same time, have made commonplace the miracles of diagnosis, surgical intervention, and rehabilitation. Medicine's internal changes and progress have also increased people's anticipation of its ready availability and its potential efficacy in regard to them as individuals. The truth remains, however, that not every treatment or operation is or can be successful. Disappointment in modern medical care increases nonetheless when, for whatever reason, it seems to fail people. Americans live in an environment of optimistic expectation about their health. One must also remember that young adults have little memory of the death of siblings or schoolmates from diseases, such as polio, that were common scourges little more than a generation ago. They are not conditioned as previous generations were to illness as a fact of life.

Indeed, for a combination of reasons, Americans have come to think differently about themselves and their health in recent generations. Holistic medicine, with its emphasis on the entire person, on a lifetime of well-being through a combination of prophylaxis and proper treatment, symbolizes a way of regarding health and related issues that is without previous parallel in world history. We have witnessed a major change in the model through which we imagine our physical functioning, the ways in which we are "healthy," and the repertoire of treatment, nutrition, and exercise that will maintain it. "Illness," for example, is currently a term used not nearly as much as "wellness." Good health and a happy life have come to be regarded as rights that should be guaranteed to the country's citizens. There is a contemporary counterpart of Rousseau's "noble savage" in today's image of the "naturally healthy" person whose innocent robustness may be corrupted by contact with health care professionals.

It is no accident, in this regard, that the vocabulary associated with matters of sickness and health has been so remarkably revised over the years. One may, for example, look in vain on a university campus for a hospital or a medical building but readily discover a center for the life sciences or health ecology systems. In these structures people are no longer considered patients receiving care for various sicknesses; they are participant-consumers selecting from the competitively arrayed services of health care providers. These transformations have a distinctively American ring to them; they seem akin to mortuaries renamed as funeral homes, or jails as correctional facilities, bombings termed "surgical strikes." While funeral homes still attend the dead, and correctional facilities continue to house criminals, health centers are now expected to do more than cure the sick and ward off illness. Americans want good health, they want it enhanced, and they have come to expect that their doctors and others can and should make this possible for them. A progressive notion, an observer might say, well suited to the development of medicine and associated health care professions. It may also, however, generate demands that, given the imperfections of the human condition and the health sciences, cannot be successfully met. If, for example, patients are conceived as consumers of health care, they are fundamentally entitled to full value of what they pay for, a fair exchange of terms of an economic relationship. The idea of an adverse outcome is increasingly intolerable in this postmodern, reimagined notion of personal health and treatment.

The difficulties are manifold because, as people come to regard health as a right, illness persists and diseases thought conquered sometimes unaccountably revive themselves even as new ones, such as herpes and AIDS, rise as terrifying specters highly resistant to treatment. Progress and certainty suddenly seem fragile entities once more. The new model finds difficulty in accommodating health and illness under the same roof.

Medicine is not an exact science. It is the very nature of doctors to venture into the dark vale of ignorance, to learn by admitting that they do not yet know everything, to proceed by experiments that fail frequently as they haltingly lead to the discovery that succeeds. Dr. Paul Ehrlich failed, for example, over 600 times before discovering a cure for syphilis. Adverse outcomes are endemic to any scientific inquiry or practice; they are built-in hazards that, despite our growing philosophical intolerance of them, abide in the name of learning. Medicine is an incomplete construction, a partial circle seeking but never succeeding in closing itself. The weather is always uncertain in such a world, almost any procedure carries a certain amount of risk, and bad outcomes are predictable. The latter are by no means proof of negligence or malpractice; often they cannot be described as somebody's "fault." They are rooted deeply in the nature of the process of science, in the nature of the mystery of existence itself.

To find adverse outcomes "unconscionable" may be an expression of legal tactics, but it does not existentially or medically establish a causal relationship between their occurrence and medical negligence. The thinking, however, that makes a malpractice suit a vehicle of "second opinion" presumes that health care is a unique universe subject to full and automatic control by medical personnel. This does not fit human or medical experience. One must posit this error-free environment as a necessary condition for rejecting the attribution of negative outcomes to chance or contingency. This is a legal way of construing reality so that every mishap is technically compensable through the tort allegation of malpractice. This paradigm is presently accepted in trial law.

Trial lawyers necessarily view medicine and other professions according to their training and traditions. They instinctively expand reasons for legal actions and develop legal strategies to support them, and vice versa. Rand Corporation researchers, for example, demonstrated that the legal strategy of increasing the number of targets for liability, either by adding defendants or by raising multiple theories of liability, resulted in more successful verdicts for plaintiffs. (Chin and Peterson, *op. cit.*, p. 50.) Lawyers search, therefore, for reasons to rationalize tort actions of negligence. That, one might say, is their business and, in concert with a public who combine high expectations about professional performance with a willingness to sue if these are not met, their expansion of the notion of negligence is understandable and predictable. The basic outlines of the original concept—negligence equals genuine professional failure—becomes, like the image of the cottage swollen out of shape by later additions, progressively more difficult to discern or even to remember. In practical terms, this means that lawyers have come to sue for bad results even though there may have been no bad medical procedure, errant judgment, or negligent treatment involved in the incident. The tort of negligence becomes the effective instrument for doing something about the negative event. In this situation the doctor, the institution, or other health care personnel, even if not technically negligent, become so legally for the purposes of seeking payment from their insurers for injured parties.

For example, trial lawyer Susan Loggans, who in a 1980 interview predicted that psychiatrists were in for a "storm of malpractice suits," asserted that the very occurrence of suicide can, in itself, be evidence of malpractice. The therapist, in Ms. Loggan's broadened legal judgment, must become the "second insurer" of the suicide risk's life (M. Holoweiko, "Here's the Malpractice Hit List for the 1980s," *Medical Economics* 57 [1980]: 59–63). She filed forty-seven suits in 1983, thirty in 1984, and fifty in 1985 against Chicago area physicians. These suits, for the most part, allege birth injury or injuries to minors rather than psychiatric malpractice (1983–1985 Index of Medical Malpractice Suits, *Cook County Jury Verdict Reporter*, Chicago, 1984–86). One might infer that she has found a new field of accusation, perhaps for business reasons of her own, in which to specialize.

Even though many think Ms. Loggan's theory is psychiatrically unfounded and unreasonable, it can, with the presently expanded notion of negligence, be made a *legally* effective accusation, that is, it may succeed in court even though, by common sense and medical standards, no real malpractice has taken place. The fact of suicide, an unhappy and untoward outcome, becomes the legal responsibility—the fault no matter what the circumstances—of the treating professional. As the head of the Department of Psychiatry at a leading southeastern medical school remarked, "If that becomes the standard, then I will have to refuse to see any depressed patients at all." The professionals of the highest repute and standing agree that not all suicides are predictable or preventable. Yet those who attempt to treat patients who contemplate suicide—a high-risk task at any time—are, through this legal outlook, held to a standard that can never be fully met. Ms. Loggan's prediction is being proved true in that the current frequency of claims against psychiatrists is estimated to be 7.4 claims per hundred doctors compared to two in one hundred in 1978 (*Psychiatric News*, November 4, 1983, and Tillinghast, Nelson, and Warren, Inc., 1985 [insurance company, personal communication]).

Similar logic lay beneath the charges of negligence brought by the men who were shot at the time of the assassination attempt on President Reagan, against John Hinckley's psychiatrist. The lawyer's complaint sought to establish that psychiatrists were responsible for the behavior of their patients, a charge that represents an extraordinary broadening of the concept of negligence.

Another new area of liability for physicians has grown out of the alleged cost-cutting second-surgical-opinion mechanism prooted by many insurers. What if a consultant's second opinion against surgery is not heeded by the primary physician and a bad outcome occurs? Such a case was recently tried in California with the injured patient awarded $667,550 following a jury trial. The plaintiff's lawyer called the decision "a breakthrough for plaintiffs. It opens up a whole new area of negligence." Ironically, the court issued an order stating that "the judgment rendered here does not relate to a breach of integrity or any lack of professional competency or training on the part of the defendant" (J. Carlova, "A New, and Growing, Malpractice Threat," *Medical Economics,* October 17, 1983). This is a clear indication of a conscious decision to do two things: Award compensation on the basis of untoward outcome and clear the doctor of negligence.

Many suits have been brought against obstetricians by parents who feel that the birth of an imperfect child is an adverse outcome for which the physician may, in one way or another, be considered responsible. If there has been no damage to the child for which the physician is truly at fault, such charges obviously offer another example of the expansion of the concept of negligence. Whatever the reasons for these developments in our culture, they have contributed powerfully to changes in our understanding and application of the notion of medical negligence. Although most Americans think negligence refers to "the omission or neglect of any reasonable precaution, care, or action," as it is defined by *The American Heritage Dictionary of the English Language,* its legal usage has pushed its meaning far beyond that to include the behavior of anybody associated in any way with an adverse medical result.

A GENERATION OF
MALPRACTICE CRISIS

Cases of medical negligence are not novel in American history
Early in his career, Abraham Lincoln unsuccessfully represente
a downstate Illinois doctor who was charged with improperly se
ting a wrist fracture. The incidence of cases was remarkably lov
however, until the middle of the 1960s. Reasons as varied an
seasoned as lawyers' opinions have been offered to explain th
steady rise in malpractice cases over the last twenty years. Som
see the sudden challenge to doctors as but one aspect of th
convulsive revolt against authority that shook the pillars of th
republic so violently in the sixties. Perhaps ignited by the murde
of the young President Kennedy in the Dallas streets, a long smol
dering firestorm of resentment broke out against authority in al
its manifestations. Medicine found itself as the first major authori
tative establishment to be placed in the dock of inquiry by a sud
denly skeptical public.

Some observers suggest that medicine had long enjoyed al
immunity to criticism and that certain segments of the professio
provoked public doubt by their willingness to exercise authorit
in fields other than their own, to become seers and prophets ir
residence on matters about which they knew little. The America

ledical Association came to be perceived by many as the gray
minence of all lobbying organizations, dominated by an elite
hose members seemed to identify excessively with the interests
f free enterprise and conservative politics than with the country's
assive social needs.

There is little doubt that organized medicine developed a big
usiness image that made it vulnerable to the savage questioning
f its expertise and territorial rights in health care in the late
xties. The work of revisionist social critics such as Ivan Illich,
ne passionate spirit of a militant consumer movement, the spread-
ig doubt about the trustworthiness of the American government
fter Watergate: all these contributed to the souring of the na-
onal mood about authority in general, and about that of medicine
a particular.

This overall cultural transformation provided a setting in which
hysicians and other professionals found that the once unques-
oned reverence for their training was stripped away and that
ney were being examined with an increasingly critical eye. Physi-
ans, according to some analysts, also became willing to testify
gainst their colleagues on issues of negligence during this period,
us facilitating the drawing of negligence charges. In the heyday
f the Great Society, these developments blended with a burgeon-
ig sense that an attentive government could provide compensa-
on for all the hazards and contingencies of life, ranging from
lness and accident to job loss and old age. At another level,
mericans felt increasing conflict about the possible development
f a welfare state for the undeserving. The national attitude was
us seeded with unresolved conflicts about issues that, to some
xtent at least, related to the quality and availability of health
are as well as the position and function of doctors in society.

Others have suggested that, as states passed laws developing
o-fault automobile insurance, the interest of many personal in-
ıry lawyers turned to the medical field, to which they had previ-
usly paid little attention. Rand Corporation researchers dispute
nis opinion, claiming that, statistically speaking, other issues, such
s the increased number of physicians, were of greater influence
a setting the scene for mounting negligence litigation. They
ontend that "pro-plaintiff changes in common law doctrine con-
ributed significantly to the rapid growth in the frequency and
everity of medical malpractice claims in some states in the early
970s" (P. M. Danzon, *The Frequency and Severity of Medical Malprac-*

tice Claims, R-2870, p. vi). These latter changes included the abol
tion of the immunity to suit once enjoyed by many charitabl
institutions, including hospitals. States that passed these and othe
legislative modifications that made it easier for plaintiffs to initiat
negligence suits experienced, according to the Rand study, "clair
costs in 1976 over twice as high as states that had adopted non
of these doctrines" (op. cit., p. vi). Not only had the mood o
the country shifted to one of systematic doubt about the profes
sions, but recourse to legal remedies for alleged professional fai
ures was greatly facilitated.

An additional reason cited by some for the increase in malpra
tice litigation is the fact that Medicare and third party insuranc
coverage enable all segments of society to obtain medical car
thus enlarging the pool of potential litigants.

The knot of causation has yet to be fully untangled, but th
increase in medical malpractice cases prompted congression;
hearings on the subject in the late 1960s. These were followe
by a study under the Department of Health, Education and We
fare, whose findings, under the signature of then Secretary Elio
Richardson, were issued in 1973. The report concluded that "De
spite the publicity resulting from a few large malpractice case;
a medical malpractice incident is a relatively rare event; claim
are even rarer and jury trials rarer still" (*Report of the Secretary
Commission on Medical Malpractice,* DHEW Publication No. OS-7;
88, Washington D.C.: Government Printing Office, January 1(
1973, p. 12). Over a decade later these words seem sanguine
not optimistic because every statistic demonstrates that the nun
ber of claims made, the dollar amount of awards granted, th
number of suits pending, and the numbers of doctors involve
have risen at a rate that can only be described as startling. Th
reality of the 1980s is that, however we name the forces tha
came together in the 1960s and despite the calm judgments o
the 1970s, the increase in malpractice litigation is now a majo
cultural phenomenon whose continued growth may have worke
irreversible changes in the nature and delivery of health care i
the United States.

How did this problem attain its present proportions and ho\
can it be analyzed so that some sense of its multidimension;
presence and effects in the nation's life may emerge? The answer
to these questions vary with the choice of a mode of analysi.
Perceiving this as a reflection of a developing consciousness abou

poor medical care, one pursues this construction of the problem, defining it as a failure of professional functioning. If, on the other hand, it is viewed as basically economic—a question, for example, of maintaining insurance coverage for doctors—then the situation must be considered very differently. Still another focus is necessary if the malpractice phenomenon is interpreted as a function of the nation's unresolved conflict about its guiding social philosophy. Yet another set of constructs is demanded in order to understand it as trial lawyers do. No one of these approaches by itself leads to a full understanding of the current critical state of medical malpractice litigation. These avenues of interpretation must be examined synoptically to appreciate what each reveals about the nature of the overall phenomenon.

Malpractice as an Economic Crisis

The malpractice crisis may be considered as a specific economic problem, bimodal in shape, which peaked, like the energy crisis, first in the mid-seventies, then seemed briefly to subside, and surged again near the end of the decade. In 1975, insurers complained that their capacity to project profits had been severely damaged because of three developments. The first was the increase in the number of malpractice suits that had been filed; the second, the great increase in the amount of dollars that had been awarded as a result of these actions. The third pressing factor was associated with what insurers termed the "long tail" of many of the malpractice suits, that is, the extensive interval that ordinarily stretched from the initial placing of a claim to its later payment either through settlement or legal judgment. For example, the St. Paul Fire and Marine Insurance Company's experience indicates that ". . . 30 percent of its claims are filed in the year of treatment, 30 percent in the year after treatment, 25 percent in the third year, 7 percent in the fourth year, and 8 percent in years five through ten" (Robert Pierce, "What Legislators Need to Know about Medical Malpractice," *National Conference of State Legislators,* July 1985, p. 5).

The "long tail" introduced an element of unpredictability, because actuaries could no longer estimate how much money they had to hold in reserve in relationship to premiums taken in to cover these potential and unresolved claims. The experience of

Employer's Insurance of Wausau illustrates the nature of the "long tail." Employer's insured the majority of physicians in New York for twenty-five years, from 1949 through 1973, during which time the total premium was $225 million. Between 1974 and 1984, indemnity payments, excluding claim expenses, were over $300 million. An additional $55 million was paid in attorney fees and other expenses. In 1984, ten years after Employer's stopped writing insurance and collecting premiums, loss payments were still more than $30 million. Over 1,300 claims remain unsettled, and new claims are being reported at the rate of over two hundred a year ("AMA Response to ATLA," *op. cit.*, pp. 8–9).

In 1975, many well-established insurance carriers viewed this as too risky a business proposition and dramatically raised their premium charges for physicians. Others withdrew altogether from offering professional insurance to doctors. The nation's doctors were faced with either losing their coverage or of paying rapidly escalating premium charges and passing these costs on to their patients.

This phase of the malpractice phenomenon was viewed even by organized medicine as purely and urgently economic, a question of finding some way to keep physicians insured at reasonable costs, and was not comprehended or responded to except in these terms. Among their responses medical associations included the establishment of physician-owned insurance companies in cooperation with local medical societies. The American Medical Association established and funded the American Medical Assurance Company as a partial reinsurer for these new companies. Coverage was thereby reestablished for doctors.

By the end of 1976, average premiums had risen 131 percent over 1973 levels (American Medical Association, Chicago, *Socioeconomic Monitoring Report* 1 [October 1982]: 7). The doctors of the country breathed a sigh of relief, protested the new premium rates, but factored them into their overall professional costs, and the crisis, much like the one that had concomitantly affected the price of gasoline, seemed to stabilize itself. Indeed, Rand Corporation researchers who restricted their analysis of the problem to statistics available only up to 1978, retrospectively described the malpractice crisis as a "came and went" phenomenon (S. Taylor, "Study Reports a Dramatic Decrease in Medical Malpractice Claims," *New York Times*, April 19, 1983). The pause in this aspect of the malpractice crisis, however, paralleled the deceptively quiet period in the energy crisis that proved to be its unlikely but ghostly twin. Both exploded again just as the 1970s were drawing to a close, each with repercussions that can still be felt in the nation's life.

While the sheiks planned their price increases in oil, the insurance companies, still attempting to adjust to increasing numbers of malpractice claims, introduced changes in their way of writing policies. Up until 1975, they had written what they called "occurrence coverage," insurance that covered a physician for all claims that arose from an incident in a particular covered year or while the policy was in force even if the claim was filed many years later. In order to offer this coverage economically, insurers had to be able to predict with fair accuracy when claims would be filed and how much would be paid out to resolve them. After 1975, insurers offered "claims made" policies that covered only those claims reported during the specific year of the policy and in the preceding years of the policy's effectiveness. By this method, insurers established rates based on claims actually reported rather than on the unreliable trajectories of projections of claims that might be filed in the future.

The initial economic result of this change in policy writing was a reduction in premium costs. Indeed, some physician-owned companies, on the basis of this methodology, were able to declare dividends that they paid to their surprised but pleased doctor members even as they reduced their premium costs. The longer "claims made" policies are in effect, however, the greater the likelihood becomes of claims being filed. The cost of such policies inevitably catches up, usually within five years, with that of "occurrence" coverage (Institute of Medicine, *Beyond Malpractice: Compensation for Medical Injuries, A Policy Analysis,* pub. no. 78–01, Washington, D. C.: National Academy of Sciences, 1978, p. 10). Lower premiums in the early years reflect the fact that the exposure for the "tail" belonged to the prior "occurrence" carriers. ("AMA Response to the ATLA," *op. cit.,* p. 11). The reduction in costs is, therefore, temporary as, in fact, it has turned out to be in the last five years for independent and physician-owned insurance companies.

Insurance premiums have increased again in response to the steadily rising number of medical malpractice suits and the amounts of awards to which these have led. This spurt in the cost of insurance premiums for physicians has revived the fear

that the economic soundness of the system is again seriously im-
periled. The price of premiums varies according to the location
and nature of a physician's specialty. For the physician-owned
company in Indiana in 1985, the average premium charged for
coverage limited to $100,000/$300,000 was $1,345 a year (Data
Report, *Physician-Owned/Medical Society–Created Liability Insurance
Companies,* Chicago: American Medical Assurance Company,
1985). In New York, the average premium charged for coverage
limited to $1/$3 million was $16,500 a year (Dena Seiden, "The
Malpractice Muddle," *Commonweal,* January 17, 1986, p. 9). Although this latter figure seems high, underwriters claim that these
rates still fall short of covering their anticipated payouts.

Leading insurance companies report that premiums for the
total medical professional liability industry increased 30.8 percent
between 1977 and 1983, from $1.20 billion to $1.57 billion, and
losses soared 144.8 percent rising to $2 billion in 1983 from
$817 million in 1979. (Best's Insurance Management Reports,
Property/Casualty Edition, selected issues 1981–84. A. M. Best
and Company, Oldwich, N. J.) This same source (January 2, 1984
issue) notes that "Medical malpractice [insurance] is reaching the
point of no return in terms of producing investment income from
loss reserves that exceeds the underwriting loss." A front page
article in the *New York Times* (January 15, 1985) entitled "52 Percent Rate Rise Is Approved for Doctor's Insurers," illustrates the
problem. As a result, Long Island neurosurgeons must now pay
an annual rate of $101,000 per year and Long Island obstetricians
as much as $82,000 annually for coverage.

The AMA reports that premiums for all physicians have increased by 44.8 percent from 1983 to 1985 and 236 percent from
1975 to 1985. The actual figure paid in total medical malpractice
premiums is in the vicinity of $4 billion dollars a year ("Response
of the AMA to ATLA," *op. cit.,* pp. 3, 5). Richard Layton, former
vice-president for marketing of the American Medical Assurance
Company, estimates that by 1985, $500 million in claims reserves
had been set aside by physician-owned companies for obstetric-
related incidents alone (personal communication). According to
A. M. Best Company, America's insurance companies anticipate
that they will eventually pay out $1.52 for every dollar of malprac-
tice premiums they take in (State Legislative Digest, *1982—Professional Liability,* Chicago: Surgical Practice Department, American
College of Surgeons, April 1983, p. 1).

Costs have clearly broken free of the control that seemed imposed by the expensive adjustments of rates in the mid-1970's. The economic dimension of the malpractice phenomenon is once again painfully salient because of the escalating costs of premiums triggered by the increase in both malpractice claims and the monies awarded. The present problem confronting the malpractice liability companies is whether or not they can continue to obtain reinsurance. Insurance companies buy insurance, called reinsurance, from other insurers to cover potential losses that may be too large to absorb. They thereby share their risk with other companies. Foreign reinsurers, such as Lloyd's of London, account for a significant share of the reinsurance market in this country. Because the market is so volatile, concern has intensified about the continuing willingness of such reinsurers to underwrite reinsurance for present malpractice carriers. Lloyd's of London, for example, has publicly expressed doubt about ever again reinsuring the once standard occurrence policy (B. Keppel, *Los Angeles Times*, Business section, June 17, 1985, p. 1).

Besides costs of premiums, physicians have increased their use of defensive measures in their practices. These include ordering more tests than are medically indicated and the increased use of consultants and other measures in response to the increased growth in claims and awards. The AMA estimates that such measures may add as much as $15 billion in costs to medical care each year (American Medical Association, Proceedings of the House of Delegates, Interim, 1983, pp. 93–102). The charges are ultimately absorbed by the consumers of health care, and while these are estimated to constitute only 1.5 percent of the total annual bill of some $250 billion, it is hardly a negligible sum by any standard. Organized medicine reenacts the Sisyphus myth in its strenuous efforts to roll the boulder of insurance coverage costs up the mountain only to have it roll back, out of control, just as it nears the summit.

The Legal Dimension of the Malpractice Crisis

If malpractice is considered under the heading of legal events then it is dealt with by legal means. In addition to the mid-1970s establishment of physician-owned insurance companies to keep coverage in place for the country's doctors, organized medicine also embarked on a massive, state-by-state program to support legislative packages that would reform the tort law that was the basis for medical negligence suits. In a 1981 interview, B. J. Anderson, associate general counsel of the American Medical Association, reflected the legal construction of malpractice by noting that the association had "isolated the tort system as the problem." This Association, employing more than twenty-four full-time lawyers, eleven of them associated with the Division of Legislative Activities, has vigorously sought reform of tort law through legislative means. "The American Medical Association," Ms. Anderson noted in 1981, "does not perceive malpractice litigation as a national problem but as a state-by-state one. There is no national solution to the problem" (personal communication). This huge effort to restrain malpractice suits through fresh enactments of law has, with mixed results, continued for almost a decade. The AMA is beginning to perceive malpractice litigation as a national problem and has recently drafted the Professional Liability Reform Act of 1985, the basis for the Hatch Bill (S. 1804, H.R. 3865), which provides federal incentives to states for tort and disciplinary reform measures.

Legislative action has been employed to achieve several main objectives. Principal among these is the elimination of the *ad damnum* clause—that is, the statement of any specific dollar amount in damage—in the text of a claim. The rationale for this change is, according to a Rand study, "that large claims may encourage prejudicial pretrial publicity, harm the reputations of defendants who are later vindicated, and distract the jury from basing its award solely on the evidence presented at the trial" (P. M. Danzon, *The Frequency and Severity of Medical Malpractice Claims*, R-2870, p. 39).

Another goal of the legislative reform of tort law has been the establishment of voluntary binding arbitration mechanisms for medical malpractice claims. There has also been an effort to limit the size of contingency fees, traditionally at least one third of the settlement, payable to an attorney from a plaintiff's award. Other attempts have aimed at the establishment of malpractice claims screening panels whose task would be to eliminate frivolous causes of action before they get to the stage of actual litigation. These and other legislative changes have been passed in a variety of states. As of July 1985, twelve states had statutes that limit health care providers' liability by either limiting the amount of recovery for certain types of damages, placing a maximum on the amount of damages recoverable, or placing a cap on provider liability through the use of a compensation fund. In October 1985, the U.S. Supreme Court refused to hear an appeal of a California case testing the constitutionality of a law limiting liability, which, in effect, upheld the constitutionality of the limits legislated (General Accounting Office, Medical Malpractice, *Report HRD-86-50*, February 1986, p. 79).

Illinois, in company with many other states, passed broad reform legislation in 1976, including several of the measures described above. By 1983, only the reduction of the statute of limitations from three years to two was found constitutional by the highest state court (J. T. Howe, "Statute of Limitations—as it related to physicians," *Chicago Medicine* 86 [1983]: 199–201).

As of July 1985, forty-one states had provisions in effect to shorten or modify the statute of limitations, that is, the period of time for filing a malpractice lawsuit after an injury occurs or should have been discovered. Interestingly, a statute of limitations formerly imposed an absolute bar on bringing a course of action. As more and more courts applied the discovery rule (where a cause of action accrues when a person discovers an injury) to medical injury cases, statutes of limitations were no longer an absolute bar, and defendants were exposed to longer and longer periods of exposure. As a result, some states are enacting a statute of "repose," which places an outer time limit on exposure. In addition, the language of the statute is also subject to judicial interpretation (American Medical Association, *State Health Legislation Report*, 13 [November 1985]: 29).

Indiana's medical malpractice act, established in 1975, was upheld by the state's highest court on the basis that the act's provisions were a reasonable and non-arbitrary manner of addressing the medical malpractice crisis. (Professional Liability in the 80's. AMA Special Task Force on Professional Liability and Insurance. November, 1984) Supreme courts differ from state to state on whether the problems presented by the medical malpractice crisis are so unique that they necessitate treating medical claims as a special class separate from other tort actions (American Medical Association, *State Health Legislation Report* 10 [February 1982]: 11).

The bulletin on pending legislation in the various states issued by the Department of State Legislation of the American Medical

Association (*Pending Bills of Interest in the States,* April 5, 1983)
illustrates the dynamic and conflictual nature of the legal approach
to the problem of malpractice. In Arkansas, several bills had been
introduced to represent the interests of trial lawyers in countering
the legislative reforms supported by organized medicine. These
included a bill that would extend the statute of limitations on
malpractice indefinitely if a physician filed a suit against a patient
to collect for services rendered; a bill that would change the status
of comparative fault, so that even if both parties are at fault the
plaintiff can recover damages attributable to whatever share of
fault could be attributed to the defendant; still another bill would
provide that interest on a judgment in any lawsuit, including those
for professional liability, would be calculated from the time the
action is filed. By 1986, none of these measures had been adopted.
Physicians in Illinois, on the other hand, introduced during the
1985 spring legislative session a series of bills aimed at strengthen-
ing the legal position of medicine, which they described as restor-
ing "fairness" to the tort system. Proposals included mechanisms
to establish screening panels, structured payment of awards, standards for expert witnesses, actions for malicious prosecution, the
elimination of punitive damages in jury awards, and liability for
plaintiffs or their attorneys who make untrue allegations without
reasonable cause. The provisions were passed and went into effect
in August 1985. Immediately, the constitutionality of these statutes was challenged, and in December 1985, Judge Joseph Wosik
of the Cook County Circuit Court found key elements of the Medical Malpractice Reform Act of 1985 to be unconstitutional. In
making his ruling, Judge Wosik said, somewhat astonishingly,
"There is no empirical data to support the claim that a medical
malpractice insurance crisis exists in the State of Illinois." ("Circuit Court Finds Malpractice Reform Unconstitutional," *Illinois
Medical Journal,* 169, no. 1 [1986]: 12). In June 1986, the Illinois
Supreme Court upheld the constitutionality of all provisions except the screening panels.

These contrasting packages of statutes symbolize the stale-
mate, frustrating to all parties, that has resulted from conceptualiz-
ing and dealing with the malpractice phenomenon on purely legal
grounds. In addition, a 1985 study that examined the impact of
several different tort reforms found that only mandatory use of
pretrial screening panels had a statistically significant association
with lower malpractice insurance premiums (Frank A. Sloan,

State Responses to the Malpractice Insurance Crisis of the
970's: An Empirical Assessment," *Journal of Health Politics, Policy
nd Law* 9 [Winter 1985]: 642–46). Nevertheless, like inexorable
pponents in some distant war, the forces on both sides regroup
fter each legislative session, count their gains and losses, and
repare to throw themselves back into a seesaw battle that so
ar has not permanently resolved any of the elements of the basic
ispute. Some observers suggest that, frustrating as these efforts
re, engaging in them gives the involved parties the sense that
ley are at least doing *something,* howsoever ineffective, to deal
ith an oppressive problem.

Other Strategies

ssociated with both the economic and legal analyses of the mal-
ractice situation are other developments designed to lessen the
ossibilities of loss through systematically reducing the risks asso-
iated with the most common causes of malpractice actions. Great
nergy and sizable amounts of money have been devoted to what
night be termed "spin-offs" from the malpractice imbroglio. A
ew specialty of risk management has, for example, emerged on
he scene. Such specialists analyze hospital environments to isolate
nd make recommendations about situations or practices that run
high risk of being associated with litigation. To this end, they
nvestigate incidence reports, initiate patient satisfaction surveys,
nd create procedure manuals designed to decrease claims risks
or these institutions. While techniques such as these may appear
lesirable ways of preventing medical injuries and, therefore, ulti-
nately beneficial to the patient, the fundamentally economic ob-
ective of risk management efforts is underlined well by Marsh
nd McLennan, a well-known hospital liability insurance firm.
They define risk management as "the results-oriented approach
o protecting the assets of a business so that its operations can
row profitably" (W. R. Fifer, "Risk Management and Medical
Malpractice," *Quality Review Bulletin* 5 [1979]: 9–13). The data
o far reported suggest that these approaches have had no effect
on preventing patients from initiating lawsuits against hospitals
op. cit., Fifer, p. 9).

Risk management techniques have also been applied to individual physicians to reduce their vulnerability to negligence actions.

These have included, for example, recommendations to keep mor
legible records in black ink and other practices that essentiall
make doctors more legally "defensible" should litigation late
be instituted against them. These initiatives, referred to as los
prevention efforts, have been widely incorporated into educationa
programs for physicians but have as yet had little measurabl
effect on reducing the total number of liability suits filed agains
individual physicians.

The amount of litigation continues to increase with a greate
number of observers suggesting that the present system no longe
achieves effectively the original intent of the tort system of com
pensation. Critics of the present fault-based system charge tha
(1) to establish fault, a considerable expenditure of time and effor
is required; (2) the legal fees consume a large percentage of award
and settlements; (3) the outcome of the claims and size of award
are unpredictable; and (4) awards and settlements are frequentl
excessive, particularly for non-economic losses such as pain anc
suffering (GAO report, *op. cit.*, p. 2).

Alternative approaches to resolving claims for medical mal
practice are expanding, although none has as yet been tested
and/or been proved successful. A medical adversity insurance sys
tem such as that proposed by Clark Havighurst and Laurence
Tancredi ("Medical Adversity Insurance—A No-Fault Approach
to Medical Malpractice and Quality Assurance," *Insurance Law Journal,* February 1974) would be funded by premiums paid by health
care providers. Patients who experience a pre-determined injury
covered by the policy would be automatically compensated for
certain expenses and losses. For outcomes and injuries not included in the policy, access to the traditional fault system woulc
remain available.

Another approach, recently introduced into Congress (H.R.
3084), and largely the work of Jeffrey O'Connell, professor of
law at the University of Virginia, describes an elective no-fault
program. Under this proposal, health care providers within a specified period of time can elect to pay a patient's net economic
losses arising from medical injury. By tendering an offer, the
health care provider forecloses the patient's right to sue the provider except in cases of wrongful death or intentional injury. This
is designed to serve as model legislation for individual states.
The costs of such a program are undetermined because the plan
has never been implemented.

Other proposals, especially those which are basically social insurance systems for medical injury, are popular but untried and untested notions for providing fair compensation for injuries sustained in the health care sector.

MALPRACTICE LITIGATION: A CRISIS GETTING WORSE

The malpractice crisis continues to expand but an essential question remains unanswered: how much real negligence occurs in American medicine and what is being done about it in an effective way?

Most critics would agree that more Americans are receiving better medical care than ever before in our history. The relevant available evidence supports the notion that most of the country's doctors are conscientious professionals, among whom the incidence of proven negligence is relatively small. Even in situations in which the defendant is judged as negligent, this assessment must also be weighed against the policy issue raised regarding jury verdicts: do the courts make awards only when negligence has occurred and to the extent of the loss actually incurred? A Rand study indicates that it is unclear whether the probability of negligence increases with the more severe injuries or whether courts tend to relax the negligence standard when cases involving severe injury are heard (P. M. Danzon and L. A. Lillard, *The Resolution of Medical Malpractice Claims: Research Results and Policy Implications*, R-2793, p. vi).

As noted previously, attempts at self-policing by removing doctors from medical staffs for reasons of incompetence or negligence by either local or state medical groups are currently often thwarted by civil litigation, frequently successful, alleging that such actions deprive accused doctors of their basic right to earn a living. Judgment on a doctor's competence has also been taken over in for-profit hospitals by entrepreneurial interests who make decisions almost exclusively on the basis of the physician's potential financial productivity.

An effort to regain regulation and control of medical practice is exemplified by legislation sponsored by state medical societies. In New York, despite amendments to the statute passed in 1975 defining the state regulation of professional medical conduct, a study group in 1981 found "numerous deficiencies" in the process. "These include: inordinate delays in the hearing of cases and the writing of opinions, inadequate resources for investigators, too many steps in the procedure for appeals, insufficient delineation of the different responsibilities of lawyers, physicians, lay persons, and administrators on the Board." (Committee on Medicine in Society, "Report of the Subcommittee on Professional Medical Conduct in New York State," *Bulletin of the New York Academy of Medicine* 61 (1985): 604–8). Illinois established the Medical Disciplinary Board in 1975, which provides for investigation of complaints against physicians which may result in disciplinary measures ranging from reprimand to revocation of license. The inherent contradictions in its functioning emerge in its rules for reporting medical malpractice claims. Professional liability companies must report not only physicians who lose malpractice suits but also those who settle a malpractice suit. Since any settlement is an agreement arrived at without the admission or denial of guilt, the act of reporting doctors who settle to a disciplinary board automatically implies negligence on their part. Lawyers and insurers agree that settlement is basically a business decision and not a reflection of a professional's competence. The intent of the rule becomes distorted in practice, generating an atmosphere of suspicion that further obscures the original problem.

That organized medicine finds it difficult to speak of or for itself in defining or evaluating the ethical and clinical soundness of the nation's medical care may be related to its taking its principal advice on the matter from counselors who necessarily define it according to their own nonmedical habits of mind, members of the insurance industry on the one hand, and members of the bar on the other. Even though it has been spectacularly unsuccessful, American medicine has until very recently remained committed to this approach. It is only beginning to define and articulate the problem as a medical challenge. A fresh look is necessary if a solution in the best interests of medicine and the public is ever to be worked out. As Nobel laureate Saul Bellow has noted, the issues surrounding the medical malpractice crisis challenge people "to think seriously and perhaps to transform their thinking on a subject they think they already understand."

Doctors' Personalities

Most doctors, along with other professional scientists, possess obsessive-compulsive characteristics. They are painstaking in their approach to problems, they worry about whether they do things correctly, whether they follow procedures exactly, whether, in other words, they carry out their duties conscientiously. They do not feel comfortable if they leave something to chance, they are not inclined to gamble, and they would rather double-check than endure the internal discomfort that follows on not doing so. While numerous horror stories exist about doctors who seem to function otherwise, the great body of American physicians— and social and physical scientists—feel the pull of the "should's" and "ought's" of their commitments. The honor of medicine, and its right to claim the title of profession, depend, in fact, on its practicioners' applied curiosity, conscientiousness, and systematic self-examination.

Gabbard suggests that the traits of doubt, guilt feelings, and an exaggerated sense of responsibility form a compulsive triad in the personality of doctors. The doubt leads the physician to go " 'the extra mile' and rule out the rare disease entity that a less conscientious person might fail to consider." At the same time, feelings that he may have missed something lead to guilt feelings from the idea that he *should* and *could* have behaved more responsibly. Gabbard suggests that the current legal pressures have exponentially "increased the physician's proneness to self-doubt and guilt feelings." (G. O. Gabbard, "The Role of Compulsiveness in the Normal Physician," *JAMA* 254 (1985): 2926–2929).

These characteristics serve doctors poorly in their attempts o diagnose and cope with the problem of increased malpractice litigation and its implications about medical negligence. Self-questioning and a readiness to criticize one's performance are not the attitudes of choice for someone who wishes to engage in a successful dialogue with others dedicated, as insurers are, to setting odds about risk, disaster, and death, or, as lawyers are, to adversarial encounters on legally defined questions.

Doctors reveal what may be generously described as naiveté in their involvement with consultants who speak languages and pursue goals quite different from those of medicine. Doctors are expected to doubt themselves and to accept that doing the best they can, they may fail anyway, and that they must learn from that failure for the future. This psychological hallmark of scientists (it may, as suggested, be found as well in physicists, chemists, engineers, psychologists, and a whole list of other persons imbued with research interests) renders them uniquely vulnerable to challenges and confrontations with others. Their willingness to entertain the doubts expressed about them by others may be the source of their strength and progress in their professional work; it is a source of weakness as they interact with those who impose a different template of interpretation on their medical activities.

As a result, physicians as individuals and in groups allow themselves to be reviewed, scolded, and, on occasions, shamed and even humiliated by those who, for whatever reason, examine their work critically. This may not indicate ill will on anyone's part; it does explain why doctors are so frustrated in trying to make progress through dealing with malpractice as solely an economic or solely a legal problem. Lawyers are accustomed to the adversarial style of grave accusations trussed in legalese and they do not make or take them personally. Insurers, whose public relations imagery depicts them as nobly and amiably dedicated to humanity, are basically businessmen who sell coverage for potential loss. They may do this with integrity of a high order but they do not stay in business long by systematically entertaining doubts about their procedures or by questioning themselves after every transaction. The very vocabulary of the profession is enlightening; insurance agents "settle," they "adjust" claims. They deal with economic realities, with the prevention of financial loss for others in a way that makes some financial increment possible for themselves. Lawyers and insurers simply do not conceive of the world or interact with it in the same way physicians do.

Physicians do take things personally, especially accusations that they have been negligent in their professional practice. So, too, they feel malpractice litigation as a referendum on their own deepest selves. As a result they become very angry at lawyers and insurers for their roles in bringing charges against them or protecting them at what they consider exhorbitant rates. At the same time, they take most of their advice and confer regularly with these other principal actors in the malpractice drama. They resemble French aristocrats embracing the revolution that overturns their world.

Physicians are instructed by such counselors to practice good medicine; if they do that, they need have no fear of the malpractice litigation specter; if they spend more time with their patients they will lessen their chances of being sued; if they warn patients in advance of all the possible difficulties and potential risks connected with a specified course of treatment; if they keep more legible records in black ink; if they are honest about their mistakes; and finally, and with great feeling, if they would learn a little humility and stop playing God, they would avoid lawsuits. Even self-styled medical sage Norman Cousins asserts that a good doctor-patient relationship is "the best malpractice insurance of all—whatever branch of medicine." (N. Cousins, "Unacceptable Pressures On The Physician" *JAMA* [1984] 252: 351–352) A review of the pertinent research literature, however, reveals that there is *no* evidence relating these behaviors to being sued or not being sued.

Physicians often feel that they are doing these things as well as they can and yet they still live in fear of possible lawsuits for what one trial lawyer described as "iatrogenesis, the undesirable side effects of medical treatment" ("MD's Hit, Attorneys Defend Tort System, Contingency Fees" *American Medical News*, 25 [1982]:3). Most doctors, following the advice given them, try harder to carry out their duties carefully only to discover that the volume of negligence suits continues to rise while their own sense of threat does not diminish. Doctors are presently caught between two forces, the law and the insurance industry, and despite their efforts to accept and integrate the advice of these huge establishments into their professional practice, they feel that things have steadily deteriorated.

The malpractice litigation situation has worsened, despite all the money spent, advice given, and earnest resolutions made, because it originates less from the character of contemporary professional medical practice than from the century old conflict between insurance and the law about the nature and means to recompense for injury. The varied analyses of malpractice by these two influential entities reflect their old antagonism on this question; so, too, does their physician-directed advice which expresses their contrasting philosophies about loss and reimbursement in our culture. The shadows cast by these contesting Goliaths on this point obscure the issue of how much true negligence may be found among America's doctors.

A Brief History of Recompense

Because of the transformation worked in American life by the Industrial Revolution, the thrust of tort law changed in the mid-nineteenth century. A New York court ruled, in 1843, that a person who used ordinary care and foresight was not liable for injury or accident that, according to the court, was "the misfortune of the sufferer, and lays no foundation for legal responsibility" (B. Schwartz, *The Law in America,* New York: McGraw-Hill, 1974). If a person was injured but could not demonstrate liability on the part of some business or other person, he or she could recover no compensation.

The common law moved, therefore, from strict liability, to a more refined understanding of fault. Cases that were concerned with unforeseeable injury were referred to court as tort for negligence. The spirit of the times arose from the philosophical explanation offered by jurists. Progress could hardly be attained if every injury that occurred in its pursuit demanded compensation. Industry would not be able to expand, the railroads would be crippled, and America would be denied the glory of its manifest destiny. Defining justice, in effect, as that which best served the national interest, the courts took stands that heavily favored industry over the individual.

Prompted by the more widespread development of liability insurance in nineteenth-century England, liability came to be defined more sharply. This insurance was applied at first to the coverage of liability of factory owners for the injuries sustained by their workers and was later extended to larger manufacturers and others who recognized the necessity of protecting themselves against the risks that multiplied with new products and services.

Workers utilized torts in their own attempts to establish liability on the part of industry because such legal action offered them their only chance to obtain compensation for work related injuries. Strongly affected by Darwinism and Spencerian social philosophy, the times were not receptive to the laboring man's pursuit of compensation. Life and the workplace tested people's fitness to survive; it was in the nature of things. Such a philosophy supported freewheeling industrial and economic progress built to some extent on the incidental suffering and loss experienced by an increasing number of human beings. As the public began to react to this imbalance, American state legislatures directed their attention to the inequities that flowed from such an emphasis of the common law.

The twentieth century has been the scene of industrial and technological progress whose natural by-product has been increased hazards for almost everyone. The revolution in transportation, for example, has created the benefits as well as the risks of automobile and airplane travel. The change from an agricultural to an industrial, and now a postindustrial, age has resulted in a new world of expanded opportunities and difficulties. Modern life, seeded with the risks of unemployment, illness, disability, and old age, has become inherently dangerous. A transforming social consciousness began to identify society as the source of many of the misfortunes suffered by people and arrived at a conclusion with far-reaching implications. If society was itself the source of risk and loss, then it should also be the source of recompense for affected individuals. This philosophy has been applied in a practical manner during this century in a series of developments that began with workman's compensation and ranged through social security to no-fault automobile insurance. Each of these developments represented an effort to guarantee compensation, irrespective of fault, for people suffering because of the multiple hazards of modern life.

Work was conceptualized as one universe, transportation another, and gradually systems of insurance compensation were developed for them. One vast universe of contemporary experience remains in which risk, mishap, and death are inevitable, that of health care. No automatic system of compensation is in place to cover the mishaps, including those tangential to treatment, such as a patient slipping on a highly polished floor, that can occur to individuals as they pass through this universe. Here we arrive at the core of the great, lumbering crisis of malpractice litigation. Lacking a no-fault system of insurance to cover the world of medical care, legal action alleging fault, as once was routinely true even for minor auto accidents, remains the principal means of access to the insurance monies that are the source of potential reimbursement. This tort action must charge negligence. That is the only language that works—as a certain password does for computers—to gain access to insurance funds. The malpractice litigation crisis stands on this invisible foundation. Negligence must be formally charged, whether authentic medical negligence has taken place or not, in order to tap the available insurance coverage. As legal scholar Bernard Schwartz has observed "the law of torts has steadily moved from a fault to a social insurance basis" (B. Schwartz, op. cit., p. 242).

The competing interests of law and insurance have merely moved their continued struggle with each other onto the grounds of health care. Lawyers' lack of interest in removing allegedly negligent doctors from practice can be explained simply: their concern is primarily with compensable mishaps rather than with the probity of medical care. The willingness of insurance companies to write higher premiums for allegedly malpracticing physicians merely reflects the nature of their business: to cover risk, irrespective of moral, ethical, or other considerations, at a cost.

The questions of the existence of medical negligence, and the proper regulation and policing of health care professionals, have been lost in the smoke and flame of the great pitched battle between the interests of insurance and law. Medical discipline is one issue. Compensation for persons who suffer injury—as a result of negligence or poor outcome—is another. In some sense, organized medicine cannot study itself adequately—or effectively sort out its malpractitioners—until the battlefield is cleared. As noted earlier, even small efforts to discipline doctors within the profession draw intrusion by the law. The bitter fight to the death between the law and insurance has distorted the nation's understanding of the malpractice litigation crisis that is indeed grave and that touches everyone, doctor and patient alike.

SIDE EFFECTS ON
DOCTORS AND PATIENTS

Americans, always profoundly ambivalent about authority figures, have in the last twenty years expressed that conflict in a spirited rebellion against professionals in every field. Doctors have been particularly vulnerable to criticism. People speak of their grievances against doctors in general while they may, in the same breath, speak admiringly of their own personal physicians. Still, as a class, doctors have been major targets of discontent: they make too much money, they don't spend enough time with you, they are too arrogant. The other side of the ambivalence is found in the pride and affection that many people still feel about their doctors, and in the high standing doctors maintain despite the heavy criticism directed against them.

There are signs, however, that the seemingly intractable problem of malpractice litigation has begun to take its toll on the nation's physicians, sapping them of their energy and deflecting them, in important areas, from practicing medicine in the way they think they should and in the manner that they feel is in the best interests of their patients. Malpractice litigation has proved to be a fierce storm that has battered the house of medicine more severely than is generally realized. As with all storms, it is indifferent about its effects, and it does not touch doctors in isolation from their daily work. In the long run, patients become the final victims of a phenomenon that has already markedly affected their doctors. Patients pay the price for increased insurance premiums, for the already far advanced changes in the doctor-patient relationship, for the retreat from research on risky frontiers, for the subtle losses in the delivery of health care that are yet to be fully and adequately calculated.

The public still hears the "horror stories" about medical malpractice, tales of vigorous persons reduced to vegetative states, for example, through physician negligence. There are highly publicized cases in the papers almost every day that rouse sympathy for maltreated patients and anger at the physicians who are portrayed, as in the film *The Verdict,* as lacking in moral and professional integrity. Members of the public are not aware, however, that the explosion of litigation has had extensive side effects on their own medical care and well-being.

It is difficult to dramatize another set of horror stories in which doctors, rather than their patients, are the characters who suffer. Such tales do exist but they are given scant attention, not so much because the public will not listen but because they have not been told. Doctors are trained to suppress their feelings, to keep them to themselves in an effort to prevent them from adversely affecting their work. Doctors who are sued for malpractice have not talked much even to their colleagues about the experience until very recently. Just a few years ago, only 11 percent of sued doctors said that they talked with any of their peers about their suit. (S. C. Charles, J. R. Wilbert, and E. C. Kennedy, "Physicians' Self-Reported Reactions to Malpractice Litigation," *Amer. J. Psych* 141 [1984]: 563–65). Organized medicine, interested in supporting the image of doctors, has hesitated, until very recently, to publicize this side of the malpractice crisis. It is not so much that medicine shrinks from its faults in public; it has, for example, openly explored the problems of the "impaired" physician in recent years. Organized medicine has been, however, reluctant to admit that negligence litigation, because of its effects on physicians, has already altered the nature and delivery of health care to the American public. That, nonetheless, is the case.

One can recount stories of physicians who, even though vindicated through court trials, find that their sense of themselves has been so affected by malpractice litigation that they can no longer practice with confidence or the legitimate sense of satisfaction they once experienced in their work. A pathologist in a far western state, for example, was accused of misreading a slide of a patient who later developed a malignant growth. He had sent the slide for verification to the Army Institute of Pathology at Walter Reed Hospital where his interpretation of the slide was supported by the nationally recognized experts there. Still, he was later accused of negligence and, although he won his trial, he found that, as a result of this experience, he became enormously anxious and indecisive whenever he was called upon to interpret similar slides, whenever, in other words, he was called upon to draw on his years of training and experience in the service of the public. Unable to function, he sought psychotherapy. He suffered personally despite his vindication, but far more striking is the side-effect that his expertise was removed from availability to the public.

One could cite the cardiovascular surgeon, an inventive pioneer in his field, who, even though cleared of negligence charges, found that the possibility of their being lodged against him again without justification made further practice impossible. At the height of his career he retired to become a gentleman farmer, his irreplaceable knowledge and expertise removed from the spectrum of health care.

Those physicians, vindicated by court trial, who continue to practice do so with a different attitude toward themselves and their patients. They feel constrained and cautious and find that a new edge of uncertainty colors their relationships with their patients, with whom many report a reluctant feeling of guardedness. Many physicians confide that they were sued by the patients with whom they spent the most time, by those with whom they extended themselves most fully. A distinguished orthopedic surgeon shakes his head as he tells of the many months he spent working with a young boy suffering from curvature of the spine. The results of the surgical implantation of straightening rods were excellent and the horizons of the young patient's life were notably expanded. Several years later the boy, grown to young manhood, crashed his car and the implanted rod was broken. He sued the surgeon, alleging that he had used a defective rod. In this example, the strands of the malpractice litigation may be observed: A favorable outcome of good, conscientious medicine that improved a patient's condition was retrospectively reinterpreted in order to achieve recompense after a later unrelated injury. Although the doctor was cleared he still experienced the impact of the accusation of negligence. He reports that he is changed in subtle ways as a result of this episode—and every patient he now sees is also affected by the caution and defensiveness that he cannot shake off.

Similar stories can be told of surgeons in other specialties who discovered that, after years of dealing with malpractice charges, courtroom vindication did not restore the self-confidence, indispensable to their work, that had been compromised by their experience of unwarranted malpractice litigation. The skills of such highly trained individuals have been removed from availability to the public. As one chairman of a department of surgery at a large midwestern hospital noted, "Doctors who are sued are never the same again, even after they have cleared their reputations in court. The problem is that they know that it might happen again at any time." Many physicians have withdrawn from specialties in which they are fully trained and accredited, because of the high risk of negligence litigation. Others have moved into different kinds of practice, often with industry, in a fashion that effectively removes their skills from the health care delivery system of their region. Others retire early, preferring to avoid the dangers of negligence charges altogether.

Obstetrician-gynecologists are among physicians most affected by the excess of litigation, and documentation of its effects on the delivery of obstetrical practice is beginning to emerge. Results from a nationwide sample of 1,646 ob-gyn specialists in 1985 reveal that 73 percent have had at least one malpractice claim against them, approximately two-thirds have increased the use of diagnostic tests, 12 percent have dropped obstetrical practice altogether, and 23 percent have decreased their practice of high-risk obstetrics. Another effect beginning to emerge is that young physicians appear to be shunning the specialties who care for high-risk pregnancies. "Of the seventy-five programs in the field, forty-five show vacancies today." ("Professional Liability Insurance and Its Effect: Report of a Survey of ACOG's Membership," *American College of Obstetricians and Gynecologists,* November 1985).

A recent report to the AMA contained information that American Medical News described as "most sobering" about the "flight from practice of many high-risk specialists" because of the litigation crisis ("Payment, Liability Issues Concern Delegates," *American Medical News,* December 20, 1985). These include one ou of every four surgeons responding to a survey of the American College of Surgeons who said that they had stopped performing certain high-risk procedures. One out of five family physicians report reducing obstetrical practice.

Counterpointing these stories of doctors whose ability to function is compromised by litigation is the fact that, after vindication, doctors are almost never able to countersue successfully. Judges have ruled that, even though they are sometimes sued without cause, doctor defendants do not thereby suffer any real loss. When physicians have attempted to sue for "malicious prosecution," the usual countersuit charge, they must prove that they suffered special damages as a result of the suit. The courts so far have determined that because the damages ordinarily listed by physicians are typical losses sustained by all physicians who are sued, they do not constitute "special damages" and, therefore, the countersuits have been unsuccessful (J. T. Howe, "Physician Countersuits in Malpractice Cases," *Chicago Medicine* 82 [1979]: 285–288).

It is known that some doctors actually found negligent nonetheless did their very best in the situation that generated the litigation. Retrospective evaluation by expert witnesses who were not on the scene, aided by convincing trial attorneys, have sometimes resulted in negligence verdicts that in other times and in other places would have been accepted as poor outcome or the human error that is integral to the practice of any profession. This small group of physicians who have experienced this outcome have not been studied sufficiently.

Researchers have also found their work clouded by the storm of possible litigation. Autopsies, a prime source of the continued learning of medicine, have diminished, partially as a result of the threat of negligence suits. Postmortems sometimes reveal disease conditions that had gone undiagnosed. Such findings may be used as the basis for lawsuits. Twenty years ago 40 percent to 60 percent of all patients who died in hospitals underwent autopsies. The figure now is 20 percent. "Ultimately," this change, says Dr. Werner Kirsten, chief of pathology at the University of Chicago, "will affect medical care. Medicine is a continuing learning process, and autopsies are an important part of that learning" (*Chicago Tribune,* May 2, 1982).

Similar concerns about the seemingly inescapable net of potential legal actions have also led to a decrease in experimental medical and surgical treatments, traditional sources of the clinical knowledge that leads to the development of improved treatment techniques. Speaking on the effects of malpractice suits, Dr. Oscar Sugar, former chief of neurosurgery at the University of Illinois in Chicago, commented: ". . . they have made life much more difficult for the neurosurgeon. . . . The threat of malpractice has inhibited the expansion of new techniques . . ." (*Scope*, University of Illinois, Winter 1980, p. 7). Physicians step back from the "risky" treatments that often have positive results. Under the threat of negligence suits, doctors are under enormous pressure always to choose the absolutely "safe" course of action. This demoralizes physicians as it dulls the incentive for professional discovery, it retards medical progress and levels care off at a mediocre plane. The ultimate losers in such a situation are the patients who could have profited from the searching, experimental medicine that keeps its cutting edge as finely honed as its ambition for excellence.

In reaction to the suit against Dr. John Hopper by the men wounded with President Reagan by Hopper's patient, John Hinkley, the American Psychiatric Association commented that making physicians responsible for the actions of their patients will only increase medical defensiveness (*Psychiatric News*, April 15, 1983). Translated into action in the mental health field, that means that many individuals who could be better treated on an out-patient basis will instead experience longer, more frequent, and costly hospitalizations. This retreat from offering the best of current treatments to all who could profit from them raises serious professional and ethical issues that deeply trouble many physicians. Here again, it is the public's access to the best of health care that is curtailed through the litigation that fundamentally forces a legal concept of medical practice to be followed.

Perhaps the aspect of health care that has come under the most intense pressure in the wake of the increase of malpractice actions is that which lies at its heart, the doctor-patient relationship. The winch of the law has been turned tightly on this traditionally privileged and highly prized interaction. The trust that is essential to its flourishing has been contaminated by the introduction of the adversarial style that, while functional in the courtroom, distorts and may actually destroy the relationship between doctor and patient. Healing, despite the technological settings of modern medicine, remains an art that is worked out in and through human relationships. As social scientist B. H. Mawardi has suggested, the practice of medicine—with all its uncertainties—may not even be possible without a good doctor-patient relationship (B. H. Mawardi, "The Doctor-patient Relationship," in *Physicians And Their Careers,* 1979 University Microfilms Inter. Cleve, 1979). The efficacy of many treatments may depend more on the trust and respect shared by doctor and patient than on any other dimension of medicine. That relationship is under severe stress that makes many doctors and patients uncomfortable with each other.

Doctor and patient may view each other as potential adversaries to the detriment of the medical care to which they are a party. Patients feel the cultural pressures to doubt their physicians and are, often to their own dismay, affected by them. Doctors, on the other hand, have grown uneasy with the possibility that the next patient with whom they deal may become a plaintiff against them in a lawsuit if something untoward occurs, even if it is not their fault. This has led to reserve and caution on both sides, a holding back that is harmful to effective treatment. This is one of the most disturbing and paradoxical side effects of malpractice litigation. Although some still describe the latter as a positive force in improving the responsiveness and attentiveness of doctors to their patients, it may, in fact, be contributing to a mechanical bureaucratization of the doctor-patient relationship. The impossible demand that this relationship be both human and error-free deepens the alienation that doctors and patients already regretfully experience. As they become more defensive with each other, the heart of satisfying and satisfactory medical treatment hardens. Both patients and physicians suffer as health care, in the name of avoiding litigation, is routinized and depersonalized.

The confidentiality of professional relationships has also been dramatically transformed in recent years. Actions in many state legislatures have created numerous exceptions and permitted broad subpoena access to formerly privileged materials. Many commentators think that traditional confidentiality, like a bold signature erased too often, is barely discernible anymore. Third parties are now also able to enter into relationships from which they were once effectively barred. Insurance companies seek access to confidential records as a condition for reimbursement for professional services, patient advocates are granted the right to review medical and psychological records and test materials, and

awyers regularly search such material for evidence on which to
base cases for negligence, fraud, or libel.

Professionals have been deeply disturbed by legal statutes that
require them, under penalty of a crime, to break confidentiality
and immediately report certain activities, such as child abuse, that
they may uncover in their work. They feel that their freedom to
practice is severely compromised by this absolute demand from
a source extrinsic to the therapeutic relationship. Yet they are
caught in a bind: While wanting to honor their traditions they
do not wish to set themselves against the law of the land. The
lords of irony winced as the nation's lawyers recently rejected
inclusion in their code of ethics a demand that they reveal knowledge of their clients' criminal activities, claiming for themselves
what they have been instrumental in qualifying in other professions—an absolute confidentiality they identify as essential to their
professional work.

The nerve center of medical practice is clinical judgment. It
has been profoundly affected by extrinsic forces such as those
connected with malpractice litigation. Through exercising individual judgments, physicians bring to bear on specific clinical situations all that has gone into making them doctors—their basic
education and training, their breadth of experience, their natural
talents and skills, along with the subtle factors almost beyond
counting that define their professional commitment.

Clinical judgment is that moment in which physicians or other
professionals distill everything they have learned into a single
choice of action. When, for example, President Ronald Reagan
was shot in downtown Washington on March 31, 1981, his then
personal White House physician, Dr. Daniel Ruge, was immediately contacted. The president was not in the surgical suite at
Walter Reed, he was in the emergency room at George Washington Hospital in downtown Washington. What should be done?

Ruge did not hesitate. Drawing on his experience in medicine
and his knowledge of the president's health, he made one of the
most crucial clinical judgments of the decade. The hospital should
proceed just as it would with any similar gunshot case that day.
He supported the treatment plan that was in place, letting the
resident doctors carry on without interfering, allowing the hospital's own rhythm and practice to proceed without interruption.
Hospital officials later praised Ruge for his calm, authoritative
decision. It contributed enormously to saving the president's life.

As in this illustration, a clinical judgment is made by a doctor solely for medical reasons in the best interests of his patient. Ruge's judgment, applauded by everyone in hindsight, could have been the right thing to do but might, for other unpredictable reasons, not have worked out as well as it actually did. Nonetheless it would have remained a wise clinical choice. It could not have been made well at all if Dr. Ruge had first to confer with lawyers, accountants, or members of the State Department. Clinical judgment is prudential rather than actuarial or mechanical; it is what being an expert involves, whether it was Eisenhower looking at the weather reports and deciding to go ahead with the Normandy landings, or a teacher sensing something special about a student in a ghetto school. Committees cannot make such decisions. They constitute the heart and soul of professional life.

Clinical judgment is presently under pressure from multiple extrinsic factors; it is often affected or compromised by legal constraints, insurance regulations, legislative actions, or even the business practices of the new "health provider" medical managers. Who controls clinical judgment, however, also controls medicine. Many physicians report that their mounting feeling that extrinsic forces impinge increasingly on their responsibility for judgment has been jarring and demoralizing to them. The classic example of clinical decisions forced by malpractice litigation is that of "defensive" medicine, the ordering of tests to cover the potential legal action rather than to carry out seasoned medical judgment. Doctors do something they do not believe should be done for reasons that are not medical in nature. Here again, what affects the doctor affects the provision of health care and, therefore, the nation's patients. The irony remains: This development occurs because of legal interpretations of what medical care should be in order to be of greatest benefit to those who receive it.

Recent evidence suggests that physicians who have been sued change their professional practices in a variety of other ways. In one sample of physicians who had been sued, 61.8 percent reported that they order diagnostic tests for "protection" in case they are sued, 28.2 percent had stopped performing certain kinds of procedures for which they were qualified but that they judged too "risky" in the malpractice climate, and 41.8 percent have stopped seeing certain kinds of patients whom they assess as potentially litigious (S. C. Charles, J. R. Wilbert, and E. C. Kennedy, "Physician's Self-Reported Reactions to Malpractice Litigation,"

Amer J. Psych, [1984] 141: 4, pp. 563–565). Nobody really knows what criteria doctors apply when making such decisions. Nonetheless, such changes in clinical practice have clear repercussions on medical care.

A more recent survey of another sample of sued physicians corroborates the above, with 48.9 percent refusing to see certain kinds of patients, 42.9 percent thinking of retiring early from their professional work, and 32 percent discouraging their children from pursuing a career in medicine (S. C. Charles, J. R. Wilbert, and K. J. Franke. "Sued and Non-sued Physicians' Self-reported Reactions to Malpractice Litigation," *Amer J. Psych* [1985] 142:4, 437–440). In addition, this research suggests that physicians who have been sued talk little about their experience with others, except within their own family circle, and often experience personally distressing symptoms, such as sleeplessness, feelings of anger, frustration, headache, and other evidences of increased stress. Many physicians also attribute indecisiveness to the experience of being sued. They also report an inability to concentrate, feel a "loss of nerve" in certain clinical situations, and decreased self-confidence in the physician role. These personal feelings associated with the stress of malpractice litigation also overflow into their clinical relationships, interfering with their ability to deliver the best of themselves to the care of their patients. Lewis Thomas, M. D., speaking of the role physicians played in his care during a recent illness, wrote "in large part my confidence resulted from observing, as they went about their work, their own total confidence in themselves" (L. Thomas, *The Youngest Science*, New York: Viking Press, 1983, p. 219).

Many physicians who have not been sued report that the *threat* of malpractice litigation motivates them to modify some of their practice behaviors. In one study previously cited, 29.5 percent of physicians who have never been sued acknowledge that there are certain patients they will not see because of the potential threat of litigation, 59.6 percent order more tests than are clinically indicated, and 32.6 percent have stopped performing certain procedures they associate with "increased risk"—that is, increased risk of suits arising from them. Many of these physicians also note that the threat of litigation is of sufficient stress that they, too—although generally to a lesser degree than those who have been sued—suffer from such disturbances as decreased self-confidence (30.9 percent), a loss of nerve in certain clinical situations

(22.4 percent), difficulty in concentrating (35.5 percent), and inde‑ cision (26.3 percent) (Charles, Wilbert, and Franke, *op. cit.*) The fact that doctors report that both the threat and reality of litigation are perceived as a personal stress is a vivid reminder of the intrinsi‑ cally human interaction that is integral to the character of the health care Americans have come to expect.

Such developments are sharply accented by added documenta‑ tion regarding the impact of the malpractice crisis on the actual delivery of health care to patients. For example, the implementa‑ tion of a well-funded effort to establish health care for the home‑ less in eighteen American cities has been hampered because according to the *American Medical News* (December 27, 1985), "The fear of litigation has made physicians leery to give their time." In a related development, two leading cancer experts report "that thousands of cancer patients may be dying needlessly each year because the fear of malpractice suits is causing doctors to under‑ treat them with chemotherapy" (Ronald Kotulak, "Cancer May Feed on Malpractice Fear," *Chicago Tribune*, March 25, 1986, p. 3). "Doctors," according to Dr. Vincent DeVita, Jr., director of the National Cancer Institute, "are frightened to death of malprac‑ tice and patients should know that because of malpractice they are often not getting a potentially curative dose of chemotherapy." In other words, the patients of America are already bearing the effects of the malpractice litigation crisis in the diminished charac‑ ter of the treatment they receive.

FINAL ARGUMENTS

The malpractice litigation crisis in not fundamentally one of insurance coverage because its basic elements transcend economic analysis or remedy. Neither is this crisis, which has reached critical mass in America, one that can finally or fully be translated into legal terms or resolved through judicial procedures. This is not to indict the indispensable tasks of the insurance business or to slight the role of law in the equitable management of human affairs. It is to observe that because these perennial antagonists have had such a large role to play in this crisis, the elements of their traditional rivalry have come to dominate our imaginative structuring of every question associated with professional liability and malpractice.

The medical malpractice litigation crisis has, in the mid-eighties, become a cultural problem that threatens the best traditions and the stability of American medicine. The shadow of potential negligence suits has fallen across the lives of every professional involved in providing health care. The latter have begun to react in ways that go beyond their own private worlds of anxiety to affect that public world of their performance as professionals. The aftershocks of the malpractice earthquake reach and touch

every person who seeks these services. Americans as patients—
or, as some prefer, consumers of health services—not only absorb
the costs of higher malpractice insurance premiums in their medical bills, but they also experience the subtler transformations that
issue from the negligence suit crisis: they lose the services of
highly trained specialists; they find that certain, once readily available medical treatments and surgical procedures are being gradually withdrawn; they learn that they may well lose in the next
generation the benefits of experimental research that they have
enjoyed so bountifully in this one; and they discover that the
quality and accessibility of health care have declined rather than
improved because of the malpractice litigation that they thought
only affected "bad doctors."

Observers may say that all professional work is stressful and
that other experts seem to manage their problems without mani-
festing the symptoms that seem to affect so many physicians. One
may note that, indeed, all professions have been under seige over
the last generation of anti-authoritarian sentiment. Few other professionals, however, deal as regularly in basic life and death questions as physicians do and as a result are seldom involved in
situations in which so much is at stake; they are not sued nearly
as often as doctors. For all the flaws that doctors may have, they
still occupy the first ranks in the parade of specialists because
their work is carried out on the borderline of health and illness,
its drama heightened by technological advance and every possibility, therefore, of mechanical failure as well as human error. In
any case, while there are suits against insurance agents, lawyers,
psychologists, and accountants, and every other group that describes itself as a profession, the number of these added together
would not approach the aggregate of suits that have been filed
against physicians. When, as leaders of the medical community
in Illinois, for example, say their member doctors must operate
knowing that 50 percent of their colleagues have already been
sued, then the atmosphere is heavy with risk, and the caution
and concern of doctors is understandable. This is translated into
changed attitudes and procedures in dealing with patients. The
patient, in other words, is the final recipient of the stress that
radiates off malpractice suits.

Other observers ask whether anyone named in a lawsuit would
react in a fashion similar to that of doctors. Anecdotal evidence

suggests that the trauma of a lawsuit—or courtroom experience of any kind—is a major source of stress for the average person. Some people, after all, complain that it is stressful just to deal with lawyers on routine matters. Litigation-associated stress is high in America because the law is now used to settle disputes, many of which were formerly handled in other less-structured ways. The results of research studies transcend the anecdotal, however, in showing the effects of malpractice litigation on doctors and the delivery of health services in America.

While organized medicine may hesitate to admit that doctors can be rendered professionally vulnerable by litigation, physicians themselves tell quite a different story. These are men and women whose skills and knowledge are not easily replaced and whose value to the American people, even if considered purely in pragmatic terms, may well be incalculable. For fully trained specialists to withdraw their talents from availability in the health care system as a result of malpractice litigation constitutes a major and tragic assault on the integrity of that system. Individual doctors may make their weary peace through varied compromises, such as early retirement or selective practice. They act as individuals; society reacts as a whole. The attenuation of health care and medical research that is already occurring in the United States leaves ordinary people as the ultimate bearers of the losses that flow from these events.

What can be done about the negligence suit crisis that already affects every American? The question needs to be rethought so that the various issues that have become intertwined can be separated and distinguished from each other. Because the crisis initially manifested itself in the rise in malpractice insurance premiums early in the 1970s, that part of the problem has been taken for the whole. This distortion has resulted, as noted previously, in obscuring the basic question about the integrity of the nation's health care.

Although law is obviously associated with medicine, it cannot rule it as if it were a conquered province and expect that medical care will prosper as a result. Lawyers' gradual assumption of control over what is or what is not an acceptable or safe medical judgment or procedure through the instrumentation of negligence suits not only destroys the basic idea of independent professionalism but also further obscures the question that the law claims

as its main concern: How many bad doctors are practicing an
what can be done to redress the injuries they cause and eliminat
their influence?

The apparent advantages of settling legal claims before the
are brought to trial must also be reinspected if there is to b
any progress in lessening the impact of malpractice litigation o
the American public. When physicians settle a case they sign
consent agreement that allows for the payment of a designate
sum of insurance funds to a claimant while it also absolves then
of any responsibility or wrongdoing in the case. Insurance compa
nies like to settle cases because they can resolve claims mor
swiftly, save the cost of extended periods of preparation and tria
and avoid what might be a judgment considerably larger tha
the settlement. A doctor or another professional is thereby free
of the burden of a lawsuit but they also lose the chance of bein
exonerated by a jury of their fellow citizens.

While settling has its attractions because it relieves the defen
dants of the ongoing stress, it also possesses certain disadvantage
beyond the obvious one of leaving the professionals in that limb
of neutralized claims in which their integrity is neither completel
damned or completely vindicated. Interestingly enough, in th
research previously quoted on the effects of malpractice litigatio
on physicians, 54.1 percent of those who had been sued felt tha
settling a case was in some way an admission of guilt while 37.
percent of the nonsued doctors felt similarly, a statistically signifi
cant difference between the two groups. Doctors' attitudes towar
settling may change once they have the actual experience of a sui

The main difficulty in settling cases in which defendants ar
certain that they have not been negligent is that it reinforces th
litigation phenomenon. If cases can be successful to the exten
that they yield a sum of settlement money even in causes tha
do not represent authentic malpractice, then they will be draw
repeatedly in anticipation of the same result. Nothing succeed
in malpractice litigation like success. Settling may only contribut
to the deadening impasse malpractice litigation has reached. Goo
cases should be brought to court and won. Nothing will brin
malpractice litigation back into perspective more effectively tha
victory in cases in which no negligence has occurred. This wil
also contribute to a more accurate definition, in the long run
of what constitutes actual malpractice.

The malpractice litigation crisis will finally be resolved onl
when the consciousness of the public is raised about its presen

complicated and misleading perception and its subtle but pervasive impact on patients themselves. As long as the question of malpractice remains in the hands of legal and insurance industry consultants, it will be answered in the actuarial and legal vocabulary. As long as organized medicine follows such counsel, it will embroil itself further in an old battle in which it has, almost without reflection, become an active partisan of insurance interests. The massive engagement between insurance and law in which organized medicine has become so expensively involved has been aimed at making doctors insurable and legally defensible, neither of which outcome is essentially relevant to whether or not they are good doctors.

Reeling under the impact of this crisis, America's doctors have begun to show the signs of stress in transformations in their professional practice as well as their personal lives. As a result, health care for the public is changing for the worse, and patients are beginning to bear the brunt of this generation-long problem. Only when the American people realize how their own interests are now at stake—and how much they stand to lose of what they have come to expect in health care—will there be even the beginning of a proper diagnosis and treatment of the malpractice litigation syndrome.

ABOUT THE AUTHORS

SARA C. CHARLES, M.D., is associate professor of clinical psychiatry at the University of Illinois Medical School in Chicago and a psychiatrist.

EUGENE KENNEDY is a professor of psychology at Loyola University and an award-winning biographer and novelist.